On Antisemitism

Solidarity and the Struggle for Justice

Jewish Voice for Peace

Foreword by Judith Butler

HaymarketBooks

Chicago, Illinois

Published in 2017 by
Haymarket Books
P.O. Box 180165
Chicago, IL 60618
773-583-7884
www.haymarketbooks.org
info@haymarketbooks.org

ISBN: 978-1-60846-761-7

Distributed to the trade in the US through Consortium Book Sales and
Distribution (www.cbsd.com) and internationally through Ingram
Publisher Services International (www.ingramcontent.com).

This book was published with the generous support of Lannan Foundation
and Wallace Action Fund.

Cover design by Rachel Cohen.

Printed in the United States.

Entered into digital printing May 2019.

Library of Congress Cataloging-in-Publication data is available.

Table of Contents

Foreword

Judith Butler

There are many ways to approach antisemitism. A study might be dedicated to understanding what antisemitism is, what forms it now takes, and how best to oppose it. Another might ask why there are conflicts about how best to identify antisemitism, and to try to situate and understand those conflicts in light of their underlying political aims. Still another might set forward the proposition that any analysis of antisemitism ought to be conceptually—and politically—linked to other forms of racism. And yet another might ask about how the demography and history of the Jewish people are represented in contemporary arguments about antisemitism, or how the history of antisemitism has changed in various times and places. Still another might ask about the conditions under which the charge of antisemitism is made, who makes it, for what purpose, against whom is it leveled and why, and how best to judge whether the charge is justified.

As one seeks to open up these important intellectual questions, one is invariably asked to respond to the urgent ethical and political questions: Is antisemitism wrong? And should it be opposed in all its forms? The simple and clear answer is: yes. While it is certainly true to say that everyone in this volume agrees that antisemitism is wrong and must be opposed, it is not at all clear whether there is more generally a single understanding of what constitutes antisemitism (which acts, practices, forms of speech, institutions) or how best to conceptualize its workings. Barring a common understanding of what antisemitism is, it is not at all clear what is being claimed when one explicitly opposes antisemitism. If we could arrive at a single or, at least, a minimal definition of antisemitism, then we would not only be able to explain what we mean when we say that we oppose it, but we would also be able to bring that definition to bear on particular cases in order to distinguish, for instance, between charges that are justified and those that are not.

In our contemporary world, there is a great deal of conflict about how to identify forms of antisemitism. First, antisemitism is sometimes cloaked as something else. It takes a fugitive form when, for instance, a discourse emerges that presumes that there is a group that owns all the banks, or that actively makes use of conspiracy theories to explain how political events take place. The word "Jew" hardly has to be mentioned to be already nefariously at work in such a discourse. The same can be said about any reference to the "blood libel"—a scurrilous rumor that has been tenaciously circulated against the Jewish people for centuries, justifying attacks on and murders of Jews in Eastern Europe. The more explicit forms of antisemitism not only subscribe to gross generalizations based on ostensible anatomical or physiological characteristics, the attribution of a "Jewish character," concocted histories, or the projection of sexual proclivities, but also engage active forms of legal discrimination, for sequestration, expulsion, or active oppression or death. Genocide is the most extreme version of antisemitism. And boycotts against Jewish businesses, especially in the history of Germany, are also clearly part of the history of antisemitism. These are all examples of antisemitism, but they do not, taken together, give us a single definition that could serve our purposes. In fact, far more important than a single definition of antisemitism would be an account of its history and its various forms: the language, the attitudes, actions and practices, the policies. That is the only way to know what it *is*, and that means we cannot expect that a single definition will hold for all cases. Or rather, if we do establish a single definition, it will of necessity be so broad that we will not be able to say immediately how and when it should be applied. After all, the charge of antisemitism depends on the ability to identify antisemitism in its various instances, and here is where the matter of interpretation does come into play.

Given the contemporary framework in which the matter of antisemitism is discussed, the conflict about how to identify its forms (given that some forms are fugitive) is clearly heightened. The claim that criticisms of the State of Israel are antisemitic is the most highly contested of contemporary views. It is complex and dubious for many reasons. First: what is meant by it? Is it that the person who utters criticisms of Israel nurses antisemitic feelings and, if Jewish, then self-hating ones? That interpretation depends on a psychological insight into the inner workings of the person who expresses such criticisms. But who has access to that psychological interiority? It is an attributed motive, but there is no way to demonstrate whether that speculation is a grounded one. If the antisemitism is understood to be a consequence of the expressed criticism of the State of Israel, then we would have to be able to show in concrete terms that the criticism of the State of Israel results in discrimination against Jews. Of course, it would be a clearly antisemitic belief to say that "all Jews" share a single political position, or that "all Jews" support the State of Israel, or even that "all Jews" are the same as the State of Israel (the State either represents "all Jews" or there is no distinction between Jews and the State—it is all a blur). The latter claim rests on a gross stereotype and fails to acknowledge the various viewpoints and political affiliations of Jewish people who have very different histories, locations, and aspirations.

Distinguishing among the very different historical trajectories of Ashkenazi, Sephardic, and Mizrahi Jews breaks up monolithic understandings of what it is to be a Jew, and so deprives antisemitism of its noxious habit of vulgar generalization. It also foregrounds the demographic and racial differences among Jews, and it calls into question the way that Jewish history is so often narrated through the lens of European history alone. That some Jews suffer discrimination on the basis of their Arab origins also foregrounds the way that both racism and antisemitism can operate in tandem, but also how intra-Jewish hierarchies are built. Doing a better job of gathering those various histories will not only disrupt antisemitic generalizations, but also replace forms of inequality with a more diverse understanding of who the Jewish people have been, and continue to be. Finally, Jews within the Diaspora and within Israel hold a wide range of views about the State of Israel and Zionism more broadly. Is that diversity of viewpoint to be accepted as part of being Jewish, or does a critical position qualify a person—or his or her utterance—as antisemitic? Just as we assume a diversity of viewpoints among Jewish people, so should we assume it about Palestinians and their allies. Is there only one viewpoint to be ascribed to Palestinians? In any case, the notion that the critique of Israel by Jew or non-Jew is antisemitic only makes sense if we accept that the State of Israel *is* the Jewish people in some sense. Indeed, that particular identification would have to be very firmly consolidated for the position to take hold that criticism of the State of Israel is hatred for, or prejudice against, the Jewish people in general. Of course, when and where those criticisms are accompanied by explicit stereotypes, there are good grounds for seeing antisemitism at work.

But what about the fugitive forms that antisemitism takes? Could we not say that the criticism is silently fueled by antisemitic hatred? That claim is a complex one, since if we accept that antisemitism has conventionally taken fugitive forms, it is clearly possible that it could provide a motivation for some criticisms. But how would one ground that interpretation? On what basis would anyone argue that they know this interpretation to be true?

Is the problem that no motivation besides hatred can be imagined for the person who criticizes the State of Israel? Or is it that only someone deeply insensitive to the historical suffering of the Jews would not "see" clearly that hatred continues, and now takes the form of the critique of the Israeli state. Whoever holds that view would have to explain whether *every* criticism of Israel is a sign of an antisemitic motive, or only *some* criticisms. What difference does it make whether what is criticized is Israeli policies, the occupation, or the structure and legitimation of the State itself? Are only those who voice the latter criticisms eligible for the charge of antisemitism, or does the charge include members of all three groups?

If modern democratic states have to bear criticism, even criticisms about the process by which a state gained legitimation, then it would be odd to claim that those who exercise those democratic rights of critical expression are governed only or predominantly by hatred and prejudice. We could just as easily imagine that someone who criticizes the Israeli state, even the conditions of its founding—coincident with the Nakba, the expulsion of 800,000 Palestinians from their homes—has a passion for justice or wishes to see a polity that embraces equality and freedom for all the people living there. In the case of Jewish Voice for Peace, Jews and their allies come together to demonstrate that Jews must reclaim a politics of social justice, a tradition that is considered to be imperiled by the Israeli state.

So under what conditions does a passion for justice become renamed as antisemitism? It cannot be that the only way to refute the charge of antisemitism in these debates is to embrace injustice, inequality, and dispossession. This would be a cruel bargain indeed. Similarly, when Palestinians call for an end to colonial rule, administrative detention, land confiscation, and violence done against their communities, are they not motivated by a desire for freedom, equality, economic and political justice? The shared Palestinian desire to be released from colonial rule is surely a reasonable desire, one that is broadly admired and valued in other decolonization struggles (South Africa, Algeria). For that desire to be renamed as fugitive antisemitism seems then to be part of a strategy to de-legitimate that struggle. It would be odd to assume that the main reason why Palestinians seek to be free of colonial rule is that it will fulfill their ostensibly antisemitic desires. The colonizer projects the desire to destroy colonial power onto the colonized, but renames it as the desire to destroy the Jewish people. The founding mandate of Hamas only amplifies this problem—and should be definitively rejected. Still, if the desire to throw off colonial power is renamed as the desire to destroy the Jew, then the Jew is equated with colonizing power (and the equation is made not by the colonized, but by the colonizer!). There is no reason to assume that Jews have to be colonizers, so the desire to overcome colonialism should be, in every instance and all sides of the conflict, disarticulated from antisemitism. Only then can the Palestinian struggle be grasped as motivated by a legitimately grounded desire to be free of colonial rule.

So to answer the question, why is antisemitism attributed to those who express criticisms of the Israeli state?, we have to change the terms of the question itself. We have been asking, under what conditions can we decide whether or not the charge of antisemitism is warranted? What if we ask: What does the charge of antisemitism do? If the charge operates as a form of power, what role does the charge of antisemitism assume in the political debate about Zionism, the State of Israel, and the Palestinian struggle for freedom? If a critical position can be discounted by calling it antisemitic, then it does not exactly answer the criticism: rather, it seeks to put the criticism out of play. When the charge functions in a spurious way to censor a point of view, it seeks to delegitimate the criticism by claiming that it is a cover for antisemitic passion or motivation. If a criticism is nothing but a fugitive and persistent form of antisemitism, then that criticism has to be censored and expunged in the same way that antisemitism has to be censored and expunged. A great deal depends on this substitution: critique of Israel = antisemitism. Taken together with that other substitution, the State of Israel = the Jewish people, it can then be argued that the critique of the State of Israel is antisemitic. And yet, if neither of those substitutions holds, then the argument begins to fall apart.

When the charge of antisemitism is used to censor or quell open debate and the public exchange of critical views on the State of Israel, then it is not exactly communicating a truth, but seeking to rule out certain perspectives from being heard. So whether or not the accusation is true becomes less important than whether or not it is effective. It works in part through stigmatizing and discrediting the speaker, but also through a tactical deployment of slander. After all, the charge can be enormously painful. It does not roll easily off the back; it does not get quickly shaken off, even when one knows it is not true. For many Jews, there could hardly be anything worse than being told that you are antisemitic, allied with Nazis or right-wing fascists in Hungary, Greece, Belgium, or Germany, or with all those who believe in the poisonous Protocols of Zion. Those who deploy the charge of antisemitism to discount a point of view and discredit a person clearly fear the viewpoint they oppose and do not want it to be heard at all. It is also a tactic of shaming, seeking to silence those for whom identifying with antisemitism is loathsome.

If I am right, then those who accuse those who have criticisms of the State of Israel of antisemitism know that it will hurt Jewish critics of the State of Israel in an emotionally profound way. They know it will hurt because they also know that the Jewish critic of the State of Israel also loathes antisemitism, and so will loathe the identification with antisemitism with which they are charged. In other words, those who make use of the accusation for the purposes of suppressing criticism actually know that the person accused is not antisemitic, for otherwise the accusation could not hurt as it does. Indeed, it does not matter whether the accusation is true, because the accusation is meant to cause pain, to produce shame, and to reduce the accused to silence. So my efforts to use reason to show how it is not necessarily justified to attribute antisemitism to those with strong criticisms of the State of Israel will doubtless not persuade. The point of the charge is not to utter what is true, but to do damage to the criticism as well as the person who speaks it. In other words, the charge of antisemitism has become an act of war.

Finally, I wish to point out how important it is that the charge of antisemitism be saved for those situations in which it aptly describes what is going on. If the charge is instrumentalized for other purposes, a general cynicism about the charge is engendered. It is considered a lie or a tactic and it loses credence as a claim. We need the charge of antisemitism to remain a strong and credible instrument against contemporary forms of antisemitism, especially when we note that swastikas have appeared at fraternities (Emory University is a case in point), that the right-wing populist parties with antisemitic agendas have won representation in governments in Poland and Hungary, where the Jobbik party won 20 percent of the vote just two years ago. One of its leaders claimed that Jews were a threat to national security. Golden Dawn continues to draw popular support in Greece. They have rallied anti-Roma, anti-refugee, and antisemitic sentiment, and maintain alliances with far-right groups in the United Kingdom, Poland, Slovakia, Croatia, Austria, and Bulgaria. A resurgence of fascist ideology is now happening in Austria, reanimating the scourge of Nazism. And the United States has now joined ranks with it. The rise of hate crimes in the immediate aftermath of the Trump election targeted Jews, Blacks, Latinos, and Arabs. Trump's racist discourse has emboldened self-avowed white supremacists to take to the streets while the mainstream media normalizes this scandal by calling them the "alt-right."

If the charge of antisemitism becomes a tactic to suppress open criticism and debate on the State of Israel, its practices of dispossession and occupation, its founding and the ongoing implications of that founding for Palestinians, then it will lose its claim to truth. It will be understood as a tactic that actually knows the untruth of what it claims. Who will believe the charge when it is used to name and oppose rising forms of fascism or actual ideologies bound up with its actual toxicity? We should not waste our words, the words we need to name and oppose forms of oppression that are on the rise with new forms of nationalism and populism. We should be trying to build a world in which injustice is named and all forms of racism, including antisemitism, are opposed as equally unjust and unacceptable. There is enough hatred circulating in the world that remains unnamed and unopposed, so it makes no sense to wage a war on critical viewpoints whose accommodation is one of the basic obligations of democracy, and when we need to understand the contemporary constellations of racism. When the struggle against antisemitism becomes allied with all struggles against racism, including anti-Black and anti-Arab racism, we will be surely on the way to building a world in which language still means, and justice names, the passion that motivates critique.

A Note about
the Spelling of "Antisemitism"

Throughout this book, we have chosen to use the spelling "antisemitism," following the advice of scholars in Jewish Studies who have made a compelling case for this spelling. While this term is used to refer to anti-Jewish sentiment, the category "Semite" was actually imposed by scientific racism, a pseudo-scientific use of scientific techniques and hypotheses to identify and classify phenotypes, and to sort humans into different races. Scientific racism often supported or justified racial hierarchies. The term "antisemitism" was notably popularized by the German writer and politician Wilhelm Marr, who used the term "Semitic" to denote a category of language that included Aramaic, Arabic, and Hebrew. Marr used this term to lend credence to his analysis of what he argued was a life-or-death struggle between Germans and Jews, a struggle that could not be resolved by assimilation.[1]

According to Yehuda Bauer, the use of the hyphen and upper case, as in "anti-Semitism," legitimizes the pseudo-scientific category of Semitism.[2] We have therefore chosen to spell the term as "antisemitism" throughout. There are contributors to this book who argue for reclaiming the term "Semite," and emphasizing, among other things, the relationship between Hebrew and Arabic that the term implies. Those contributions retain the spelling of "anti-Semitism." We do not want to minimize this analysis: it is crucial to understanding that the European invention of antisemitism saw European Jews as "others," more like Arabs than Europeans, in the context of a civilizational and orientalist discourse. As contributions to this book make clear, as we fight antisemitism, it is essential that we fight Islamophobia and anti-Arab racism with equal vigor.

Introduction

Rebecca Vilkomerson

This book was written in the spring of 2016. Just before it went to press, Donald Trump was elected president of the United States. In the weeks following his election, what has been termed the "alt-right" movement—but is really just another name for white nationalism and supremacy—has moved with startling speed from the very fringes of US discourse to the center of the government. In particular, the early appointment of Steve Bannon, formerly the editor of Breitbart News, to the position of chief strategist in the Trump administration is an indicator that the racism, misogyny, Islamophobia, and antisemitism of the white nationalist movement is gaining proximity to power. Antisemitism is a key tenet of the movement, and in addition to an upsurge in physical attacks and acts of harassment toward Muslims, queers, and people of color in the wake of the election, there has also been an upswing of Nazi-themed graffiti and publicly expressed anti-Jewish sentiment.

At the time of this writing, we know very little about the era to come. While the open antisemitism that has emerged is absolutely appalling, we continue to be most urgently concerned by the policies targeting Muslims and immigrants that were a key element of the presidential campaign and are under serious consideration by the new administration. At the same time, the acquiescence and even support for Trump and his appointments by a number of mainstream Jewish institutions is opening a new conversation about how support for Israel and support for Jewish people are not only not equivalent, but sometimes at odds. In fact, a noxious stew of Islamophobia, antisemitism, and racism is emerging that remarkably converges on one point: support for Israel.

We hope that this collection will be useful in providing context for not just the current moment, but where we have been and where we are going. Regardless of what happens next, one thing we know for sure: it is the responsibility of all of us to renew our resistance to all forms of bigotry and oppression.

In 2004, Jewish Voice for Peace (JVP) self-published a modest volume entitled *Reframing Anti-Semitism: Alternative Jewish Perspectives.* At that time JVP was a small Bay Area organization, but the question of how to disentangle the actual antisemitism that still exists in the world with the way that accusations of antisemitism are used to suppress the conversation about Palestinian rights was already a challenge.

In the years since, while the political conversation about Israel/Palestine has shifted enormously, the questions raised in our earlier book are as relevant as ever. JVP is now an organization with national reach and scope. At the time of this writing, we have sixty-five chapters around the country, over 210,000 online supporters, 300,000 Facebook followers, and 10,000 dues-paying members. We have a Rabbinical Council, an Artist and Cultural Workers Council, an Academic Advisory Council and a Labor Council—providing many different paths into membership in JVP and opportunities for action depending not just on where we live but on our deepest professional and vocational affiliations. We are working in partnership with a Jews of Color/Mizrahi and Sephardi Caucus, which is leading us in confronting the ways in which we have not dealt with issues of racism, internal oppression, Ashkenazi dominance, and the erasure of the Mizrahi/Sephardi experiences inside JVP and in the Jewish community more generally.

In short, we have a new commitment to create a community that is a true reflection of the reality of who makes up the Jewish community. We are struggling toward a new model for a Jewish institution in this country—one where we strive to be a place where you can bring your whole self. Several members of the councils and chapters as well as the abovementioned caucus are represented in this book.

When our first book was published, the Palestinian call for global solidarity through Boycott, Divestment and Sanctions (BDS) had not yet emerged, let alone gained the strength, victories, and mass support that it has today. And in the past few years the latest manifestation of the struggle for Black lives in this country has renewed the discourse about white supremacy and the intersectionality of struggles for justice in our own country and around the world.

But in the same period, perhaps in response to the growing strength of the movement for Palestinian rights, there have been increasing efforts by those that unconditionally defend Israel to include criticism of Israel as part of the definition of antisemitism. Dubbed the "new antisemitism," it defines Israel as the "Jew among nations" in order to shield it from criticism, and has gained broad acceptance in the intervening years, leading to a dangerous blurring of lines that equates criticizing the actions of a state, Israel, with hatred of Jewish people.

So while much has changed, much is still the same. On campuses, in churches debating divestment, and in our own communities the same quandaries are still in play: how to talk productively about antisemitism when so often the accusation of antisemitism is used as a cudgel to repress substantive discussion, and whether criticizing Israel is antisemitic.

This new volume aims to offer something new in response to the current moment. It includes a multiplicity of Jewish experiences in the United States, and also looks at antisemitism from beyond the Jewish perspective, including how antisemitism and accusations of antisemitism affect other movements.

And for the first time, we are offering our own definition of antisemitism (see Appendix I). For too long, many of us have been reluctant to dive into the debate about how to distinguish true antisemitism from criticisms of Zionism or Israel. Accepting that frame of the debate in itself seemed to endorse a fundamental suspicion of the movement for Palestinian rights that is neither called for nor appropriate. We also felt strongly that the endless debates about the definition of antisemitism would detract from necessary attention to the state-sponsored systemic violence and structural power of Islamophobia, anti-Black and anti-immigrant sentiment, and all forms of prejudice and bigotry that demand our immediate and sustained attention.

But by doing so, we realized we were allowing a definition of antisemitism to prevail that can shield Jews—especially those with white or class privilege—from examining our own roles in oppression in the United States and in Israel/Palestine, is often used to justify or excuse Israeli human rights abuses, and that intimidates and silences people who aren't Jewish from speaking out on one of the most pressing issues of our time. We hope that with this book we are offering an effective tool for serious consideration of antisemitism in its proper context.

Of course, that does not mean that the pieces in the book are in lock step. This collection has a definite point of view: each author who contributed takes as a starting point that fighting for Palestinian rights is part of the framework of our commitment to justice. But that being said, there is dialogue and tension among the pieces, including contrasting approaches and conclusions that we hope will make the public discussion of antisemitism and related topics both richer and deeper.

One thing that comes through loud and clear in several of the chapters, especially those not written by Jews, is the extraordinary fear of being called antisemitic, and just how damaging that accusation can be, so much so that there is one glaring omission in this collection: despite the enormous amount of activity on campuses, the Palestinian students we asked felt they could not run the risk of harassment and retaliation if they publicly described the first-hand experience of what it is like to be a Palestinian student accused of antisemitism. Not only is the collection the poorer for it, but it is a sobering reminder of what is at stake in these discussions—for Jews and non-Jews alike.

We hope that this collection will be of value to multiple audiences. It is certainly for those who may be new to this issue and are grappling with these questions for the first time, or who may be interested in what people active in the movement for justice in Palestine think about antisemitism.

But most of all this book is for our movement—our members, our allies, our partners—everyone who takes as their core principles that equality, freedom, and human rights are for everyone. It is an exhortation not to give up the fight—to take antisemitism seriously as part of a movement for justice but also to have real open conversations about what it is and what it is not, to break through fear, silence, and the hegemony of the approach to antisemitism in this country.

It is for everyone who works so tirelessly and bravely, whether in the face of their own communities' opprobrium or in the face of fear of state repression. We dedicate this book to you.

Finally, heartfelt thanks to each and every one of the authors included here, who took on these questions with such seriousness and thoughtfulness. Your work is making an enormous contribution to a much-needed discussion. Adam Horowitz offered generous and constructive criticism at a crucial stage of the process and Dorothy Zellner brought immense rigor and a sharp pen to the manuscript, as did our summer fellows Josh Strassman and Emma Tasini, who helped with fact-checking. Enormous thanks to the JVP staff team—Tallie Ben Daniel, Natasha Perlis, and Rabbi Alissa Wise (in addition to me)—who made this book possible by shepherding it from conception to completion with attention to every step in between. Tallie and Natasha in particular have led us all so gracefully throughout the process.

Finally, much gratitude to Haymarket Books, which enthusiastically took on the challenge of a book like this one with its characteristic dedication. We are deeply grateful to be able to offer this collection with the Haymarket imprint, and look forward to the discussions we hope it will inspire!

Part I:

Histories and Theories of Antisemitism

Antisemitism Redefined: Israel's Imagined National Narrative of Endless External Threat

Antony Lerman

For activists battling daily against the abuse of antisemitism to stifle free speech on Israel/Palestine, on university campuses and in Jewish religious and communal bodies of all kinds, it may seem something of a luxury to dwell on the reasons why contemporary understanding of antisemitism has become so politicized, bitterly contested, and controversial. But if we don't take time out to examine this question, the crucial task of devising effective means of fighting the serious antisemitism that continues to exist is made much harder, and the development of sound arguments to undermine the highly influential efforts to brand any comment about Jews and Israel as antisemitic is greatly weakened.

For those of us who have been studying and combating antisemitism for decades, it's hard to believe that anyone born since the end of the Cold War hasn't known a time when Israel was *not* at the center of discussions about the state of current antisemitism. Today, it's self-evident that practically no discussion about current antisemitism takes place without Israel and Zionism at its center. And judging by the vast number of books, pamphlets, articles, and conferences on the subject of Israel and Zionism as the principal targets of antisemitic discourse and action, this trend is widely welcomed.

When I first started monitoring and studying contemporary antisemitism close to forty years ago, there was, broadly speaking, a shared understanding of what antisemitism was. And Israel was hardly ever mentioned. True, historians differ over a precise definition—quite understandably, given that the term was coined only in the 1870s, and was then used to describe varieties of Jew-hatred going back two thousand years. But I would argue that, in practice, during the first three or four decades after the Second World War, antisemitism was commonly linked to the classical stereotypical images of "the Jew" forged in Christendom, adopted and adapted by antisemitic political groups in the nineteenth century and further developed by race-theorists and the Nazis in the twentieth century. That process of reformulation and revision did not end with the Holocaust. The most significant development in antisemitism after 1945 was the rapid emergence of Holocaust denial. Interestingly, while it seems some began to refer to this as "new antisemitism," no attempt was made to produce a fundamentally new definition of antisemitism to encompass it. Researchers and academics analyzing and writing about the phenomenon had no difficulty in seeing it as essentially a new manifestation of a consensually defined, multi-faceted antisemitism.

How the Shared Understanding of Antisemitism Has Been Undermined

Today, not only has that consensus broken down and Israel is promoted as the central object of antisemitic hate, but something much more far-reaching has occurred. A fundamental redefinition of antisemitism has taken place. And the term that most fully encapsulates this redefinition is "new antisemitism."

The term itself actually is not very new and has been applied to a variety of rather different phenomena. But from the late 1970s it increasingly came to be somewhat loosely applied to forms of criticism of and hostility to Israel especially emanating from the Arab world, and use of it grew. However, in the last few decades, and especially since the beginning of the twenty-first century, those who use the term to describe what they believe is a real, existing phenomenon have tended to identify with a far more specific understanding of what it means, as in this quote:

> In a word, classical antisemitism is the discrimination against, denial of, or assault upon the rights of Jews to live as equal members of whatever society they inhabit. The new antisemitism involves the discrimination against, denial of, or assault upon the right of the Jewish people to live as an equal member of the family of nations, with Israel as the targeted "collective Jew among the nations."[1]

This definition, which appeared in the above formulation in the *National Post* on November 9, 2010, was produced and has been publicly proclaimed countless times by one of the key figures in dissemination of the term since the 1970s, the Canadian professor of law and former minister of justice in the 2003–6 Liberal government, Irwin Cotler.

The "new antisemitism" is seen by most, but by no means all, of those who give it credence and promote its use as synonymous with anti-Zionism; as such, they find it not only in the Arab world but also in the political left, anti-globalization movements, jihadist and Islamist movements and the Muslim world more generally, the Palestinian Solidarity Campaign, the left-liberal press, antiracist groups—the list is long. Crucial in providing the "new antisemitism" notion with legitimacy and erroneously taken by its proponents to be *the* European Union definition of antisemitism was the "working definition" of antisemitism published by the now-defunct EU Monitoring Center on Racism and Xenophobia (EUMC) in 2005. This 514-word document contains a key passage giving examples of critical discourse about Israel that it says "could" be taken as antisemitic. In addition, Natan Sharansky, former right-wing Israeli government minister and currently chairman of the Jewish Agency for Israel, popularized a parallel "formula" for identifying when critical comment on Israel constitutes antisemitism, which is commonly known as the "three Ds": demonization, delegitimization, and (applying) double standards. This was incorporated in the widely referenced US State Department definition of antisemitism, which also draws heavily on the EUMC "working definition."

The concept of the "new antisemitism," or "new antisemitism theory" as it is sometimes called, contains the radical notion that to warrant the charge of antisemitism, it is sufficient to hold any view ranging from criticism of the policies of the current Israeli government to denial that Israel has the right to exist as a state, without having to subscribe to any of those things that historians and social scientists have traditionally regarded as making up an antisemitic view: hatred of Jews per se, belief in a worldwide Jewish conspiracy, belief that Jews generated communism and control capitalism, belief that Jews are racially inferior, and so on. Given that the definition of the "new antisemitism" is fundamentally incompatible with any definition relying on elements that historians deem to make up an antisemitic view, for anyone who agrees with the definition of the "new antisemitism," it's but a short step to conclude that it replaces all previous definitions, and then further to argue that no other kind of antisemitism exists. This may seem bizarre, but Bernard-Henri Lévy, France's most prominent and possibly most influential public intellectual, could, with his trademark portentousness, confidently make such a claim in his 2008 book, *Left in Dark Times*, writing that antisemitism of the twenty-first century would be "progressive"—meaning essentially left-wing hatred of Israel—or not exist at all.

It's not as if there are no perfectly serviceable definitions of antisemitism that would cover genuine instances where critical discourse about Israel and

Zionism is clearly antisemitic. One such is the work of the Oxford University academic Dr. Brian Klug, a leading expert on modern uses and abuses of the term "antisemitism." Klug emphasizes that to the anti-Semite, "the Jew" is "not a *real* Jew at all" and therefore, as in his following short definition, should always appear enclosed in quote marks: "At the heart of antisemitism is the negative stereotype of 'the Jew': sinister, cunning, parasitic, money-grubbing, mysteriously powerful, and so on. Antisemitism consists in projecting this figure onto individual Jews, Jewish groups, and Jewish institutions." He fleshes out this imagined "Jew" as the anti-Semite would see him:

> The Jew belongs to a sinister people set apart from all others, not merely by its customs but by a collective character: arrogant yet obsequious; legalistic yet corrupt; flamboyant yet secretive. Always looking to turn a profit, Jews are as ruthless as they are tricky. Loyal only to their own, wherever they go they form a state within a state, preying upon the societies in whose midst they dwell. Their hidden hand controls the banks, the markets and the media. And when revolutions occur or nations go to war, it's the Jews— cohesive, powerful, clever and stubborn—who invariably pull the strings and reap the rewards.[2]

Klug then extends the definition to cover discourse about Israel and Zionism by arguing that "if [a] text projects the figure of 'the Jew' directly or indirectly (a) onto Israel for the reason that Israel is a Jewish state, or (b) onto Zionism for the reason that Zionism is a Jewish movement, or (c) onto Jews, individually or collectively, in association with either (a) or (b), then that text is antisemitic."[3]

Klug acknowledges that applying these definitions to real phenomena is by no means always straightforward. But that does not justify the abandonment of what would have been seen as a reasonable consensus definition of antisemitism thirty to forty years ago. And make no mistake, this is also not an argument about semantics, but rather about coming to terms with changing political realities—on the one hand, as Klug does by building on accumulated academic knowledge; on the other hand, as proponents of the concept of the "new antisemitism" do by abandoning almost all of that for reasons of national, ethnic, or religious identification and loyalty, as well as political ideology.

So How and Why Did We Reach This Point?

There was never any basis in fact for Lévy's 2008 prediction. A cursory glance at antisemitism monitoring reports from the time proves that it was an absurd statement to make. Today, with indisputable hard evidence of the persistence of far-right antisemitism in Europe, as well as the revelation of the role of Jew-hatred in the thinking of the Norwegian mass murderer Anders Behring Breivik, Lévy's rhetorical flourish looks even more ridiculous.

One of the main drivers of the discussions that led to formulation of the "new antisemitism" idea was the passing, in 1975, of UN General Assembly Resolution 3379, equating Zionism with racism. (It was revoked in 1991.) Remember that at the time support for Zionism and Israel was still broadly seen as a progressive and liberal cause in the West. Quite a number of the African and non-aligned countries that voted for 3379 had good, if fairly low-key, relations with Israel, a policy Israel's then-socialist government had pursued to improve its international position. So the apparent snub to Israel by these countries and the perception among Jewish and non-Jewish supporters of Israel in the West that Israel was losing its status as a progressive cause provoked much soul-searching and consternation. In Jewish and Israeli circles the dominant response was not to see any flaws in Zionism but rather in those attacking it and Israel, so one of the main questions being asked was: What was the relationship between anti-Zionism and antisemitism?

While some writers, academics, and commentators were convinced from early on that Arab hostility to Zionism and Israel was antisemitic, during the 1970s and 1980s there was considerable debate and reasoned disagreement about the validity of the charge. Political and ideological considerations played a relatively small part in the conferences and seminars increasingly taking place to discuss the issue. But what began largely as a series of intellectual and academic discussions gradually changed character as pro-Israel advocacy groups, the World Zionist Organization, multi-agenda major American Jewish organizations (including the Anti-Defamation League, American Jewish Committee, and American Jewish Congress), and Jewish communal organizations monitoring and combating antisemitism took up the matter. Mounting international criticism of Israel was having a major impact on their work.

What started organically, therefore, morphed into a planned campaign to create a coalition of mostly Jewish activist academics, pro-Israel and national representative bodies in the Jewish Diaspora, and the aforementioned major American Jewish organizations to take the discussions in an increasingly political and ideological direction, linking anti-Zionism and antisemitism ever more closely. A key player in and growing influence on this campaign was the Israeli government, pursuing a new policy since the late 1980s, through its then-recently-established Monitoring Forum on Anti-Semitism. The policy aimed at establishing Israeli hegemony over the monitoring and combating of antisemitism by Jewish groups worldwide. This was coordinated and mostly implemented by Mossad representatives working out of Israeli embassies.

The policy served to bind Diaspora communities more closely to Israel, their self-appointed "defender against external threats"; to promote Zionist immigration by using highly problematic data on antisemitic manifestations to stress the fragility of Diaspora Jewish communities; and to portray Israel as equally in the firing line of antisemitic attack by increasingly linking criticism of Israeli policy with antisemitism.

I had close personal experience of the role the Mossad played in establishing Israeli hegemony over the monitoring and combating of antisemitism. While I was director of the Institute of Jewish Affairs (IJA) and its successor, the Institute for Jewish Policy Research (JPR) in the 1990s, I founded and was principal editor of the annual *Antisemitism World Report*, the first objective, independent, country-by-country survey of antisemitism worldwide. The London Mossad representative dealing with antisemitism made it clear to me that they were very unhappy about our independent operation and then tried to pressure us into either ceasing publication or merging our report with one that the then-new Project for the Study of Antisemitism at Tel Aviv University, headed by Professor Dina Porat and part-financed by the Mossad, was beginning to produce. I vigorously resisted the pressure, as I recalled in my book, *The Making and Unmaking of a Zionist*: "I tried to persuade the Israelis to allow us to operate without interference, but was given short shrift by the Mossad representative at the Israeli embassy in London and by the Israel ambassador [Moshe Raviv] himself," with whom I had met, together with the chairman of the IJA, to discuss the matter in 1994.[4] Notwithstanding, we continued to produce our report and continued to come under pressure from the Mossad. A year or two later, I made a further effort to persuade them to end their attempts to undermine our work—which they were having some success in doing as certain Jewish antisemitism monitoring bodies in other countries succumbed to Mossad demands that they cease to provide us with information about developments in their countries. In 1994 the IJA had severed its connection with the World Jewish Congress and had entered into a relationship with the American Jewish Committee (AJC), which was very keen to be associated with our *Antisemitism World Report*. The head of the AJC's Israel office at that time was Dr. Yossi Alpher, former head of the Jaffee Center for Strategic Studies at Tel Aviv University, but more important, he had been a Mossad officer for twelve years, leaving the agency in the late 1970s. Alpher and I developed a good working relationship and he fully understood the value of the independent antisemitism work we were undertaking. He offered to use his good contacts with the Mossad to broker a meeting between me and the Mossad official responsible for overseeing the agency's role in centralizing global Jewish monitoring and combating of antisemitism. This meeting took place in Tel Aviv, but to no avail. The exchange was polite, but he had absolutely no intention of relaxing pressure on us. We soldiered on, but the obstacles placed in our path proved too onerous to allow us to continue, and publication of our *Report* in book form ceased in 1999.

During the 1990s there was some ambivalence about and opposition to this policy in Diaspora communities, largely because of growing evidence that traditional antisemitism was declining, which meant that effective challenges to "new antisemitism" thinking could still be mounted. Moreover, the policy was suspended by Prime Minister Yitzhak Rabin during the few years of optimism surrounding the 1993 Oslo Accords, as he did not want to be constrained by too close a relationship with the increasingly right-wing American Jewish Israel lobby in negotiations taking place to achieve rapprochement with the Palestinians.

Events in the year before 9/11 already appeared to lend credibility to the idea of the "new antisemitism." The collapse of the Camp David negotiations in July 2000 (presented by Israel and its loyal supporters as a Palestinian betrayal), the outbreak of the second Palestinian intifada in the autumn, and the anti-Israel and anti-Jewish manifestations at the UN Conference on Racism in Durban in August–September 2001 were all explained as evidence of a deeply rooted, extreme, irrational anti-Zionism, seen by pro-Israel loyalists as conclusive proof that Israel was now incontrovertibly the "Jew among the nations." When the Twin Towers were destroyed and the Bush administration moved rapidly to frame its response as declaring "war on terror," it was inevitable that Israel, under the leadership of a national unity government led by Prime Minister Ariel Sharon, would seek to identify itself ever more closely with the United States as a fellow victim of Islamist terror—indeed, as the prior victim. Al-Qaeda's ideology, which, in part, jointly demonized America and Israel, and also Jews in general, provided the Zionist right with even more justification for its argument that the "new antisemitism" now posed the greatest threat to Jews since the Holocaust.

This became the dominant narrative among Jewish and Israeli leaders and the wider and growing neo-conservative commentariat, which included prominent journalists and columnists as well as prominent academics. The Israeli government, reflecting the country's political drift to the far right, was again very publically linking Israel's fate with Jews worldwide and stepping up its leadership role on the antisemitism question, this time with the fuller cooperation of Diaspora Jewish leaders, many of whom were more in sympathy with Israel's harder-line political direction than they were when the country was led by Rabin. In these circles, the "new antisemitism" discourse was now in the ascendant and was rapidly acquiring the status of a new orthodoxy. This was not only in political forums, the media, and public debates, but also at academic conferences and seminars, in academic articles and books. Inevitably, being so intimately connected to a controversial political issue—the Israel-Palestine conflict—discussion of the issue of antisemitism became more politicized than ever before.

Antisemitism was thus recast as principally anti-Israel rhetoric emanating largely from Muslim sources. That rhetoric figured prominently in various forms of media in European countries with relatively large Jewish populations, like France, the United Kingdom, and Germany, and was sometimes directed at Jews because of their support for Israel, but also because Jews and Israelis are often seen as one and the same. This—together with an increase in antisemitic incidents ascribed to Muslim perpetrators—led Jewish establishment leaders to see the Islamist elements in Muslim communities as a direct threat to Jewish security. Some extended that fear to Muslims more generally. Despite the fact that the growing sense of Jewish belonging in Europe in the 1990s stemmed in great part from the success of multiculturalism and the positive influence of the culture of universal human rights, blame for Muslim hostility toward Jews was now put down to multiculturalism's alleged failure to integrate Muslims and the perception that human rights values were being applied to all minorities except Jews. Both were seen as responsible for allowing the unrestrained attack on Israel to proceed unchecked. Add to this the fact that Israeli leaders were only too ready to redefine the Israel-Palestine conflict as a religious war, and it was but a logical step for Israel to come to be seen, in Slavoj Žižek's words, as "the first line of defense against the Muslim expansion."

Meanwhile, the far right had been undergoing a process of self-sanitization: playing down its antisemitic past and distancing itself from Holocaust denial, and refocusing its animus toward immigrants, but Muslims in particular. By the early 2000s, a new far-right strategy emerged, exemplified by the National Alliance (AN) in Italy, the former neo-fascist party headed by Gianfranco Fini, who reached out to the Italian Jewish community to apologize for the party's "former" antisemitism and to express support for Israel, all against the background of a supposed shared understanding that Muslims were now the common enemy.

While some evidence emerged of Jews publicly identifying with far-right groups in France, Austria, and Italy, it never amounted to very much. More significant, however, was the far right's increasingly warm pro-Israel rhetoric, which began to be looked upon favorably by the right-wing Zionist parties in Israel and their sympathizers in the Jewish Diaspora. Geert Wilders, in his capacity as leader of the Dutch populist, anti-Islam Party for Freedom, visited Israel in 2008 and has been back a number of times since. Leaders of four other far-right parties—the Belgian Flemish Interest, the Austrian Freedom Party, the Sweden Democrats, and a new German anti-Islam party, Freedom—visited Israel in late 2010 and were warmly received by settler leaders and other far-right Zionist politicians. And yet these parties had by no means abandoned their antisemitic roots.

Although the far right in America does not have political representation of the kind found in Europe, the same anti-Muslim, Israel-loving, anti-liberal, deeply reactionary phenomenon is highly prominent in the powerful evangelical Christian organizations, which play such a major role in influencing political debate and policy, and in some very influential sectors of the Republican Party. Many American Jewish Zionist leaders have welcomed evangelical support for Israel, ignoring its apocalyptic eschatology and its rigid adherence to the necessity of the fundamental disposability of Jews to bring about the Second Coming. This acceptance that support for Israel and Zionism trumps any underlying, if muted, antisemitism is made easier for sectors of the American Jewish community because Israel's government and most Israeli politicians see this Christian Zionism as an almost unalloyed benefit to Israel's defense of its position in the Middle East and internationally.

It has become quite clear that in the battle against what right-wing populists see as the creeping Islamization of Europe, Israel is on the front line. But it's not only right-wing populists in America and Europe who see Israel playing this role. A mélange of Jewish and non-Jewish columnists, public intellectuals, think tank specialists, and mainstream politicians, who would firmly reject being labeled "far right," express similar views and harsh criticism of the Muslim community for not tackling the extreme hostility toward Jews and Israel found in its midst. This kind of alliance can be found in America, the United Kingdom, France, and elsewhere.

The parties in Israel's governing coalition have been encouraged by the range of anti-Islam forces lining up behind the state. They have seen this as giving external backing to far-right Zionism's ideological project to put anti-democratic bills before the Knesset designed to reinforce the exclusively Jewish character of the state, brand Palestinian citizens of Israel as the internal enemy if they don't accept Israel as the Jewish state, restrict the activities of human rights groups, undermine academic freedom, and curtail freedom of speech. The failure of supposedly more moderate political leaders and of the parliamentary system as a whole to turn back this mounting anti-democratic tide has led respected commentators, academics, and former military and security personnel to see the growth of deeply disturbing signs of incipient fascism.

Many Israel-supporting Jews with progressive political views now find themselves between a rock and a hard place. As supporters of a two-state solution to the Israel-Palestine conflict and opposed to settlements and the occupation, finding themselves in the company of the far right is the last thing they would have expected, whether in Europe, America, or in Israel. And yet many such Jews are convinced that the threat of a left-wing-plus-Islamist "new antisemitism" is severe, and in maintaining their Zionism or pro-Israelism, they are merely stuck with unsavory allies. Some Jews have simply chosen to cut themselves loose from their traditional progressive moorings. Others, who simply refuse to join the anti-Muslim bandwagon and reject the post-9/11 Clash of Civilizations "you're either with us or against us" type of choice they feel they are faced with, are left high and dry. If they consider allying themselves with dissenting Jews who have doubts about or reject Zionism, reject the "new antisemitism" thesis, and refuse to put support for the policies of an occupying power above the human rights of an occupied people, they are liable to face the hatred and vilification of Zionists whose arguments contain more than a hint of "some antisemitic logic." As Žižek writes: "Their ... figure of the Jew ... is constructed in the same way as the European antisemites constructed the figures of the Jew—he is dangerous because he lives among us, but is not really one of us."[5]

From very early on in the development of the Zionist movement, Jewish opponents of Zionism were attacked using antisemitic stereotypes. For example, when Theodor Herzl, the founder of modern political Zionism, angered by anti-Zionists, painted the weak ghetto Jew, in his 1897 essay "Mauschel," as the bad Jew who speaks with a Yiddish accent, a "scamp," "a distortion of the human character, unspeakably mean and repellent," interested only in "mean profit," he was using antisemitic attributes. To a great degree the use of such demonizing language largely disappeared from mainstream intra-Jewish discourse because Zionism appeared to achieve such hegemonic dominance among Jews everywhere. But as dissenting views became more prominent in the last twenty to thirty years, so the language used to attack dissidents became ever more strident, once again appropriating antisemitic phraseology, as in, for example, the right-wing British columnist Melanie Phillips's description of the founding signatories of Independent

Jewish Voices as "Jews for genocide." Zionists have always understood full well that antisemitism helped advance the cause, even as they promoted Zionism as the solution to the scourge of antisemitism. Exploiting this dualism today is absolutely central to far-right Zionist ideology and to right-wing Zionism's Jewish and non-Jewish fellow travelers.

It should be clear by now that where the "new antisemitism" label is applied to criticism of Zionism or where anti-Zionism is described as "bigotry against Jews," what those who speak in defense of Zionism mean by it varies greatly. Their definitions may be simplistic, as in "support for the existence of the Jewish state of Israel." They may emphasize its political and ideological sub-movements, each signified by a prefix to the word "Zionism": "labor-," "socialist-," "revisionist-," "religious-," "cultural-," "liberal-," etc. They may stress its quest for freedom: "the national liberation movement of the Jewish people." Or prioritize the connection with the Jewish Diaspora: "the principle that the state of Israel belongs not only to its citizens but to the entire Jewish people." While there may be some partial historical relevance to some of these definitions, and others may reflect what many Jews feel about their connection to Israel, they ignore Zionism's actual historical trajectory and what it has become. In reality, one form of Zionism triumphed, marginalizing all others: the political Zionism promoted by David Ben-Gurion (and many other Zionist leaders), Israel's first prime minister, who struggled to create a sovereign Jewish state in historic Palestine. But once this was achieved, Zionism did not stop there. Creating a sovereign Jewish state turned out to be—some would argue that it always was—an ongoing project, taking on a religious, messianic, and increasingly open right-wing, ethnocentric character that required the continuous dispossession of the indigenous inhabitants, the Palestinians, both within the pre-1967 borders and in the occupied Palestinian territories. Whether the path of maximalist nationalism and settler colonialism this Zionism has taken was inevitable from the beginning is open to discussion, though both aspects of Zionism were present from the inception of the modern Zionist movement. But the key point here is that this Zionism is the only form of Zionism that has any agency today, making irrelevant all the constructions of Zionism by those who propagate "new antisemitism" theory, which are designed to spread the net of the "new antisemitism" ever more widely. As even the prominent liberal Zionist Peter Beinart, former editor of the *New Republic*, acknowledges, bigotry is what characterizes today's Zionism: it denies Palestinians the right to vote, it denies them the right to live under the same law as Jews, it strives for permanent control over them and opposes Palestinian statehood or any kind of genuine Palestinian national self-determination. Deflecting perfectly legitimate criticism of and vociferous opposition to this viewpoint by labeling it "antisemitism" simply won't wash.

Understanding the Wider Context Is Crucial

Since 9/11, the growing popularization of the redefinition of antisemitism as hostility to the State of Israel has given license to Jews and Zionists to act according to the maxim "My enemy's enemy is my friend." The forging of links between the Israeli far right and Islamophobic far right groups in Europe, embracing the position of Israel as the front line against the Islamization of Europe, turning a blind eye to the antisemitism of Christian Zionism, entrenching the exclusivity of Jewish nationalism in Israeli law, and demonizing Jewish dissenters using antisemitic rhetoric have all been made possible by placing Israel at the heart of what is considered antisemitism today. It is all of a piece with the ethno-national and ethno-religious exclusivism that was part of Zionist ideology from the beginning of political Zionism.

Today, the redefinition of antisemitism is proving of great value in Israel's pushback against the Boycott, Divestment and Sanctions (BDS) movement, a nonviolent means of pressuring Israel to abide by international law. By constantly branding BDS as antisemitic, using the argument that "it's boycotting Jews just like the Nazis boycotted Jews in the 1930s," the Israeli government, its propaganda machine, Zionist organizations, Israel advocacy groups, and leaders of Jewish communal organizations exploit continued public sensitivity to accusations of antisemitism and in the process seek to delegitimize groups working for a just solution to the Israel-Palestine conflict. They are also shameless in turning murderous jihadi attacks on Western targets, in which there is often an element of violent ideological Jew-hatred as experienced tragically by Jews in France, Belgium, India and elsewhere, into proxy attacks on Israel, claiming that the "Jewish state" is the real jihadi target and that Israel is therefore in the front line in defending "Western civilization" against this onslaught.

In the day-to-day struggle against the abuse of antisemitism, understanding and drawing attention to this wider context is crucial. A great deal is at stake.

There *are* instances when a discourse critical of Israel and Zionism displays clear antisemitic characteristics, but the wholesale redefinition of antisemitism that turns Israel into "the Jew among the nations" makes it impossible to maintain any distinction between legitimate criticism and the negative stereotyping of Jews, which using the symbols and images associated with classic antisemitism to characterize Israel or Israelis amounts to.

There are very worrying signs of the persistence and intensification of traditional antisemitism. For example: the rise of openly antisemitic political parties such as Golden Dawn in Greece and Jobbik in Hungary; indications that the new or sanitized far-right, populist Islamophobic parties have Jews in their sights too; continuing high levels of antisemitic sentiment in some countries; broader anti-migrant feeling leading to more mainstream parties and authoritarian regimes deploying a more nationalist, exclusivist, Christian rhetoric inimical to minorities in general, Jews included. The defense minister in the new right-wing Polish government thinks that *The Protocols of the Elders of Zion*, the tsarist antisemitic forgery, is probably genuine. Given these developments, the unjustified exclusive stress on Israel as the principal or only target of antisemites today is therefore dangerous for Jewish populations across the globe.

Serious, high-level monitoring and analysis of current antisemitism—or for that matter also Islamophobia, anti-Black racism, and so on—is fundamentally important for a healthy liberal society. But what the redefinition of antisemitism has done is virtually destroy the possibility of maintaining objective academic discussion of the problem. Certain highly influential American, European, and Israeli entities—the so-called academic institutes, think tanks, self-styled Jewish human rights groups, and defense organizations—dealing with current antisemitism are deeply infected with Zionist ideological and political bias and exist principally to promote new antisemitism theory. While there are some bona fide, objective institutions researching antisemitism, their work and the entire field is overshadowed by the propagandistic, Israel-focused, Islamophobic public advocacy of the others.

Reverberations of the degradation of scholarly approaches to contemporary antisemitism have extended far and wide. A detailed study published in May 2015 by JPR, respected as an independent think tank of the British Jewish community, slams the Jewish authorities for being responsible for the absence of "professionalism, objectivity[,] expertise," and "definitional clarity" in attempts to make sense of the recent distressing antisemitic manifestations in France and the United Kingdom. There's no "intelligible plan to inform [Jews] about what they should actually do." In such circumstances, conclude the authors, no progress can be made in "policy development" to confront the threat. I would argue that the Jewish authorities' intense and almost exclusive focus on the "new antisemitism," evident in other countries too, is largely responsible for this situation since plans to combat it essentially involve shoring up Israel advocacy, not dealing with actual reasons for the antisemitic manifestations to which the JPR refers.[6]

Finally, we can now see with great clarity how the emergence of "new antisemitism" theory was central to Israel's steady shift to the right from the 1970s onwards. The eventual domination of messianic, ethno-religious Zionism, which placed exclusive control of Israel/Palestine from the Mediterranean to the Jordan at the center of an illiberal, authoritarian ongoing national project that has developed an increasingly fascistic character, required a narrative of endless external threat to the security, demographic viability, and national culture of the state. A distorted and manipulative use of Jewish history—centuries of antisemitic persecution, pogroms, but principally the Holocaust—was pressed into service to justify colonization and unending repression of the Palestinians. The result has been increasing defensiveness, a strengthening sense of Jewish victimhood, a disdain for the complex situation of Jewish populations around the world, and even more reliance on an America that the Netanyahu government has made clear it does not trust. This is a high price to pay for treating as a victory the undermining of the shared understanding of what constitutes antisemitism.

Palestinian Activism and Christian Antisemitism in the Church

Walt Davis

This essay focuses primarily on the role of Christian beliefs in generating and perpetuating anti-semitism. However, the essay concludes by citing some of the most egregious Christian actions against Jews throughout the centuries, actions that directly flowed from those beliefs.—Eds.

Unjust social systems are sustained by false narratives that justify and fuel separation, prejudice, discrimination, and violence. Contemporary narratives that rationalize racial and ethnic strife around the world may be too numerous to list, but surely Western Christian antisemitism must be placed at the top of any list. How ironic that the Zionist narrative, which sustains Israel's conquest of Palestine, originated in response to the lethal Christian narrative.

After World War II, some liberal Christians began major theological revisions in response to the Holocaust. Two of these revisions remain in conflict with each other. The first is a firm repudiation of the doctrine of *supercessionism* (the idea that in Christ God had replaced the "old covenant" with the Jews by a "new covenant" with the church). The second is a reinterpretation of certain biblical texts so as to endorse modern political Zionism at the expense of justice for Palestinians.

Palestinian solidarity activists believe it is essential to support practical tactics such as the nonviolent Boycott, Divestment and Sanctions (BDS) movement to end the occupation and anti-Palestinian discrimination. I believe it is also necessary to refute both the Christian ideological narrative that fuels antisemitism and the Zionist ideological narrative that drives the oppression of Palestinians and makes BDS necessary. In fact, our work in the pursuit of justice requires that we help birth a new narrative for *all* the Abraham-ic faiths—one that moves beyond exceptionalism and "othering"[1]—because some elements in all three religious narratives continue to fuel injustice and violence against outsiders.

Is Antisemitism in the Eye of the Beholder?

In late 2014, a small group of rabbis and Presbyterian pastors began meeting periodically to discuss reactions by rabbis and members of their congregations to the June 2014 decision of the Presbyterian Church (U.S.A.) to divest from Caterpillar Inc., Hewlett Packard, and Motorola Solutions. The rabbis reported that many of their congregants think that Presbyterians are anti-Jewish.

After several meetings listening to the rabbis' objections to the divestment decision, one of the pastors laid out the Presbyterian case for nonviolent resistance in the form of divestment, citing decades of brutal and systemic violation of Palestinian human rights. The moderator asked the rabbis how this explanation of the case for divestment made them feel. One rabbi responded, "It makes me afraid." Other rabbis nodded in agreement.

Palestine activists often experience accusations of antisemitism as deliberate maneuvers to silence criticism of Israel and stifle solidarity with the Palestinian movement for equality. This interpretation is not farfetched. There is plenty of evidence to support the claim that some mainstream Jewish organizations *do* use false charges of antisemitism to silence criticism of Israel.[2] Members of these same organizations sometimes justify any and all actions by the State of Israel, no matter how egregious, as necessary for Israeli security and Jewish survival.

However, in the case of the Jewish-Presbyterian dialogue described above, a different understanding of the fear expressed by the rabbis is suggested by philosopher Martha Nussbaum. Emotions, Nussbaum declares, are *narrative-dependent*. "Emotions are not feelings that well up in some natural and untutored way from our natural selves. . . . We learn our emotions in the same way that we learn our beliefs—from society. . . . They are taught, above all, through stories. . . . Emotion itself is the acceptance of, the assent to live according to, a certain sort of story."[3] In other words, the fear prompted in the rabbis by the discussion of the BDS movement can be seen as an emotion that has been learned over time by internalizing the dominant narratives to which they have been exposed over the course of their lives.

Nussbaum's insight into the deep connection between emotions and beliefs does not mean that the stories we live by are innocent or value-neutral. We are not excused from examining the ethical consequences of our personal and social narratives. However, an ethical critique of our inherited narratives is very difficult when the dominant narrative is persistently reinforced by our primary community, the community in which we want to feel a sense of belonging and inclusion.

Important questions arise from the recognition of the interdependence of stories and emotions. What is antisemitism? Are some definitions of antisemitism subjective and relative, existing "in the eye of the beholder"? Is fear embedded in every personal and social identity when the collective narrative and political system reserves rights and privileges for the in-group that are denied to out-groups? If the stories we live by are so fragile that we must defend them with dogmatic fundamentalism while refusing to examine their consequences for other peoples, do the stories themselves enhance or diminish us?

Western Christian Antisemitism

Even if some antisemitism is subjective, the sordid history of Western Christian antisemitism provides much evidence that Christian antisemitism has been a vicious objective reality composed of forced separation, prejudice, discrimination, and violence against Jews in general. Political Zionism emerged in the nineteenth century largely as a response to the fear produced by this centuries-long collective Jewish experience.

Three theological doctrines within the Christian narrative have been used to justify and inflame violence against Jews throughout the centuries. These doctrines illustrate a poisonous tendency in Christianity and perhaps in many faith traditions: when political or religious institutions sacralize conflict by defining it as the will of God, some followers of that faith lose all moral constraints on violent human inclinations.

Early Christian-Jewish Conflict

The early Jesus movement was entirely Jewish, centered in Jerusalem, firmly rooted in Jewish law, and located in temple-based worship. This began to change in the mid-30s CE,[4] when Saul of Tarsus, a Pharisee and persecutor of the Jesus movement, converted to Christianity and became Paul, "the apostle to the gentiles." Paul established Christian congregations in many parts of the Roman Empire as well as in Rome itself. As Christianity established itself outside Palestine, it became Hellenized, losing some of its Jewish roots.

Judaism and Christianity each taught that its believers (and no others) belonged to the one, true, chosen people of God. The two religions competed with each other for members, often using inflammatory accusations against each other. When Christians gained access to imperial power in the early fourth century under the Emperor Constantine, the exceptionalist claims of Christianity proved lethal for Jews as well as for those Christians whom the church deemed heretics.

Deicide

If Jesus is the Son of God, as Christians claimed, then killing Jesus was equivalent to killing God. "You killed the one who made you live. Why did you do this, O Israel?" wrote Mileto, the bishop of Sardis, in the mid-second century. Bishop Mileto was referring to Matthew's version of the life of Jesus. According to Matthew 27:25, during the trial of Jesus, Pilate judged Jesus to be innocent of the charges against him, but the people demanded his execution, declaring, "His [Jesus'] blood be upon us and upon our children." Over the centuries the accusation of deicide has served as a major pretext for the persecution and slaughter of Jews by Christians.

Replacement of the "Old" Covenant
with a "New" Covenant

From the earliest times the Jesus movement claimed that Jesus of Nazareth was the long-awaited messiah, and that in him God had fulfilled the "old" covenant made with Abraham and Moses, and replaced it with a "new" covenant. Thus, Christians had replaced Jews as God's chosen people. In his letter to the Philippians (2:9-11) written from prison in Rome about 62 CE, Paul incorporated a confession of faith used widely in worship by early first-century Christian communities: "God has highly exalted him [Jesus] and bestowed on him the name which is above every name, that at the name of Jesus every knee should bow ... and every tongue confess that Jesus Christ is Lord."

Some forty years later the writer of the gospel of John placed a similar claim in the mouth of Jesus himself: "I am the way, the truth, and the life. No one comes to the Father except through me" (John 14:6). In the mid-third century, Cyprian, bishop of Carthage, institutionalized this claim by declaring *extra ecclesiam nulla salus* (outside the church there is no salvation). For centuries this doctrine would justify and inflame witch-hunts, pogroms, and wars against Jews and others who remained outside the dominant church.

In the beginning this exceptionalist Christian claim may not have been very threatening to Jews, who at the time had much more socioeconomic power than Christians within cities throughout the Roman Empire. However, the security of Jewish communities suffered a major blow in the early fourth century when the Emperor Constantine had a vision: if he turned the cross of Christ into a weapon of conquest, he could conquer his enemies and unite the empire under one religious ideology. Soon after Constantine consolidated imperial power, Jews were forbidden to proselytize. Later, Jewish proselytizing became a crime punishable by death.

God's Punishment of the Jewish People

By the early fifth century some influential church leaders, including Bishop Ambrose of Milan, were "openly concluding that the ... continued existence [of Jews] could no longer be justified."[5] Augustine, bishop of the important Roman city of Hippo in North Africa (and the most influential Christian theologian in the entire history of the church), publicly opposed his mentor Ambrose. "Do not slay them," Augustine admonished. Jews are dispersed by God, he said, "as witnesses to the prophesies which were given beforehand concerning Christ. . . . God himself protects them." Jews, Augustine taught, must be allowed to survive but never thrive. Their backs must be "bent down always."[6] Therein lay the Augustinian catch-22: the Hebrew Scriptures [the Old Testament] provide proof of Christianity's divine origin. Jews deny the divinity of Christ because they are blinded by God and, therefore, punished by God. At the same time their universal state of misery serves a higher purpose by warning others against rejecting the Christian God.

Augustine's position became the official position of the Western church from the fifth to the twentieth century, reiterated from time to time by numerous theologians and church officials. When Theodor Herzl convened the First Zionist Congress in Basel in 1897, a prominent Christian periodical commented: "According to the sacred Scriptures, the Jewish people must always live dispersed and wander among the nations, so that they may render witness to Christ not only by their Scriptures . . . but by their very existence."[7] The Augustinian theological rationale justifying the humiliation, impoverishment, and persecution of Jews was not formally retracted until the Second Vatican Council in 1965, when the insidious role of Christian antisemitism in the perpetration of the Nazi Holocaust was generally recognized.

Two Modern Forms of Christian Disrespect for Jews and Judaism[8]

Christian Zionism has roots in seventeenth-century Protestant theology. In our time it takes two major forms. The first is conservative and fundamentalist; the second is liberal and interfaith. Both appear on the surface to be strongly pro-Jewish.

The most visible contemporary spokesman for the fundamentalist brand of Christian Zionism is Rev. John Hagee, founder of Christians United for Israel (CUFI). In spite of CUFI's substantial political and financial support of Israel, these Zionists have little intrinsic appreciation of Jews or Judaism.[9] Instead they regard the State of Israel as an instrument of God to hasten the eschatological End Time when Jesus will return to earth for the final judgment. On Judgment Day Jews who opt for Jesus will go to heaven while those who remain Jews will be relegated to hell.

A liberal Protestant form of Christian Zionism also provides uncritical theological and political support for the State of Israel, but for different reasons.[10] Stung by guilt and shame for the Christian contribution to the Holocaust, liberal Christian Zionists have embraced a pro-Israel historical narrative and concentrate on building friendly relationships with Jewish neighbors in the United States. In the past this has required silence in regard to Israel's treatment of Palestinians, thus abandoning the prophetic task of justice that is central to both Judaism and Christianity. Neither of these expressions discriminates against Jews; neither threatens bodily harm; but I would argue that both are deeply disrespectful of Jews and Judaism and in that sense verge on being antisemitic.

Recently we have begun to see signs of more authentic interfaith dialogue, including mutual accountability and support for a single standard of human rights applicable to all peoples.

Repudiating Religious and Nationalist Exceptionalism[11]

In the first section above, we examined the subjective and relativist dimension of accusations of antisemitism and identified their source in emotions derived from narratives of personal and collective identity. This does not mean that because some definitions of antisemitism are "in the eyes of the beholder," they are innocent or without atrocious consequences. Some definitions of antisemitism can perpetuate objective forms of oppression. The report by JVP entitled *Stifling Dissent* documents the well-organized campaign to silence criticism of Israel on US campuses, thereby undermining freedom at home as well as in Israel itself.[12]

If emotions rest upon beliefs, as Nussbaum claims, "then they can be modified by a modification of belief."[13] New emotions actually *require* new narratives.

Only a Christian narrative that is free of exceptionalism, then, will bring an end to the theological roots of Christian antisemitism. The same applies to Zionist and Islamist narratives that justify and fuel prejudice, discrimination, and violence. For decades, theological as well as political forms of exceptionalism have been evident in the role of US and Israeli public policy vis-à-vis support for the occupation and the dispossession of Palestinians from their ancestral lands.

As a response to the horror of World War II, a universalist narrative based on equal rights for all peoples (and for every person) has gradually taken root in the consciousness of humanity. Legal frameworks were built following the war—the International Declaration of Human Rights, the Geneva Conventions, international treaties, and international law. Economic and cultural globalization and the end of colonialism around the world have ushered in a welcome alternative to the historic theologies of particularism, an alternative that does not nullify the variety of human identities but expands them within a larger form of universal human identity. This new narrative rejects exceptionalism and the othering of persons and groups who are different from those who hold economic, political, and cultural power. Most religious traditions retain a mix of conflicting narratives, some stressing our common humanity, others claiming special privilege for the "chosen." The new narrative has grown out of the ashes of war and blossomed by drawing upon both religious and secular traditions of commonality and universality. The Israel-Palestine Mission Network of the Presbyterian Church (U.S.A.) was mandated by the denomination to "engage, consolidate, nurture, and channel the energy of the Presbyterian Church (U.S.A.) toward the goal of a just peace in Israel/Palestine." The Mission Network recognizes that this mandate includes combating Christian antisemitism and all other forms of ethnic and religious discrimination. The Network has stated:

> Although contemporary Christians are not responsible for the sins of our spiritual ancestors, we are responsible for combating the perpetuation of those sins in our time. Genuine reconciliation between Christians and Jews requires the recognition and vigorous renunciation of Christian anti-Jewish rhetoric and behavior. This task includes developing sensitivity to hearing some of the texts within the Bible itself as examples of anti-Jewish rhetoric and being careful in the congregation's worship and work to examine and correct how those texts are taught and understood."[14]

Today our task is to recognize that in an interdependent global community, exceptionalist ideologies and emotions have outlived any usefulness they may have once had. It is time to replace narrow, exclusive ideologies with inclusive religious and national narratives. Rabbi Brant Rosen, cofounder and former cochair of the Rabbinical Council of Jewish Voice for Peace, has provided a simple screen for identifying and correcting the exceptionalist narratives embedded in our scriptures and worship liturgies. Rosen writes: "To put it plainly, a voice that affirms claims of theological superiority in the name of one people cannot be the voice of God."[15]

To apply this screen to civic, national, and international declarations and ceremonies, it need be modified only very slightly: "To put it plainly, a voice that affirms claims of superiority or special privilege in the name of one people cannot be just or true."

For adherents of the Abrahamic faiths, the task of reforming our narratives will not be easy, but we must nevertheless rise to the challenge with energy, creativity, and compassion. The alternative is never-ending animosity and violence.

Christian Atrocities against Jews through the Centuries

Narratives contain beliefs about insiders and outsiders that religious and political authorities transform into doctrines, which they then teach and enforce. Over time these doctrines morph into popular dogmas about the nature of reality itself. In times of stress the dogmas provide intellectual and emotional motivation for the use of righteous violence against outsiders. The following examples demonstrate a pattern of Christian antisemitism from the earliest days of Christianity until now. These and dozens of other Christian atrocities against Jews over the centuries are described in greater detail in the award-winning book by James Carroll entitled *Constantine's Sword.*

414 CE: A Christian pogrom in Alexandria wipes out the Jewish community.

429: The Jewish patriarchate of Israel is abolished by order of Rome.

694: Building on the teaching of Augustine of Hippo, a church council in Toledo declares Jews should be "subject to perpetual serfdom."

1096: Pope Urban II launches the First Crusade to recapture Jerusalem, which Muslims had conquered three and a half centuries earlier. A hundred thousand volunteers signed up to go to battle wearing the sign of the cross in order to purge the Holy Land of infidels and heretics.

The first group of "others" to be targeted were Jews throughout the Rhineland. These were Europe's first large-scale pogroms. In 1096 five to ten thousand Jews were killed at fourteen different sites in the Rhineland. Church law required bishops and popes to protect the lives of Jews. But Christian mobs often ignored the pleas of church officials. Over a thousand Jews who sought protection in the courtyard of the archbishop of Mainz committed suicide rather than submit to the mayhem of the mobs.

1099: Marauding Crusaders herded Jews into a synagogue in Jerusalem, then burned them alive.

In his letter to the people of England, Bernard of Clairvaux, who would become the organizer of the Second Crusade, echoed the catch-22 of Augustine: "The Jews are for us the living words of scripture, for they remind us always of what our Lord suffered. They are dispersed all over the world so that by expiating their crime they may be everywhere the living witnesses of our redemption. . . . If the Jews are utterly wiped out, what will become of our hope for their promised salvation, their eventual conversion?" [16]

1144: In England Jews are accused of "blood libel" (ritual murder of a Christian child, followed by the use of the child's blood in perverse rituals to mock the Christian Eucharist). Like a virus, similar accusations were made elsewhere in 1147, 1168, 1171, 1182, "and again and again after that, all over Europe, and even into the twentieth century."[17]

1146: The Second Crusade is launched. Callixtus II issues a papal bull, *Sicut Judaeis*, forbidding the use of violence to force Jews to convert. Over the next four centuries, twenty popes would find it necessary to reissue *Sicut Judaeis*. But among the people, Christian teaching like that of Augustine and Bernard undermined these papal bulls.

In Bohemia in **1163,** Breslau in **1226,** and Vienna in **1267,** Jews were accused of poisoning wells. In **1321** they were accused of a conspiracy to poison every well in France. Many were burned at the stake and all Jews were expelled from Paris.

The Inquisition

1215: The Fourth Lateran Council resolves to eliminate heresy.

1231: Pope Gregory sets up roving Dominican and Franciscan courts designed to try people for heresy.

1242: An edict requires Jews to attend the proselytizing sermons of Dominicans and Franciscans, and the Talmud is burned in Paris.

1252: A decree by Pope Innocent IV permits torture.

1302: The papal bull *Unam Sanctam* repeats the formula of the Council of Nicaea in 325: the Church is "one, holy, catholic, and apostolic." Now the ideology and the institutions of absolutism are in place.

1349: The Black Plague is attributed to well-poisoning by Jews. The Plague killed twenty to twenty-five million people (one-third of the European population) including Jews; nevertheless, Jews were the scapegoats. In response, some three hundred Jewish communities were wiped out. The mobs "merely acted out in practice a hatred which the church taught in theory."[18]

June 1391: Rabble-rousing sermons by Ferrant Martinez of Seville led to the massacre of hundreds of Jews and the conversion of synagogues into churches.

Hundreds more were killed in Valencia in July and in Barcelona in August. Pogroms spread to dozens of other cities throughout the Iberian Peninsula.

1492: After decades of violence, Ferdinand and Isabella order the expulsion of Jews from Castile and Aragon. "We have been informed by the Inquisitors . . . that the mingling of Jews with Christians leads to the worst of evils. . . . The only efficacious means to put an end to these evils consists in . . . [the] expulsion [of Jews] from our kingdom."[19]

During the Protestant Reformation:

In **1523** Martin Luther condemns the inhuman treatment of Jews and urges Christians to treat them kindly, hoping they would convert to Christianity. However, in **1543**, toward the end of his life, Luther wrote an essay entitled *On the Jews and Their Lies*, declaring that the Jews are a "base, whoring people, that is, no people of God, and their boast of lineage, circumcision, and law must be accounted as filth." He also wrote, "Their synagogues and schools [should] be set on fire, their prayer books destroyed, rabbis forbidden to preach, homes razed, and property and money confiscated."[20]

Seventeenth to Nineteenth Centuries: Certain Reformed theologians become obsessed with the doctrine of predestination. Distinctions between the saved and the damned reinforce doctrines of Christian exceptionalism in some Presbyterian seminaries and congregations.

1930s–1940s: Nazi officials use earlier Christian declarations of antisemitism as propaganda to support the "Final Solution."

1965: The Second Vatican Council of the Roman Catholic Church adopts *Nostra aetate* (Declaration on the Relationship of the Church to Non-Christian Religions). Implicitly, this declaration rejects the official Augustinian doctrine of antisemitism mentioned above.[21]

The history of Western Christian antisemitism is deep and wide. It was a major cause of the Holocaust. Today, Christians must not only admit this inheritance, but also struggle to rid the present of the biblical, theological, and liturgical sources that provided an excuse for antisemitism and all forms of the othering of those who are not Christian. One example of current attempts to deal with these issues is the annual Hosanna Preaching Seminars for clergy, sponsored jointly by the Israel-Palestine Mission Network of the Presbyterian Church (U.S.A.), Friends of Sabeel–North America, and Kairos USA.[22]

Black and Palestinian Lives Matter: Black and Jewish America in the Twenty-First Century

Chanda Prescod-Weinstein

We ought never forget that there are Jews who do not like blacks and blacks who do not like Jews. Ignoring this reality, and refusing to fight against it, allows its eventual development into terrifying final solutions. . . . But the recent American obsession with anti-Semitism from blacks seems more and more to be a deliberate attempt to avoid and obscure the nightmare of white supremacy in this country.
—Julian Bond, "Introduction," *Strangers & Neighbors: Relations between Blacks & Jews in the United States*

In the American context, the most ironical thing about Negro anti-Semitism is that the Negro is really condemning the Jew for having become an American white man—for having become, in effect, a Christian. . . . One must ask oneself, if one decides that black or white or Jewish people are, by definition, to be despised, is one willing to murder a black or white or Jewish baby: for that is where the position leads.
—James Baldwin, "Negroes Are Anti-Semitic Because They're Anti-White," *Black Anti-Semitism and Jewish Racism*

One and The Other

One day I might be listening to white Jewish members of my temple condescend to a Black visitor who has spoken to us about Black community struggle, the next I am arguing with some Black people about inappropriate comments and assumptions about Jewish people. The biases against Jews that Black non-Jews inherited from Christian Europeans can make for awkward and painful family gatherings. Two years ago, my husband and I gave up membership in an otherwise liberal temple in part because the temple president's husband attacked me for saying that the outcome of the Trayvon

Martin trial reflected a racist America and not just a racist Florida. A Black Jew knows that there is no winning on either side of this prejudice, just different levels of losing.

Not all Jews are white. Not all Blacks are gentiles.[1] For those of us who are Black and Jewish, these facts are painfully obvious, but to those outside of this intersection, we are often invisible. As the likely victims of both anti-Jewish and anti-Black racism, Black Jews bear the brunt of knowing the simultaneous reality and fear of both. Black Jews uniquely know well that anti-minority prejudice of any kind is a danger that can translate into deathly violence.

Indeed, a quick Google search of my name will pull up as a top-ten search result the headline "MIT Jew Fellow Attacks Whites, Foundations of America." The caption under my photo in this "article" on a neo-Nazi website says, "Chanda Prescod-Weinstein: The new voice of Black America has a hooked nose." When articles like this were first being circulated, my inbox was filled with e-mails about Blacks and Jews. "Hitler should have finished the job," I was told by someone who is presumably a gentile. A local white Jewish lawyer e-mailed to say I was an embarrassment to Jews everywhere. Another email was an essay about the destructive presence of Jews in society.

Eventually I was forced to seek advice about personal security measures. Is it because I'm Black or is it because I'm Jewish? It is clear from the e-mails that it is because of both.

Even so, I have never feared that I would be a victim of everyday American state violence because of my Jewish identity. I have always feared that anti-Blackness would be the reason that I or someone in my family would be killed by police or a vigilante acting with the state's blessing. In an incident in front of my house, a white man was threatening to call the police on our Black FedEx delivery man for no reason—in essence a threat of state-sanctioned violence at his behest—and this had me fearing for my safety and that of the FedEx employee, not because I am Jewish but because we are both visibly brown-skinned and curly haired.

Many self-identifying liberal Americans naively assumed that the election of Barack Obama meant the United States is no longer a white supremacist state. Unfortunately, the continued mandate of white supremacy in our nation is unquestionable, and not only because of the subsequent election of a presidential candidate who won on a primarily racist platform and ran a campaign led by an explicit white supremacist. Interactions with the state and state violence prove the case that the country operates as one that works in the best interests of whites, most especially rich ones, and not for the interests of Blacks or, for example, Native Americans such as the Standing

Rock Sioux Tribe. A poor white woman can point a gun at the police, tell them to shoot her, and live. Meanwhile, a Black man can try to walk away from the police and be shot eighteen times, most of the shots taken after he is lying on the ground bleeding out. The American power structures identify with white people, not Black people. We call this white supremacy. For a nation with a diverse population to identify as being the representative of only one citizen group is to engage in a form of supremacy. In the "democratic" Jewish State of Israel, Jewish supremacy reigns. Israel's sole identification with its Jewish citizens—by self-identifying as the Jewish state—is a form of supremacy akin to American white supremacy.

Therefore, it is impossible to describe the relations between Jewish and Black people without making Israel and Palestine a major point of reference. Recent discourse about anti-Semitism on college campuses has reproduced old narratives about non-Jewish Black American anti-Jewish prejudice (aJP).[2] But any discussion of aJP must recognize that Jewish supremacy—in the form of Zionism applied to the State of Israel—enables the reproduction of anti-Jewishness. Israel has significantly shaped Jewish American identity both through the promise of Right of Return (or as it is commonly known, *aliyah*) and through the way white Jews have interacted with the Zionist[3] state's discourse about race and belonging. These forces have also shaped the boundaries of Jewish and Black co-solidarity in the last eighty years.

If we allow Zionist Jewish supremacy to succeed in its anti-Palestinian project, it empowers and legitimizes the fundamental concept of supremacy, which in turn endangers Blacks in the face of white supremacy, a hateful structure that has and ultimately will continue to target white Jews as well.[4] Anything that gives energy to the idea that supremacy is ever appropriate always puts those of us who are minorities at risk. Blacks and white Jews therefore must, for the sake of all our lives, work together to combat supremacy, whether it is white, Jewish, or anti-Jewish.

The Tent of Whiteness

One must be wary of the ways in which the prejudices that we are socialized into help us to magnify the problematic behavior of a few, or those on the fringe, in order to assign their beliefs to an entire people. Treating any ethnic or racial group as a monolith is itself a fundamentally prejudiced analytic starting point. White Jews often treat Black people in this manner when addressing non-Jewish Black anti-Jewish prejudice. There are legitimate critiques of Black aJP: for example, when considering the views and actions of the Nation of Islam (NoI). On the other hand, the existence of the NoI and any other Black purveyors of aJP must be distinguished from legitimate criticism of the Zionist State of Israel by Blacks expressing solidarity with Palestinians.

The easy thing to say is that Jews and Blacks are equally capable of harboring prejudice toward one another. It's harder, especially for white Jews, to acknowledge that white supremacy changes the power dynamics associated with those prejudices. James Baldwin's query about murdering Jewish babies can be contextualized by the analysis of Julius Lester, who is a Black Jew: "In America Jews became white because there existed a people called Blacks."[5] My parents were afraid to introduce me to my dad's grandfather, an escapee from Polish anti-Jewish pogroms and a founding member of the Teamsters Union, worried he would reject "a Nigger baby." (He didn't.) The power of white Jews to participate in white supremacy and therefore to become fully integrated into mainstream society is predicated on the painful status of Black America, which is ever trying to climb out of the Constitutional status of three-fifths human. Black anti-Jewish sentiment may be prejudiced, but white Jewish anti-Blackness comes with the full force of white supremacy at its back, making it violently racist.

Moreover, one of the things that American Jews almost universally have in common is a serious dislike of statements that begin with, "The Jews . . ." It's the kind of statement that's quite similar to, "I'm not racist, but . . . ," because it is usually completed by an assertion that is completely racist. We implicitly understand for ourselves that, as a minority that has for most of history been marginalized in the places where we existed, we are not a monolith but rather a diverse group of individuals with a partially shared history and to varying degrees commitment to the idea of Jewishness and Torah. Yet, in the discourse about Black anti-Jewishness, the same individuality and diversity of Black people is typically disallowed.

In this sense, it does not matter that most American Jews are descended from people who read Jewish press that was extremely supportive of civil rights for Black Americans and which saw Black Americans as the "Jews of America" It is hardly relevant that Jewish organizations often partnered with Black civil rights organizations, or that some white Jews were visible leaders within and supporters of the civil rights movement. As white American Jews moved from the non-white working class into a comfortable white middle class, as Baldwin noted, they became increasingly resistant to challenging the status quo that now made them comfortable. Defending Black people eventually came to be at odds with defending the newfound residency in the "tent of whiteness" of most American Jews. Whereas white supremacy had previously been a very clear danger to white Jewish people, it apparently came to serve their needs.

To make themselves comfortable with this betrayal, many white Jews have maintained a powerful historical narrative about their significant and meaningful contributions to the African American freedom struggle. In a sense, much of the community rests on the laurels of activist Jews long dead and gone.[6] It should be evident that the broader Jewish community would never respond to anti-Jewish animus in this way. For as long as aJP continues to exist, we must combat it because again, as Baldwin and Bond both remind us, terrifying final solutions are on the other end of it. Yet somehow this same sensibility of confronting anti-Blackness does not exist, and this is primarily due to the way the disempowerment of Black people financially and socially benefits—at least in a superficial sense—anyone who lives and breathes under the tent of whiteness.

This assimilation of white Jews is inextricably tied to the rise of the Zionist State of Israel, and therefore is also tied to the Palestinian struggle and Israeli policy toward Jewish and non-Jewish Black immigrants. Not only have the various successes of the Zionist mission (including the creation of Israel in tandem with the expulsion of Palestinians) shaped Jewish entitlement and empowerment in the American establishment, it has also created ever more opportunities for Black people to be suspicious of Jews and Jewishness. As Zionists continue to demand a conceptual unity between the Zionist enterprise and thousands of years of Jewish identity and history, it becomes harder and harder for outsiders—gentiles—to tell racist Zionism and Jewish identity apart.

Naturally the question then follows: can Jewish Americans support Israel's existence in its current form and remain immune from holding the idea that supremacy is sometimes acceptable? And if they cannot, are Jewish Americans therefore susceptible to supporting and maintaining white supremacy? Since white supremacy gives power to a kind of Black nationalism that is anti-Jewish in nature (such as the Nation of Islam) and a white nationalism that is both anti-Black and anti-Jewish (the Ku Klux Klan, among other organizations), it seems there is a clear connection between Jewish American support for Israel's current form and the production of harmful and sometimes violent anti-Jewishness in the United States.

Linking Black Lives to Palestinian Lives

Ultimately, non-Jewish Black American aJP must be understood in the context of a legacy of white Jews both participating in and profiting from anti-Blackness, as well as the nature and tone of Jewish participation in the struggle against anti-Blackness. In connection, Black pro-Palestine solidarity must be recognized as a challenge to the relationship between supremacy abroad and supremacy at home.[7] As described elsewhere, there are not only conceptual linkages but physical ones. American police have been trained by Israeli organizations in methods of control that are often deployed against Black communities, for example in Ferguson. During South African apartheid, Israel bucked against Black American (and other) calls to protest anti-Black human rights violations and instead collaborated with the state's racist leadership.

Moreover, growing awareness of the social structure within Israel's internationally recognized borders has changed the conversation for many Black Americans. The stratification of rights is not simply Jews vs. non-Jews. Orthodox rules about who can claim Jewish identity in Israel are out of sync with who may make *aliyah*. Thus, one may be entitled to Israeli citizenship due to their Jewish heritage, but be unable to legally marry within Israel. Meanwhile, citizens of Arab and African heritage (regardless of their Jewish identity) are more likely to live in impoverished communities, attend schools with minimal educational funding, and have negative socioeconomic outcomes.[8] For Black Americans, this is an all too familiar social hierarchy, with the whiter or lighter-appearing people at the top of an uneven power structure. What we call Jim Crow in the United States shares a relationship with what Palestinians and Jewish solidarity activists are increasingly calling apartheid in Israel.[9]

Beyond Israel's legal borders, a long list of human rights violations including an openly segregationist set of policies makes the comparison with Jim Crow richer. Palestinians attempting to transit into areas currently defined to be "Israel" are subject to differential treatment from Jewish Israelis, who are more free to move through checkpoints. Shootings of Palestinians by the Israeli Defense Forces where there are potentially specious claims that the victim possessed a weapon are not unusual. Arrests and long-term detentions of Palestinians based on questionable charges, or with no charges, are increasingly frequent, with one recent case involving a twelve-year-old girl who was incarcerated for months.[10] The parallels with the Black American experience with police murders, mass incarceration, other forms of state violence, and resource poverty are impossible for many Black American activists to ignore.[11] This has generated a sense of connection with the Palestinian cause that has little to do with a dislike of Jews or Judaism and much to do with a dislike of racist, colonialist oppression.

In effect, much of what Zionists have labeled as "anti-Semitism" from the Black community is in fact pro-Black pushback against the white supremacist nature of the occupation of Palestine. Pro-Palestine campus (and other) activism, where there has been clear solidarity and linkage with Black Lives Matter, is a natural outcome of recognizing a nationality-independent pattern of abuse. When Zionist activists have recast this organizing as anti-Semitism, they have inhibited our collective capacity to fight back against real anti-Jewish prejudice. Moreover, the frequent accusation that pro-Palestine organizing is in fact endangering Jews threatens to erase the reality of Black experiences with violence by comparing criticism of an armed state with Black suffering at the hands of an armed state. White Jewish assimilation into the tent of whiteness empowers this specious comparison and endangers what is bold and beautiful about the precepts of *mitzvah* (good deed), *tzedek* (justice), and *chesed* (compassion) in Judaism.

The Threat of Black Anti-Jewish Prejudice

Saying that Black critiques of Zionism cannot be accurately labeled aJP or "Black anti-Semitism" does not deny the existence of real non-Jewish Black aJP. It is real in the old Negro spiritual "De Jews Dun Killed Jesus." It is real in passing comments from Black acquaintances such as, "The Jews have a history of leaving Black people out of Hollywood films." It is real in the way that Jewish participation in white supremacy is sometimes magnified in the minds of Black folks relative to non-Jewish white supremacy, while the victimization of Jews at the hands of white supremacy is rendered invisible or harmless.

Another example of real Black aJP is the anti-Jewish ideology of the Nation of Islam to which some Blacks subscribe. As Baldwin and Bond both remind us, any hint of anti-Jewishness has as its ultimate conclusion "terrifying final solutions," and we should all be wary of the danger presented by any person, much less organization, that perpetuates the idea that Jews are the devil. My own personal experiences with NoI members include being harassed for betraying my "fellow people" by wearing a Jewish-identifying symbol, the Star of David, and also being told on the street in response to, "I'm Jewish, so no," that, "We are not like *that* anymore." Even so, I am cautious, aware that a man, regardless of race or religious affiliation, may feel entitled by patriarchy to harass me.

Problematically, in the discourse about Black aJP, the NoI is given power that it simply does not hold. The NoI is not nearly as influential as the people who cry "Black anti-Semitism" like to suggest. Many if not most Black people reject the NoI wholesale. Julian Bond has written about the humiliation of being asked repeatedly to decry the Nation of Islam every single time they said something anti-Jewish.[12] Indeed, the NoI is an interesting case of "Black anti-Semitism" to consider, since so few Black Americans associate with them or even relate to their way of doing things. Many, like me, are naturally suspicious because of Malcolm X's dramatic exit from their fold and their apparent complicity in his murder. It remains unresolved whether NoI's leader, Louis Farrakhan, knew of the assassination plot, but it seems that he did. Others, especially Black women, question what a patriarchal organization like NoI has to offer them. Queers, of course, are completely excluded.

This speaks to something inconveniently true for hawkers of the "Black anti-Jewish" narrative who point to the NoI as an example: the NoI is a fringe organization that, while dangerous, is hardly representative of Black Americans and importantly, unlike the Nazis/German National Socialists in the 1930s, is completely incapable of taking the reins of power in the United States. There are a few reasons why this is impossible:

1. The NoI is ideologically bound not to work with white people, much less white power structures. This makes aspirations to governance difficult, and there has never been an attempt by NoI to join the ranks of federal government.
2. The NoI is unable to integrate the American majority into its anti-Jewish community narrative because most of America is not Black, and they are a Black nationalist organization.
3. Structural white supremacy in the United States dictates that should the NoI ever reconsider its lack of aspirations to governance, their very existence itself would be made impossible.

Certainly there are NoI members who would dispute the capacity of American power structures to successfully squash any NoI attempt to rise to power. Indeed, that might have been more difficult in the 1960s when Elijah Muhammad was at the height of his influence among Black Americans. But in the meantime, Black America has found some more freedoms and many more leadership/organizing options than it previously had.

NoI has survived as an organization by reneging on its threats of violence. Simultaneously, Farrakhan has become more keen about public relations. NoI has softened on matters of patriarchy, supporting a woman's right to choose when and with whom she has babies and encouraging NoI members to "love the sinner" but "hate the sin" of homosexuality. My inner queer rejects that as something to be excited about, but intellectually I recognize the progress. And it is certainly the case that the NoI's anti-Jewishness has become less visible, perhaps because of deals being made with the Church of Scientology, which surely includes many white members of Jewish descent.[13]

But one should not have to reassure white Jews that the NoI is not an all-powerful dangerous entity. Point two above highlights what ultimately distinguishes the NoI from the Nazis in their capacity to wreak havoc on Jewish lives. Under American white supremacy, white Jews are largely welcome in the tent of whiteness. Since anti-Jewish sentiment is considered to be a very fringe and deeply racist viewpoint within the tent of whiteness, non-Jewish white people would feel threatened by any aggression against white Jews by any group of Black people. Yet white sensibilities becoming threatened by the very existence of Black individuals to the point of murder—a definitive white supremacist reaction—and that fact is evident in all of the police shootings that occur. There will be no union between Jewish-hating Black people like the NoI and a white majority—or even an unusually powerful white minority— any time soon. White supremacy forbids it.

NoI's brand of Black nationalism will never be given the necessary oxygen by white people to grow and thrive. But arguably, Black Americans will not give it much oxygen either. Notwithstanding the high attendance at NoI-organized marches in Washington, DC, the alternate options now available for emotional and organizational outlets, such as through the many organizations that make up the coalition known as Movement for Black Lives, are significant and appealing. This is not difficult for anyone to understand intellectually. It can be harder for some white Jews to accept emotionally that there is not an easy boogeyman here. But an inability to recognize that, compared to the Nazis, the NoI is and will continue to be relatively powerless is also tied to an unwillingness among white people, including white Jews, to reckon with the extreme power of American white supremacy. Which, ironically, is what leads so many NoI members to join its ranks in the first place.

White Jews could help devastate the hold that NoI has over many Black people by joining and promoting the effort to end anti-Blackness. In a world without anti-Blackness, no Black person would be driven to join an organization that purports to empower them at the expense of Jewish people. The failure to recognize this is inextricably tied to the fact that fighting anti-Blackness requires acknowledging that white Jews benefit from inclusion in the tent of whiteness. A decision by white Jews to leave or help to dismantle that tent could significantly transform Black Americans' experiences and views on the role Jews and Jewishness play in their own lives and the national story.

Building Solidarity

White Jews have gained from white supremacy because they have been able to pass for white and gentile in broader society. And although one does not need to be white to participate in and uphold white supremacy, in American society white Jews in the modern era have been given the historically unusual opportunity to maintain their cultural distinctiveness without being victimized by structural inequality. Ashkenazi Jewish immigrants have recognized that they are on the safe track into mainstream America's carefully guarded tent of whiteness.

Still, white supremacy is a danger to us all because it justifies violent hatred. Jews who attend temple during high holy days know this. In the United States, police guard us while we celebrate the new year and recommit ourselves to an ethical Jewish life. In parts of Europe, we show our ID and traverse a path marked by a series of locking doors in order to enter our holy spaces. Jews should know that white supremacy is a danger not just to Black people and people of color, but to white Jews as well.

The shared fate of Jews and Blacks was recognized early on by the Yiddish American press, which often referred to Black Americans as "the Jews of America."[14] It was not until the end of the tragic *Shoah* and the advent of Israel's formation as a state that some Jewish focus on oppression turned away from the internal racialized dynamics of America and toward Israel's state-building enterprise. One intriguing question that this raises is whether as American Jews became enmeshed with the act of colonial state-building in Israel, they became more sympathetic with the American act of state-building relying on anti-Black and settler-colonialist domestic policies.

Looking back through the Jewish legacy of opposing state violence against Black Americans in the early- to mid-twentieth century, it is perhaps surprising to see widespread support for the same in Israel now, both against Palestinians as well as African migrants. Moreover, Black solidarity with pro-Palestine campaigners shares such strong similarities with Jewish pro-Black activism that in some sense it is surprising that so many (Zionist) Jews now identify this work as threatening evidence of anti-Jewish prejudice. A more productive interpretation would be one that requires Jews who see things this way to reconsider their relationship with state violence in their name, both at home in the United States as well as abroad in the Jewish State of Israel. Supporting the existence of this kind of violence in Israel is at minimum tacit approval of the tactics that are similar to those used against Black Americans and sometimes reproduced with Israeli assistance in the United States.

White Jews cannot oppose American white supremacy without addressing the need for solidarity with the victims of supremacy abroad. For Black Jews and the rest of the Black community, a failure by white Jews and all Jewish American communities to actively confront, oppose, and end white supremacy is a matter of life or death, just as a failure to end Jewish supremacy is a matter of life or death for Palestinians. But perhaps it is just as urgent that white Jews confront both white supremacy and Jewish supremacy for their own sake. If there is any lesson that one hopes white Jews have learned in the last century, it is that we never know who will end up in the crosshairs next. The willingness of many mainstream Jewish organizations and Jewish writers in popular publications to strongly criticize and even fully reject the 2016 Movement for Black Lives platform because of its use of the word "genocide" in relation to Palestine worryingly suggests that for many, allegiance to Jewish supremacy trumps a commitment to human rights. Some of these same organizations immediately expressed a desire to work productively with a President Donald Trump in the days after his election, despite indications that his electoral success was predicated on the coalescence of voters around racist, white nationalist messaging that could have an adverse impact on Jews of all races.

Intersections of Antisemitism, Racism, and Nationalism: A Sephardi/Mizrahi Perspective

Ilise Benshushan Cohen

Writing about antisemitism is hard. I would rather a non-Jewish ally write about it, so they might be forced to reflect more closely on it and come to grasp some of its complexities, including from my perspective as a Sephardi/Mizrahi Jew.[1] As a Jewish person, I constantly navigate the feeling of "is this important enough" and weigh this against an eagerness for confronting oppression.

The history and legitimate claims of antisemitism are important to acknowledge. Defining European Christian antisemitism is critical to create a shared understanding in justice movements of its history and how it operates. Some Jewish people are afraid their safety could be revoked at any moment.[2] These fears sometimes exist even in places where Jewish people are relatively safe.[3] This internalization of antisemitism affects the health of Jewish communities and can lead to erasure, powerlessness, and other forms of domination toward people including minoritized Jews.

Growing up, I was taught that antisemitism operated on its own, separate from other oppressions, but even in childhood I understood that I did not experience it that way. Because my last name is Cohen, I am assumed to be Jewish, never Christian. I am also wrongly assumed to be Ashkenazi, and am treated differently when I assert my Sephardic identity. As a young Sephardic/Mizrahi Jew, I saw the power that (white) Ashkenazi Jews had over Sephardic Jews in the United States and Israel. At the same time, because of how I present as white-passing, I also navigate the world differently than other Jews and non-Jews of color.

The urgency to define what is and is not antisemitism and its reliance on racism/Orientalism calls for (white) Christians to take responsibility and reflect on the foundation of what produced and maintains these oppressive ideologies that target non-Christian and non-white communities. Unfortunately, within mainstream US Jewish communities and the Israeli public, antisemitism is projected whenever there is a critique of Israel. In the face of Jewish communities silencing debate, it is essential to separate out what is antisemitism versus a critique of nationalism. We have to be honest about calling out Ashkenazi dominance and white Christian antisemitism and racism in the movement for Palestinian rights. Exposing these systems of domination allows us to work toward liberation from being oppressors and victims.

European Christian Antisemitism

To describe antisemitism, imagine a triangle with the white European Christian elite on top, some European Jews in the middle, and those with less money and/or racial privilege on the bottom. When those on the bottom are dissatisfied with the status quo, they look directly above them to those who are being used as agents to implement and carry out policies responsible for their oppression. This is why white Jews have been perceived as socially and economically privileged regardless of their class position.[4] Rather than addressing the ruling class's policies as the problem, white or white-passing Jews in the middle are blamed for the oppression of the lower classes. Jews are used to divert the anger of the oppressed away from the ruling elites, which has repeatedly led to direct violence against Jews in Europe whether by collective punishment, expulsion, or attempted genocide. This serves the ruling class well, because they are not targeted. The elites can then remain in place until the next group is used for scapegoating.[5]

This is primarily an Ashkenazi Jewish experience. Jewish discourse sometimes gives a false impression that antisemitism operates alone, that it is not interdependent with other systems. Though my Sephardic Jewish ancestors experienced antisemitism in Christian Spain, it was part of a Christian- and European-centered orientalist ideology that was directed at Muslims as well. Focusing on a European Christian context also fails to give a sense of Sephardic Jewish lives in Muslim and Arab lands. Nor does this history address the kinds of *Jewish* orientalist and racist thinking that determines which Jewish people are worthy of power and which are seen as inferior.[6] It is imperative that we understand our safety as deeply linked to combating racism, white supremacy, and Christian hegemony.[7]

Internalized Antisemitism and Domination

Since many (white) Jewish people in the United States are perceived as having "made it" and participate in this "middle agent" role,[8] it is often difficult to mark antisemitism as an oppression worth addressing. However vulnerable they may feel,[9] white or white-passing Jews gain status while knowingly excluding others. They use upward mobility and assimilation for their own benefit as hedges against antisemitism, uncritically accepting such privileges. They allow people of color to be excluded, help keep structures of white supremacy in place, perpetuate racism, and internalize attitudes and practices of domination. This happened with the implementation of the GI Bill and housing redlining after World War II.[10] Some Jewish people may see these accommodations as steps toward equality, even though Blacks and Latinos were left behind.[11] Some Jews believe that being a victim historically or currently does not require you to look at your own privilege and how it harms others. One way internalized superiority functions is by calling out antisemitism while refusing to address effects of imperialism, patriarchy, white supremacy, and Christian hegemony on others. Because Ashkenazi internalized domination looks at antisemitism solely within a European context,[12] this directly affects Sephardi/Mizrahi Jews and Jews of color by rendering our personal and family experiences invisible.[13]

Antisemitism Requires Orientalism and Racism

Antisemitism does not operate alone. It only exists in the context of other oppressions, since its purpose is to act as a pressure valve for the anger of the oppressed majority. In Europe this was about white Christian peasants and workers. In the United States, the racialized class system means that it's integrated into white supremacy, but it is also used to divert the anger of white working-class Christian people while the Christian ruling class gets off unscathed.

As a Sephardic/Mizrahi Jew I was taught that there was only enough room to be a victim of antisemitism, not racism or Orientalism.[14] I internalized a specific Jewish victim point of view. The discrimination I experienced was minimized and my history erased. Growing up, I understood clearly that I had a limited space in which to be a Jew, which did not sit right with me. I had many family members who perished in the Holocaust, and in my experience attending a Jewish day school, antisemitism and attempted genocides of Jewish people were central themes that we learned from early childhood. But I could never explain the targeting I felt from within my community. I knew to be wary of the outside world, but as a young person I did not expect the constant dislocation because of my Sephardic identity. Yet I was proud to be Jewish because I was Sephardic. The Atlanta Jewish world where I grew up was inconsistent; it claimed to be an accepting community while it denied my heritage and experiences. Ashkenazim enjoyed our food, made fun of our superstitions, occasionally appropriated our prayers or traditions, and even commented jokingly in racist and hurtful ways about our "inferiority"—they actually still do this; even close family friends of mine are guilty. Meanwhile, this marginalization gave me insight and a feeling of connection with Palestinians who resist and struggle against discrimination and oppression. Sephardi/Mizrahi Jews continue to be targeted in visible and invisible ways by both antisemitism and Orientalism/racism.[15]

I was also taught that Israel was my home, even though I was raised in the United States, born to a Sephardic family that had settled in Turkey via various places including Egypt and Lebanon, later migrating to the isle of Rhodes and Cuba. When I lived in Israel for high school and university, and then as a working young adult, I witnessed the intensity of racism, exploitation, and marginalization of Sephardi/Mizrahi Jews and Palestinian citizens. Living with Palestinian citizens and working closely with Ashkenazi and Mizrahi Jewish communities, I saw the neglect of resources and infrastructure in education, health, and community services for Palestinian citizens; felt and heard the fear, hostility, and racism toward Palestinians by Israeli Jews; and saw the induced poverty in Mizrahi neighborhoods and mixed communities.

Most Jewish people and non-Jews who support the State of Israel don't know that since the 1950s, the majority of the state's population has been Sephardi/Mizrahi,[16] at the same time that Arab-ness and Middle Eastern–ness were being attacked and rejected so that the State of Israel would be identifiably a European (not Middle Eastern) Jewish state.[17] The ability of Sephardi/Mizrahi Jews to negotiate multiple identities throughout the Arab, Muslim, and Ottoman world is what for centuries kept these communities, including my own family, alive. Yet the Ashkenazi establishment and majority Ashkenazi population do not acknowledge that there is something to learn from Sephardi/Mizrahi Jews and the notion of home—it is possible to be home in the region without asserting dominance and superiority.

Having witnessed Israeli racism, I felt intense grief about *my home*, this "Jewish" state, with its unjust economic and social policies fueled by feelings of superiority over others: Jews over Palestinians, Ashkenazi over Sephardi/Mizrahi Jews, secular over religious. This became more intensified with Ethiopian Jewish immigration in the 1990s as Ethiopians became a new underclass. The state clearly did not represent me as a Jew; I did not fit in. So why would this state be the solution to antisemitism if it could also dominate Palestinians and Jews like me?

Mainstream US and Israeli Ashkenazi consciousness is not concerned with identifying and addressing orientalist and racist behavior, attitudes, and actions with the same rigor and hypervigilance as they do antisemitism. This indifference can produce a lack of sympathy for claims against antisemitism and also further marginalize Jews of color, including Sephardi/Mizrahi Jews, as well as non-Jews of color because Ashkenazi dominance is not disrupted. When Jewish fear is used to justify strategies of domination toward non-white Jews and other people of color, I believe white Jewish people, in some way, lose their right to claim a victim status. Being vigilant about racism is a critical component of addressing antisemitism.

Foundations of Antisemitism/Orientalism/Racism

Earlier, I contextualized a perspective on European Christian antisemitism.[18] However, it is imperative that when talking about antisemitism we look at its Christian and European roots and the role of white Christians in the movement for Palestinian liberation.

When white Christians[19] specifically are working for Palestinian liberation, it is essential to ask whether they are aware that antisemitism and Orientalism, including anti-Arab racism and Islamophobia, were (re)produced by Christian European hegemony and white supremacy. These struggles and oppressions are deeply intertwined with the histories of European imperialism, colonization, Christian dominance, and patriarchy. This past continues to influence the present. White US Christians can decide whose side they are on in Israel/Palestine without ever having to acknowledge their historical and current role in antisemitism and Orientalism and how these ideologies simultaneously target European Jewish and Arab and Middle Eastern bodies.[20] One might ask, how do Christians contribute to resolving this conflict when they fail to acknowledge their role in establishing and maintaining these ideologies?[21]

At times, white Christians may feel a sense of kinship and unity with Jewish people because of "shared" Judeo-Christian values[22] while supporting structural oppression toward people of color. At other times, when white Christians are working in solidarity with Palestinians and against Islamophobia, antisemitism can sometimes emerge.[23] White Christians can try to absolve themselves by supporting the "underdog" of choice, but without ending their participation in these two systems pitted at one another, their Christian dominance and these systems remain in place. In what ways does our liberation depend on white European Christian refusal to participate in and align with these structures?

In Palestine-Israel, there are multilayered oppressions that Palestinians face regardless of religion. The United States has its own distinct forms of structural and institutional racism that it enacts on communities of color. Some white Christian allies with whom I have worked have an awareness with which to think about privilege. Yet even while acting righteously, they may do something that is also harmful by feeding antisemitism. The Christian ideological foundation that rejects Judaism and Jewish people or finds Jews useful in a historical way but not palatable in the present is challenging to unravel. Even the insignificance of Jesus[24] for Jewish people remains incomprehensible to some white Christians and Christians of color. While Christians of color clearly see the racism of the Israeli military occupation, they don't necessarily address the problematics of European-based Christian supremacy.[25]

False Antisemitism, Jewish Silencing, and Gatekeeping

Ashkenazi Jews who make false claims of antisemitism see themselves as victims. Ashkenazi Jewish leadership, having internalized a Western identity and rejected a Middle Eastern one, describes itself as struggling against the Palestinian/Arab "oppressor" and the "Eastern-ness" of the non-European-Ashkenazi Jews.[26] Palestinians are blamed for antisemitism and Mizrahi Jews are barriers to being seen as "Western." Both groups are seen as obstacles[27] to a Western or European identification. However, while Israel makes claims of antisemitism, it has kept millions of Palestinian people in occupation for almost fifty years, segregated Palestinian citizenry, and marginalized and contained the majority Middle Eastern Jewish population since its inception.

How can claims against the state and its actions become understood as critiques of nationalism and exclusion rather than as antisemitism? It is urgent that we all reflect more clearly on the realities of the state, and Jewish responsibility to speak out about the abuses of power toward other communities. How does the model that describes European antisemitism change or become irrelevant when the ruling class are white Ashkenazim? The conversation then starts to become one about racism and nationalism.

After living in Israel, I couldn't keep silent about my experiences there. A rabbi told me publicly that I could never be a Jewish leader because I was critical of Israel. As a Jewish person in my mid-twenties, I felt as though someone had ripped open my heart and told me that the Jewish community had no use for what I learned. I recovered from this dislocation emotionally and spiritually by showing my leadership: speaking truth, gaining knowledge, asking questions, facilitating other people's exploration, and taking action for justice. To be a proud Sephardic Jew, I had to reject a worldwide Jewish nationalism that believed Jewish people are more important than others. Hidden in that was the message that Ashkenazi Jews were more valued than Sephardi/Mizrahi Jews. Therefore, I made a commitment as a Jewish leader to fight against unjust Israeli policies, against power differentials, and for space for Jewish differences.

I was recently invited to speak (separately) by a Hillel student and by a Hadassah group, then un-invited when they chose to cave into pressures from constituents and to enforce organizational policies of blacklisting Jewish Voice for Peace. I felt sad for the Hillel student who wanted to expose himself and his peers to multiple narratives on Israel/Palestine and was prevented by Hillel leadership and policies. As a professor, I find it criminal to control the information that students are exposed to, instilling fear rather than curiosity. As a Sephardic Jew, I am offended that Hillel leaders are pursuing racist behaviors by cutting off deeply needed conversations about power and Jewish responsibility, stifling critical consciousness and commitments to social justice.

When I received the voicemail from the Hadassah organizer canceling my talk, I was hurt. I called immediately, striving for any opportunity, even a small crevice, to talk informally with people, to share personal stories and research. Decades of this silencing and the Jewish community's refusal to engage with multiple Israeli, Palestinian, Jewish, and Arab narratives points to Orientalism and racism. Their members don't have to think about or take responsibility for the repression of Palestinians because it does not directly affect them. This is what privilege affords Jewish people who silence critical debate about ethical issues.

Even after I spent twenty-five years doing Israel/Palestine work, living in the region, and doing research at the PhD level, these organizations still attempt to silence and marginalize people like me. By calling JVP antisemitic, they use silencing tactics and take advantage of white supremacist attitudes that deny their role in maintaining oppression in the United States and in Israel. Rather than highlighting Hadassah's own history of public health initiatives in Palestine as an opportunity to address one of the longest public health crises, the Israeli military occupation of Palestine,[28] they act as though they are victims being targeted by Palestinians and the Arab world, without ever taking stock of their participation in this crisis.[29]

During the Gaza assault Operation Protective Edge in the summer of 2014, JVP-Atlanta asked to meet with the Atlanta Jewish Federation.[30] They only allowed us to meet them in the parking lot, afraid that we would take over the building. Even though I was furious and felt demeaned, it was gratifying to think about how afraid they were of us coming to make a simple request: to issue a public statement that *Palestinian lives are equal and as valuable as Israeli Jewish lives.*[31] Though the Federation claimed to value all lives, they never agreed to make this statement, which speaks for itself. To them, the Jewish state was under assault and Palestinian humanity and life under military occupation and siege was seemingly irrelevant. This behavior silences Jews who were devastated by Israeli human rights violations and loss of life in Gaza during the assault,[32] not to mention the impact on Palestinians in Gaza and the ongoing siege on the Gaza Strip.[33]

Many Jewish people are taught to be hypervigilant about critiques of Israel that may problematically be assumed to be antisemitic. Ongoing false claims of antisemitism make it impossible for those who stand outside (or even inside) the Jewish community to identify what is antisemitic because the community itself so clearly shows its alignment to Orientalism through anti-Arab racism and Islamophobia. For example, Rabbi Shalom Lewis, an Atlanta rabbi, gave a Rosh Hashanah sermon in 2014 that was deeply Islamophobic and bordering on a call for genocide.[34] Though JVP-Atlanta sent open letters to the rabbi, his board, all other Atlanta rabbis,[35] the main Atlanta Jewish institutions, and the Muslim community, the Jewish community never publicly condemned this sermon.

Unfortunately, many claims of antisemitism are coming from mainstream Jewish organizations, like the American Jewish Committee, that have hardly done deep analysis of anti-Jewish oppression in relation to other forms of oppression. The language of antisemitism is sometimes used as a buffer to support repressive policies in Israel toward Palestinians that also affect marginalized communities here, and in the United States that same language is used to shut down intersectional activism that legitimately exposes oppressive practices and policies.[36] This becomes a form of gatekeeping instead of confronting injustice or bigotry. Jewish people in positions of power have historically used Jewish gatekeeping or racist disciplining[37] to exert control over communities that criticize Israel by claiming antisemitism or by threatening to withdraw from important shared work in social justice.[38] This creates inauthentic relationships and isolates Jewish people by building alliances with individuals and organizations who might not necessarily understand historical and current antisemitism or who may quietly resent attempts at gatekeeping.

False Antisemitism as a Tool of Nationalism

Dominance and violence are not unique to Israel. And I did not grow up with the idea of Israel being a nation like all others: committing violence against vulnerable populations through patriarchy, heteronormativity, gender and ethnic oppression, class disparity, and militarism. However, nationalism is dependent on establishing a dominant identity. The state's power is often used to marginalize and exclude rather than protect vulnerable populations. It harnesses and deflects power, scapegoats people, and produces enemies. Though sometimes there is accommodation for marginalized peoples, states continue to operate with these destructive nationalist tendencies.

The Ashkenazi-led nationalist enterprise to create a nation-state for the Jewish people did not address how dominating and dispossessing Palestinians was *ethically wrong*. Nationalism doesn't function ethically since it is bound up in loyalty to a geographical location and an identity that must produce and maintain superiority. In Israel, antisemitism and racism are powerfully linked through nationalism. Insisting on the Jewish character of Israel produces the idea that any critiques toward the state are antisemitic rather than merely anti-nationalistic.

It is problematic that a state that identifies as Jewish has the right to assert antisemitism when it enacts discriminatory policies upon not only its own Palestinian population but also its minoritized Sephardi/Mizrahi/Ethiopian Jewish population.[39] The state practices authority through various forms of oppression. Writer Iris Young classifies forms of injustice into five categories, which are helpful to understand the specific types and conditions of domination: "violence, exploitation, marginalization, cultural imperialism, and powerlessness."[40] Israel refuses to acknowledge or end these practices or forms of oppression.

The distorted claims of antisemitism rely on racism. As part of a general anti-Arab and Islamophobic mistrust and hatred stemming from an orientalist perspective, Palestinians are imagined to have no legitimate claims, only a desire to harm Jews. Meanwhile actual Palestinian victimization by military occupation, discriminatory laws, marginalization, and criminalization are invisibilized. Distortions are also presented in the way that Sephardi/Mizrahi migration to Israel is presented. Anti-Jewish oppression in the Arab and Muslim world is highlighted in order to advance a specific "rescue" narrative, further codifying a nationalist identity: *Mizrahi Jews came to Israel as refugees, were absorbed as citizens, and lost their properties in the Middle East. Therefore, this "population exchange" counters Palestinian refugee claims. Arab governments should absorb these Palestinians and compensate them as Israel did with Mizrahim.*[41] However, Mizrahim were never compensated. Rather than address specific wrongs that Sephardi/Mizrahi Jews faced, Israel tries to justify continued Palestinian dispossession. In doing so, the state employs their stories for nationalist purposes while enforcing marginalization of these communities.

An anti-nationalistic critique, however, allows healthy questions to be asked and promotes resistance to the erasure of marginalized histories. This kind of critique confronts state violence and insists on equal rights for everyone. The Israeli state and Jewish organizations that support its policies of containment, occupation, and violence insist on its Jewish rather than its national character.[42] People who critique the state are then accused of antisemitism because of this insistence on Jewishness. However, this is not actually antisemitism; it is a critique of nationalism and its violent pursuit of domination. This accusation attempts to silence necessary critiques of occupation and discriminatory laws and prevents a genuine conversation about Israeli policies toward Palestinians, whether citizens of 1948, refugees, under occupation in the West Bank, or under siege in Gaza.[43]

Calling critiques of Israel antisemitic dilutes real antisemitism toward Jewish people who need allies with power to address it in their communities and the larger society. Erroneous declarations can confuse or manipulate those who would speak out against antisemitism by convincing them that they are harming Jewish people and aren't knowledgeable enough to know the difference between antisemitism and abusive state policies. This confusion is hazardous because allies don't then know what is genuine or not to struggle against. These false claims simultaneously buy into state racism toward Palestinians,[44] marginalized Jews,[45] and other people of color,[46] and into conceptions of white supremacy including its dependence on Islamophobia and anti-Arab racism. For example, some white Christians find it more comfortable to align with Israel than with Palestinians perceived to be not only "Arab," but also "Muslim."[47] Some white Christians are not concerned with Palestinian Christians because their "Arabness" is seen as negating their Christian-ness. Many Evangelical Christians, though they may show support for Israel as a Jewish state, do so *not* out of concern for what happens to Jewish people—but because of their eschatology that necessitates Jewish *return* to the land in order for the rapture to take place.[48]

Professions of antisemitism can mask the racist and supremacist policies of Israeli nationalism, specifically those affecting Palestinians. By reifying Israel as the "Jewish state," significant Israeli human rights abuses and other forms of repression get dismissed. More dangerously, the Israeli government markets legitimate critiques as a threat to the existence of the Jewish people. These declarations of Jewish identity and antisemitism also make the assumption that marginalized Israeli Jewish communities are not also negatively affected by Israeli policies. The Israeli government *claims* that the BDS movement is an existential threat to Israel and the Jewish people, while it concurrently engages in everyday violence that in fact threatens Palestinian existence.

These dishonest assertions perpetuate the historical interplay of antisemitism and racism. Instead of addressing this interplay, Israel reaps benefits while blaming those most affected by its nationalist policies of exclusion. In aligning with Judeo-Christian values, where European and Jewish identities are deemed superior, Israel also adopts a dehumanizing colonialist mentality and reproduces orientalist tropes used against Middle Eastern people. When Israel relies on orientalist thinking, then racism, class oppression, sexism, and militarization become essential to maintaining its national identity.

The contradiction of assimilation and marginalization within Israeli policy and action indicates a rupture in antisemitic claims where the Jewish state itself mistreats its Jewish population. Upon arrival to the state, many Mizrahim were placed on the "armistice line" borders. Their bodies and communities became the buffer zone for cross-border violence between Israel and surrounding Arab nations. Some Mizrahim dealt with this by internalizing a European Jewish "Zionist" identity, understanding themselves as protectors of the state, preventing Palestinians from returning to their homes. This loyalty gained them a false sense of belonging. Mizrahim generally remain marginalized: exploited as cheap labor, relegated to peripheries, subjected to racist and classist tropes, and criminalized.[49]

As a southern Jew, I learned that assimilation was the enemy.[50] Assimilation is a nationalist goal that erases and consumes one's culture, encouraging one to benefit from discrimination toward unassimilable others. Israel itself is a project of assimilation rather than of uplifting difference; Jewish people, regardless of background, are expected to assimilate into a standard Israeli Jewish (Ashkenazi-centric) national identity. For African/Arab/Middle Eastern Jews this assimilation comes at a high price if at all, whereas Palestinians and African refugees cannot.

Israel has also utilized militarism to substantiate a nationalist identity, prioritizing this over other strengths.[51] It was and continues to be a valuable asset to the United States and the West by sharing and exporting military expertise,[52] and ghettoizes itself in the region by relying on these relationships.[53] To validate its self-conception as a victim, Israel makes surrounding Arab and Muslim countries and Palestinians into scapegoats for its condition of isolation, while it invests itself as a "Western" strategic player in the Middle East. Israel asserts military dominance regionally and yet separates itself from the Arab world and Mizrahim to keep from being identified with its region. The United States has been a dishonest peace broker as it continues to support the occupation of Palestinian lands and has done almost nothing to pressure Israel to end its siege of Gaza.[54]

Ashkenazi Dominance and Racism in the Movement for Palestinian Rights

"Ashkenazi dominance" is language that some US Jews of color use to describe their experiences with Ashkenazi Jews.[55] In Israel, Ashkenazi elitism has been confronted since the 1950s Wadi Salib Riots and the 1970s Israeli Black Panther movement.[56] Though the Israeli critical left actively opposes the occupation and highlights human rights violations, the Ashkenazi left does not necessarily reflect on its dominance and racism. Working within a framework of human rights and international law does not necessarily imply an antiracist and anti-colonial analysis, which is problematic.[57] The erasure of other Jews is traumatic and contradicts work on human rights. Without this analysis, Ashkenazim are not tackling the underlying roots of oppression nor the language, attitudes, and practices that have a strong impact on Sephardi/Mizrahi/Ethiopian Jews and other people of color.

An Ashkenazi-Israeli human rights activist and colleague of mine denies that Ashkenazi superiority and racism exist. I asked him during a heated discussion to reflect on this privilege; he dismissed it as unworthy of attention. His refusal was hurtful and disappointing. He ignored the fact that even if some people achieve a more acceptable status in society, they do so at a price, undermining their power and perpetuating their second-class citizenship. He accused me of essentializing Mizrahim, while he targeted Mizrahim for their learned internalized racism toward Palestinians. Rather than use his position of privilege to further the Mizrahi struggles for equality, he preferred to blame them for supporting Israeli nationalist right-wing politics that refuse to acknowledge Palestinian human rights, collapsing years of Mizrahi history and resistance in a deeply offensive way.[58] He felt no requirement to understand the context of the Israeli occupation and discrimination toward Palestinians and non-Ashkenazi Jews as it is tied to Orientalism, racism, and his unmarked identity. His failure to reflect on his position and privilege relieves him of responsibility to counter state racism, not only toward Mizrahim but Palestinians and other marginalized groups.

Antisemitism and Racism by Allies in the Movement

Racism and antisemitism are daily realities where I live, and the ones who perpetrate these oppressions are sometimes people who are actively working on Palestinian liberation as allies. It's challenging to acknowledge people's good intentions when they fail to reflect on their own acts of bigotry and supremacy.[59] I am usually one who can gently address issues and intervene when someone has crossed the line. However, these kinds of attitudes are not "moments" but fit into patterns of privilege and attitudes of superiority.

Insulting rhetoric about "Zionists" with antisemitic undertones can replicate some oppressive behaviors. When one says "Zionist," does it refer to someone who supports Jewish nationalism favoring Jewish people over Palestinians, or any Jewish person not actively working against Israeli occupation and repressive policies toward Palestinians? When "Zionist" is used as a marker and has a "dirty" connotation, even I, who have a commitment to Palestinian liberation, shudder at the underlying tones and meanings.

Sometimes the antisemitism is clear. I recently received an email in response to a program I was organizing on the policies of dispossession of the Jewish National Fund. This person, who received my email through a local peace and justice listserv, urged the Jewish leadership in the West to examine the role of Zionists in "horrible acts of terror." According to him, "Zionists" should be blamed not only for what is happening in Palestine, but are also responsible for heinous actions including "creating and funding ISIS" and "creating Boko Haram."[60] He ends with scapegoating Jews and a threat of genocide: "These acts committed by Zionists in the name of Judaism will eventually be revealed to the world with terrible consequences for the Jewish people as they did in Europe during WWII."

Sometimes antisemitism is less direct. In a Facebook post, a white colleague of mine, raised Christian, active in Palestinian solidarity, posted an article called "'Holy Spirit' Almost Serves Up Holy Dinner at Kruger."[61] He reveled in an African man partially being mauled by lions in Kruger National Park, by saying how efficient that "some Zionists in Africa are feeding themselves to lions."[62] The activist assumed the man's ideological "Zionist" identity because he was a follower of "Zion Christian Church." The name "Zion" for this South African denomination, however, is influenced by its and other African churches' historical connection to a religious Christian city in Illinois, called Zion City.[63] Regardless of whether this kind of "Zionist" has any ideological connection to the Israeli state, it is problematic to celebrate anyone being mauled. My colleague's "joke" was riddled with antisemitism and racism, glorifying violence against a racialized African body, while using this tragedy as a vehicle to attack "Zionists" without defining the term. This article and the photo may not have been true at all. However, it doesn't change the analysis of what was said on Facebook. This post continues to be an example of the intersections of antisemitism and racism by an activist for

Palestine. Because this white ally benefits from Christian dominance and whiteness, he does not have to analyze the antisemitism and white supremacy implicit in his celebration of a "Zionist" African man. Meanwhile, as a committed *ally* for Palestinian liberation, what does it mean when one is entrenched in racist and antisemitic attitudes?

Unfortunately, these two solidarity allies don't see how the struggle for Palestinian justice intersects with struggles against antisemitism, internalized dominance, and racism. Though working for Palestinian rights is not an antisemitic cause by any means, among some people there is still ignorance, confusion, and a tendency toward using racist and antisemitic tropes that harm people of color and Jewish people.

Demanding Liberation

As a Mizrahi/Sephardi Jew, I depend on my allies to speak out and act when antisemitism and racism arise and to notice their participation in oppression. I expect in-depth understandings of how the construction of racism targets Arabs and how Christian hegemony targets Muslims [and Jews]. These expectations are not always met. Jewish people like me, whose ancestors survived because they lived in the Arab and Muslim world, and who recognize the intersection of racism and antisemitism, don't see addressing the injustices toward Palestinians as a threat to Jewish survival. We see addressing injustice as key to ending antisemitism and racism, colonization, imperialism, and all forms of domination. By doing so, we remain as allies against structural oppression, refusing to be pitted against each other.

What are the linkages among antisemitism, internalized Jewish oppression, and Orientalism/racism when we talk about Sephardi/Mizrahi/Ethiopian Jews and non-white Ashkenazi Jews? They intersect and need one another to function—and they share being affected by ideologies of superiority (Christian hegemony, Ashkenazi dominance and white/western supremacy). We must disrupt these ideologies, expose their foundations, and refuse to participate in them. This requires Ashkenazi Israelis in positions of power to stop using antisemitism and victimhood as a shield while implementing repressive and discriminatory practices as a mechanism of control over Palestinians, minoritized Jews, and other people of color. They must reflect on the harm that these false antisemitic claims and racist attitudes produce. This also requires US white Ashkenazi and white-passing Jews to refuse these hegemonic narratives and reject privileges that undermine marginalized communities.

I believe that the liberation of Sephardi/Mizrahi Jews is dependent on

Palestinian liberation. Though histories and circumstances are different, the desire for freedom and justice is the same. I seek a rupture from the normalization of whiteness, patriarchy, and European and Christian hegemony. Each of us has to be willing to face our culpability around domination, investigate how we perpetuate these systems of aggression, and grapple with the notions of safety and fulfillment that reject holding on to abusive power. We must consistently refuse to sell out another's freedom for what we think might be our own, and instead engage justly in the world knowing that our liberations are essential and inextricably linked.

On Antisemitism and Its Uses

Shaul Magid

Antisemitism is when gentiles hate Jews too much.
—Jewish-Hungarian proverb

They once asked R. Hayyim Halberstam, the grand rebbe of Sanz, what he thought about antisemitism. The rebbe responded, "Aren't you glad the bad people hate us?"
—Shlomo Carlebach*

I

There is a saying that antisemitism has existed as long as Jews have. It certainly is a paradoxical, and in some way self-serving, comment. Historically, it is certainly up for debate even as David Nirenberg in his learned *Anti-Judaism: The Western Tradition* traces a trajectory of anti-Judaic sentiment from ancient Egypt (obviously long before there were "Jews" or "Judaism") to the present. Nirenberg is as interested, perhaps even more so, in anti-Jews as he is in anti-Judaism and is careful to state up front that for him, anti-Judaism is not *by definition* antisemitism (he makes this distinction in the book's introduction). The latter is more likely an amalgam of anti-Judaic sentiment left over from Christendom mixed with race science and racial theory as it took form in nineteenth-century Europe.[1] Unfortunately, Nirenberg's comprehensive study is too often used for polemical purposes he did not intend. I would like to suggest that this is part of the problem. It is not only troubling that antisemitism exists, as it certainly does, it is also troubling the way that we have, in some macabre way, become dependent on it (that comment itself could misconstrued as antisemitic!). Some of our reactions to antisemitism seem like the kind that follow a car crash, when we can't look away even as we are horrified at the carnage we see. Millions of dollars are poured into Institutes for the Study of Antisemitism. Conferences and endowed university lectures on

---

* The author heard this orally from Carlebach.

antisemitism proliferate in Jewish Studies programs around the country. This is not to say antisemitism should not be a subject of academic inquiry. Indeed it should, just as other ideologies of hate and genocides should be examined and carefully studied. But I think there is something else happening here as well. For some, antisemitism has become a major source of Jewish identity, what I have elsewhere called "Negative Judaism."[2]

This essay largely does not address antisemitism *per se* but engages the way antisemitism is used in the American Jewish struggle to come to terms with a critique of Israel. While I fully acknowledge that antisemitism is a real and troubling phenomenon and its continued existence should capture the attention of all who care about humanism, freedom, and justice (Jew and non-Jew alike!), the use of and relationship to antisemitism among Jews both as part of and distinct from the Israel question is still also a legitimate subject of inquiry.

It remains true that if the problems facing Israelis and Palestinians and the Arab world more generally were resolved tomorrow, antisemitism would still exist. But that fact does not negate the importance of examining the Jewish *relationship* to antisemitism, how it may function in the Jewish psyche and the internal Jewish conversation, and the ways in which a certain dependence on antisemitism is unhealthy for Jewish flourishing.

In this essay I will address what I see are the contours of the complex Jewish relationship to antisemitism in the contemporary Jewish world that includes the ways in which criticism of Israel has been framed by some as an exercise in conscious or unconscious antisemitism or, when practiced by Jews, aiding and abetting antisemitism. I will suggest that this framing is partially the result of an unspoken fusion between Israel (or reflexive support of Israel, what I call pro-Israelism) and Jewish identity, especially in the Diaspora, that ironically is shared by some anti-Semites who use the same fusion for the perpetuation of antisemitism. The fusion of Israel and Jewish identity has become a kind of dogma of American Jewish civil religion that not only suppresses any significant critique of Israel by Jews but also prevents Diaspora Jewry from developing a sense of its own worth apart from the place where it chooses not to live.[3] I further suggest that the accusation of "antisemitism" waged against some critics of Israel is often an example of "cultural shorthand," suggesting we often talk about one thing when we really mean something else that is more difficult to confront.

II

Where did antisemitism come from? Many theories have been proposed, from the purely theological "Esau hates Jacob" motif that dominates classical religious texts to one of the various theories of antisemitism suggested by Theodor Herzl that antisemitism is largely an economic perfect storm whereby Jews, as excluded "others" in pre-modern Europe, were much better prepared to confront the vocational changes of the Industrial Revolution after emancipation.[4] Herzl hoped Zionism would solve that problem by significantly decreasing the number of Jews in Europe, thus diminishing the competitive edge that aroused such animus. Herzl's view was surely a minority opinion among Zionists. Most Zionists, from Leo Pinsker to Max Nordau and Ber Borochov (and even Herzl in other writings), suggested that antisemitism was something more endemic to European society. In fact Pinsker in his 1882 *Autoemancipation* rejected the term "antisemitism" for "Judeophobia," believing antisemitism to be a full-blown mental disorder that required a more clinical term to describe it.[5] The perennial nature of antisemitism has persisted to the present such that contemporary thinkers such as Ruth Wisse and (somewhat differently) Meir Kahane argue, anyone who is really surprised that the Holocaust happened wasn't paying close enough attention to history.[6]

While defining antisemitism, or locating its origins, is a veritable cottage industry in Jewish and European Studies, it is a questionable exercise in regards to clarifying matters that have contemporary relevance. The term only becomes operative in the 1880s "as a designation for particular individuals and groups demanding an end to recently adopted legal arrangements that had, to their minds, granted Jews undue influence over cultural, social, economic, and political life in their country."[7] Subsequently, it has been defined in so many ways and can mean so many things that the relationship between the term has ceased being descriptive and has taken on an objective reality all its own. Below I do not engage in defining the term but rather look at how it functions and what that might say about those inside the Jewish community who use it.[8]

In the latter decades of the twentieth and first decades of the twenty-first century, the popular and to some extent scholarly focus on antisemitism has turned from Christian Europe, where it still exists in disturbing ways, although largely in veiled form, to the Muslim world where it is raging.[9] There is some irony here because while it is true that Islam has a variegated relationship with Jews and Judaism, beginning with Mohammad's complex relationship with the Jews of Medina, historically Islam has treated Jews who lived under their domain better than Christians. While the Quran certainly contains anti-Jewish verses that are now too often being exploited toward political ends by Islamist clerics (medieval Jewish literature has some pretty harsh things to say about Islam and Christianity), for centuries Jews were protected minorities in Muslim lands, and often treated better than Christians.[10] The sudden upswing in Muslim antisemitism (one can see its modern prehistory in the Mufti's relationship to Hitler) coincides with its resistance to the political reality of Israel, both in terms of the Jews' historical claim to the land between the river and the sea (the land of Israel, the State of Israel, or Palestine) and the widely held view in the Muslim world that Zionism is a form of colonialism (during the First Gulf War, Saddam Hussein once referred to George H. W. Bush as "a Zionist"). It is also the case that Islam is still reeling from its loss to Christianity in the Battle of Vienna in 1683, which was preceded by the destruction wrought by the Mongol invasion of Islamic lands in the 1250s. While this was a long time ago, collectives have long memories of victimization, as any Jew who has ever recited the Passover Hagadah certainly knows.[11] The effects of colonialism, which in one way had nothing to do with the Jews and in another way had something to do with them, are still operative in the Muslim psyche in the Middle East. What I mean is that the Jews didn't come to Erez Israel as colonizers in the conventional sense, they did not come for the benefit of their home country. And by the 1930s most came as victims of persecution. But they were largely seen as colonizers by the Arab inhabitants of the land. And to some degree they treated those inhabitants as colonizers did. This is all meant not to excuse but to describe. Whether one defines colonialism purely empirically (like Alan Dershowitz) or phenomenologically (like Edward Said) there is a link between Muslim antisemitism and the Arab world's attitude toward the Israeli nation-state.[12] The nature and extent of that link remains open to scholarly debate. In my view, while Muslim animus toward the Jews certainly plays a serious role in anti-Israel sentiment, to exclude the impact of colonialism is to conveniently ignore an essential part of that complex equation.

Therefore, when one writes about antisemitism today, especially in the Muslim world, one cannot avoid Israel. And when one defends Israel today, one cannot avoid the extent to which it informs, rightly or wrongly, certain forms of Muslim antisemitism. For these reasons, in 2016 one cannot easily talk about antisemitism as if it can be severed completely from Israel. In a way, this is what Israel wants, and it is what anti-Semites want—and therein lies the problem.

III

Progressive groups such as J Street or Jewish Voice for Peace who are openly critical of Israel (and in the case of JVP, support BDS) often get accused of being "anti-Semitic," aiding and abetting anti-Semites, or being called "self-hating Jews."[13] Since antisemitism is no longer openly tolerated in polite American conversation (arguably less tolerated than racism) the accusation serves as a conversation-stopper.[14] If group X is deemed antisemitic, there is little tolerance for them in the American public square. In this regard, antisemitism is more than an accusation of unwarranted animus toward Jews; it has become a way to control the Jewish conversation. It moves from being a way to *locate* hatred to being a tool to *define* it.

Part of this phenomenon may be due to what Judith Butler claims is the problematic "full and seamless identification of the Jewish people with the State of Israel."[15] Decades earlier Charles Liebman made a softer claim but one that is not much different in substance when he wrote, "Israel has become instrumental to one's American Jewish identity. Israel, and concern for Israel, are preeminently a symbol of Jewish identity."[16] It should be noted that the fusion of Israel with Jewishness was not always a position from the right. In the late 1960s and early 1970s, the student movement called the Radical Zionist Alliance, which included many young Jews on the left, made a similar equation. One of its founders, Chava Katz, wrote in 1970, "To talk about being pro- and anti-Israel is like saying, 'Are you pro- or anti-yourself?'"[17]

Today the identification of Israel with Jewishness takes many forms, spoken and unspoken. It is often deployed as a defensive posture against the critique of Israel, especially against the occupation. For example, in December 2015 Israeli ambassador Ron Dermer prepared gift packages of products manufactured in Israeli settlements in "Judea, Samaria, and the Golan" (intentionally not distinguishing between areas that are occupied by Israel and the Golan Heights, which is annexed by Israel). He said, "This year I decided to send a gift for the holiday that would also help combat BDS." Defending his gift choice Dermer said, "Regardless of why they support BDS, the fanatics and fools are simply promoting a *new antisemitism*. Once *Jews* were singled out and held to a different standard than other peoples. Today, *the Jewish State* is singled out and held to a different standard than other countries" (italics mine).[18] The unjustified singling out of Jews that has been emblematic of antisemitism historically is now transferred to an entire nation-state whose exercise of power (whatever one thinks of the occupation, it is certainly an exercise in power) is now often rendered as a self-defensive act of victimization not unlike the Jews who suffered persecution throughout history. For Dermer, to criticize Israel, including the occupation, amounts to blaming Jews for their persecuted state historically. To be critical of Israel regarding the occupation is to be anti-Israel and to be anti-Israel is ostensibly to be antisemitic. On this reading the State of Israel has not solved the problem of the exilic Jew (antisemitism) but simply transposed the problem to the nation-state. Israel's retention of the Jews' victimized status by equating a disempowered people with an empowered nation-state illustrates the failure of Zionism to achieve the normalization many of its founders hoped for. Part of this is certainly due to Israel's contested regional status but part may also be due to Israel's continued traumatized condition, which, while understandable, is also detrimental to the continued flourishing of Jews and Judaism worldwide.[19] Comments suggesting that Israel, or perhaps the Jews, live in a perpetual state of 1938 made by some Israeli politicians only perpetuate a state of trauma that is used to excuse otherwise problematic behavior. This is not to deny that some anti-Zionism is indeed veiled antisemitism—it surely is—it is only contesting Dermer's implication that it is so by definition.[20]

The identification of Zionism with Jewishness has a history, one that it is far too complex to summarize here. One could argue it reaches back at least to David Ben-Gurion and the articulation of "negation of the Diaspora," the notion that the safety of the Jews—the very survival of the Jews—is dependent on a Jewish nation-state.[21] Thus to criticize the nation-state—even without fully delegitimizing it—can be construed as an expression of antisemitism "in effect if not intent"[22] because it is an act that threatens not only the nation-state but the entire Jewish people. For those who advocate this position, a Zionism-Judaism equation that constitutes a kind of doctrinal rather than empirical neo-negation of the Diaspora (since many of its adherents *live* in the Diaspora!), the works of Daniel and Jonathan Boyarin and Judith Butler are viewed as a modern form of identitarian heresy precisely because they undermine the very equation that serves as the cornerstone of the identity of many American Jews. In more "theological" times, heresy was that which undermined God's covenant with Israel by, for example, questioning the axiom "Torah is from Heaven," divine providence, or other doctrinal principles. In today's "identitarian" times, heresy is that which undermines Jewish survival and if Jewish survival is inextricably tied to Israel, then questioning Israel is threatening Jewish survival. Heresy is thus Jewish collusion with antisemitism. Traditionally, heresy threatened the covenant between God and Israel—today heresy threatens Jewish physical survival.[23] On this reading, "Judaism-Zionism" has thus in some way become a post-Holocaust civil religion, a crass way of understanding Emil Fackenheim's 614th commandment ("not to give Hitler posthumous victories"), not in addition to the 613 but too often in place of them.

In addition, this identification of Jews and Israel/Zionism is interesting because it is made by many ardent defenders of Israel as well as equally ardent anti-Semites. Defenders of Israel use it to claim that Zionism is the only legitimate form of contemporary Jewish political identity, and thus a deep critique of Zionism becomes a kind of anti-identity; and anti-Semites use it to draw from earlier antisemitic schema about "Jews" and make them applicable to Israel. In some sense, both sides *need* this identification to make their case. This should be no surprise as we know Zionists and anti-Semites in Europe during Herzl's time and also during the lead-up to the Second World War had some common goals (e.g., both wanted Europe to be *Judenrein*, albeit for different reasons and of course not in the same way). If the connection between Jews and Israel serves to fuel both sides, what is the cost to sever that linkage—for Zionist Jews and for anti-Semites? Put differently, what if Zionists did not fold Jewishness into Zionism such that a critique of Zionism would amount to an act of anti-Jewishness or antisemitism? This is not to say that that critique sometimes isn't, only to say it isn't *by definition*. The price for American Jews would be high in terms of perpetuating Jewish identity. Undermining Zionist hegemony—i.e., the support of Israel as the *sine qua non* of diasporic Jewish identity—would likely throw American Jews into a quandary. "Why be Jewish?" Whether intended or not, Zionism has reached hegemonic proportions in American Jewry in part because religion has ceased functioning as the engine that drives Jewishness; vibrant forms of diasporic Jewish secularism have not found strong enough footing for those who reject religion; and the Holocaust moves from memory to history. In short, today it is arguably the case that Diaspora Jews *need* Zionism at least as much as Zionism *needs* Diaspora Jews. Without a series of alternative identity possibilities, the price of severing Zionism from Jewishness in America may be too high. But it may be necessary nonetheless.

And what of anti-Semites? If anti-Semites could not point to Israel's policies and cry "Jews!" because Jews themselves, even those who support Israel, do not by definition claim Israel as the dominant part of their Jewish identity, what impact would it have in anti-Semites making their case in the twenty-first century, a century where the stench of the Holocaust still lingers? Could they fuse Israel to "Jews" as easily if Jews themselves do not identify support of Israel with Jewishness (even for those who support Israel)? While it may have little impact on real anti-Semites who will find any excuse to excoriate the Jews (and Israel), it may be productive for those who are not anti-Semites yet find Israel's policies abhorrent and cannot find any room inside legitimate Jewish discourse to voice their views. This is not to blame Israel here for collapsing Judaism into Zionism because in many ways it is understandable for Israeli Jews to view Zionism as the centerpiece of their Jewish identity, because their cultural, religious, political, and familial life is rooted in the place they choose to live. With Diaspora Jews, it is a bit more precarious. Diasporic Jewish pro-Israelism is the support of a place in which those Jews choose not to live. And making pro-Israelism the foundation of diasporic Jewish identity results to my mind in a thin form of identity that is not sustainable over time.

And as I mentioned above, antisemitism would certainly continue to exist without the identification of Israel with Jewishness. Yet it is still legitimate to ask: How do some of Israel's polices regarding the occupation and some antisemitic responses to Israel's actions enable each side to justify its own position?[24]

IV

When I was a student in yeshiva in Jerusalem and Brooklyn in the 1980s, it was common for some ultra-Orthodox Jews I "learned" with to call secular Jews, even Conservative and Reform rabbis, "anti-Semites." While one may easily scoff at the egregiousness of this accusation, it does have an ideological basis. For these Jews, basing their views largely on the teaching of Saadia Gaon, Israel is a covenanted nation *only* because of Torah.[25] The American ultra-Orthodox publishing house Artscroll defines Jews as a "Nation of Torah" to contest the more secular notion of peoplehood as Zionism, as secular Diaspora Jews understand it.[26] If Jews abandon the Torah, or distort it beyond recognition, they sever the covenant and thus endanger Israel (this is also why R. Yoel Teitelbaum, the Satmar Rebbe, held that Zionists were basically "anti-Semites").[27] Thus those who abandon Torah, or distort it, are exercising a kind of antisemitism in a world where Torah and Jews are fused. One can see this view in contemporary Israel as well. When some Gaza settlers chose to wear yellow stars or use the phrase of "not going like sheep to slaughter," as they were being removed from their homes by the Israeli military during the Gaza disengagement in 2005, the symbolism of the Israeli army as anti-Semites was precisely the point of their intervention.[28] For those settlers, Jewishness, the Jewish people, and the sanctity of the land of Israel were fused such that those who came to remove them from the land or those in favor of territorial concessions in Israel/Palestine more generally were anti-Semites.

And yet I think reasonable people can agree that secular Jews, or Zionists, are *not* anti-Semites, even for those that hold those equations. So, too, those who protest against the occupation, even many advocating BDS, or a one-state liberal democratic Israel, are not anti-Semites, certainly not *by definition*, even for those who disagree with them. Certainly anti-Semites may support these alternatives but the support of them alone does not constitute antisemitism.[29] I am arguing here that the accusation of antisemitism in these domains is, rather, often a tool of control that emerges when one form of Jewish identity become hegemonic and thus deems all others a threat to the Jews. In some way it is a consequence of identitarian totalitarianism.

V

Above I stated that one way of coming to terms with the accusation of antisemitism as a reaction to anti-Israelism or anti-Zionism is to see it as an example of "cultural shorthand," saying one thing while meaning another. We can try to understand this state of affairs in a more nuanced way by looking at other areas of Jewish life where a similar phenomenon occurs.

Exogamy, or intermarriage, is one of the most talked about issues in contemporary American Jewry. Following the 2011 Pew poll that found that among non-Orthodox American Jews almost 70 percent intermarry (when we include Orthodox Jews it is about 58 percent), American Jewish institutions have been pouring resources in trying to understand the phenomenon and discuss its implications. One very thoughtful contribution to this growing literature is Jennifer Thompson's recent book *Jewish on Their Own Terms: How Intermarried Couples are Changing American Judaism.*[30] An ethnographer by training, Thompson explores what she calls "thinking *with* intermarriage" as opposed to viewing it as a "problem" or "crisis" that requires a solution (the solution being diminishing intermarriage). Discussing a series of articles that focus on the "crisis" of intermarriage and the responsibility of Jewish social networks, Thompson writes, "Yet in the discussion of social networks, the term intermarriage does not simply mean 'couples that include one non-Jewish spouse.' It means 'couples who are assimilated'—that is, those who are disconnected from Jewish communities, organizations, and practices. In this cultural shorthand, not all assimilated Jews are intermarried, but all intermarried Jews are assimilated."[31] She argues that when American Jews talk about intermarriage they are really talking about assimilation, even as she cites a recent study in Boston where about 60 percent of intermarried Jews in the Boston area are raising their children as Jews (how they and others interpret what constitutes "raising children as Jews" is of course another matter).

This notion of "cultural shorthand," talking about one thing when one is really talking about something else (and knowing the reader can fill in the blank space in between), is a common way communities struggle to come to terms with things they have less control over by talking about things that they ostensibly have more control over. The fear of intermarriage for many American Jews may really be a fear of assimilation, but assimilation is such a deeply rooted dimension of the American Jewish experience, so difficult to locate much less control, and such an integral part of Jewish success in America, that intermarriage, something even many assimilated Jews fear, is an easier way to attract attention. But when intermarried Jews raise families that are either "Jewish" or partly so, it undermines the shorthand.

Cultural shorthand may be one way antisemitism is being used today among American Jews. When some Jews call Jewish supporters of BDS, or a one-state solution, or even an end to the occupation and the evacuation of settlements, "anti-Semites" (or abetting anti-Semites) it may really be an exercise in cultural shorthand for the unraveling of the Zionist-Jewishness fusion, or at least the lack of an ability to police it. On this reading, these progressive Jews are only "anti-Semites" within the hegemonic Zionist-Jewishness orbit. That is, if Zionism (which is often really not much more than "pro-Israelism" or Israel advocacy as an identitarian act) is identical to Jewishness, what Arthur Hertzberg called a "substitute religion," then challenging Zionism is an attempt to undermine the Jews.[32] Ergo antisemitism. The accusation of antisemitism as a policing tool to discredit these Jewish progressives may be a desperate effort to maintain the Zionism-Jewishness identification without which Jews would have to reconstruct new forms of identity.[33] It is in some way less a fear of what will happen to Israel as what will happen to American Jews. When new forms of diasporic identities are posited, be it in the work of the Boyarins, Judith Butler, or numerous others, they are quickly deemed illegitimate precisely because Israel has become a substitute for Torah (or other forms of Jewish identity) even, or especially, for Jews who don't live there. So when pro-Israelists call JVP or Jewish BDSers "anti-Semites" it is no different, nor less egregious, than when my yeshiva friend called secular Jews anti-Semites or when R. Yoel Teitelbaum called Zionists anti-Semites. The accusation of antisemitism (or abetting antisemitism) may be a form of cultural shorthand, a way to avoid confronting a much more complex problem of constructing Judaism or Jewish fidelity outside the conventional Zionist orbit. And by using the term as cultural shorthand it actually makes it easier for real anti-Semites to continue to function because they become part of a more diffuse and shallow use of a malady worth addressing in a more serious and careful manner.

In sum, today Jews are facing a series of interlocking problems and challenges that include but also exceed any external threat to their existence or the existence of the State of Israel—for example, the increased rise of Muslim antisemitism worldwide, Israel's electoral move to the right (which I do not think is simply reactive), the de facto annexation of Palestinian territory (that is, the disappearance of the occupation that makes two states impossible), young American Jews' increasing lack of romanticism when it comes to Israel, the failure of *hasbara* (pro-Israel public messaging), Israel's attempt to "explain" and "justify" the Israeli-Palestinian conflict, the rise of the "nones" (American Jews with "no" religion), and the simultaneous disassimilation of parts of American Jewry (even the intermarried and their children) without adequate diasporic-identity alternatives. The fear that love of and support of Israel that held Jews together for the past decades is unraveling has given rise to the misuse and sometimes even irresponsible accusation of antisemitism, or charge of aiding and abetting anti-Semites. While David Nirenberg may be right that antipathy for Jews has been around for millennia, even in places where no Jews lived, and even by those who likely never met a Jew (i.e., Shakespeare), extending that to argue for perennial antisemitism which, of course, makes the Jew, or Jews, not responsible for their behavior, is in my view not only a misreading of Nirenberg's *Anti-Judaism: The Western Tradition* but an attitude that moves outside the biblical, prophetic, and Jewish tradition. It is the Hebrew prophets, after all, who strongly made the case to the Israelites that they are ultimately responsible for their fate. Most of those prophets were rejected in their time; some were even imprisoned or banished. Yet today their words are a part of Jewish liturgy and chanted weekly in synagogues. In some way we, just like much of their original audience, too easily and perhaps unwittingly reject their approach in regards to collective responsibility.

What Judaism, especially in America, might look like if the Jewish-Israel-antisemitism triad were severed is an ongoing question, one that has been the subject of continued study from the 1980s until today.[34] While relevant to our topic, rehearsing these discussions is beyond the scope of this essay. In my view, to properly fight antisemitism we must intelligently locate what it is, which also means understanding what it is not. The loose, sometimes irresponsible, invocation of the term "antisemitism" may silence polite conversation. But it will not silence history.

Antisemitism, Palestine, and the Mizrahi Question

Tallie Ben Daniel

As a Mizrahi Jewish person, I am often shocked by the ways mainstream US Jewish histories and cultural scripts erase Mizrahi experiences and histories.[1] This erasure becomes even more acute when discussing antisemitism. In this essay, I argue that in order to have a comprehensive analysis of antisemitism that truly tackles the operations of power in the United States, one must not only take Mizrahi experiences and analysis into account, but also account for the existence of the State of Israel. The essay starts by thinking through some of the more ubiquitous understandings of antisemitism, then moves to a brief analysis of Iraqi Jewish experiences and their relationship to the conventional understanding of antisemitism. Finally, the essay takes on one of the "alternative" definitions of antisemitism, and argues that it too participates in the erasure of Mizrahi experiences. The essay concludes by asking how we can link our analysis of antisemitism to both the global struggle for Palestinian rights and to the fight against the marginalization of Mizrahi Jewish communities.

The first, and perhaps most popular, understanding of antisemitism in the United States is one I have come across both in mainstream Jewish institutions and in more alternative leftist spaces. It goes something like this: antisemitism began, so the story goes, with the scapegoating of Jews in ancient times, because of the Jewish adherence to monotheism, culminating with the destruction of the Temple by the Romans; continued through the spread of Christianity and the Crusades, manifesting in accusations of blood libel; and endured through the social and economic discrimination of the Enlightenment in the form of "the Jewish question." That was followed by pogroms, culminating in the Holocaust. Antisemitism, then, has always been with us and always will, and we have to live with this legacy. Jews, as perennial social outsiders, are blamed for economic and social problems associated with money or the media or other powerful, disembodied forces. In some cases, this story ends (happily or otherwise) with the creation of the State of Israel in 1948. Of course, in some interpretations, the violence in Israel/Palestine (or any criticism of Israeli policy) is further evidence of antisemitism.

While this is obviously overly succinct, I wonder if those reading this would have any trouble with this as a summary of the history of antisemitism. Although missing nuance, I am going to assume that for most, this encapsulates the major events. And the final conclusion must be that antisemitism is a problem that has always been with us, and will always be with us.

This narrative sits uncomfortably with me, and has for a long time. There are three major reasons: first, as an Iraqi Jewish person, this narrative often erases the experiences and histories of non-European Jews. Like all religious minorities, Jews are incredibly diverse, and there have been significant Jewish communities all over the world, not only in Europe. Second, in a US context, this narrative of antisemitism can lead to seeing it as a kind of urtext for other forms of racism, which often lets white US American Jews off the hook when confronting white dominance and structural racism. Third, this narrative, in this form, often ends with a justification for the dispossession of Palestinians— the establishment of the State of Israel was necessary, so the story goes, to correct for the centuries of antisemitism. Antisemitism, in this interpretation, is ongoing and unfixable because Jews are always outsiders, and in Israel, Jews can be the majority, and so never have to worry about such violence again.

Of course, any casual follower of Israeli and Palestinian politics should know that the establishment of the State of Israel in 1948 did not mark an end to violence. Rather, Palestinian communities worldwide commemorate the establishment of the state in 1948 as the Nakba, or "catastrophe," a military event that decimated Palestinian villages and created the second-largest refugee population in the world.[2] The Jewish majority in Israel is maintained only through dispossession, deeply unequal laws, and a demographic war against Palestinians.[3] The establishment of Israel created a new Jewish identity, in which every Jewish person, for better or worse, is hailed by the Jewish state. For some Jewish people, this relationship is one of liberation and triumph, or is characterized by a sense of belonging, even if they don't physically reside there. For others, this relationship is one of trauma and discrimination, and/or painful culpability, as the Israeli government continues to maintain systems of oppression and discrimination against the Palestinian people. And I should point out that the relationship of Jews worldwide to Israel is not limited to those I've outlined here, nor are any of these relationships mutually exclusive. But regardless, a relationship is seemingly unavoidable.

Yet, when we talk about antisemitism, even in spaces that are ostensibly aware of the occupation and displacement of Palestinians, European experiences are presented as the template for all Jews, everywhere, along with a cautionary tale of the unchanging, endless, permanent, or cyclical nature of antisemitism. We also live in a world where Western Europe, and Western European history, is dominant, so the tropes that characterize European antisemitism—like conspiracy theories in which Jews are secretly in control of financial systems or the media—are dominant as well. I do not doubt that antisemitism exists, nor do I think we should let it go unchecked. But I want an analysis of antisemitism that interrogates, rather than replicates, the Eurocentricity of the current most common narrative.

The Experiences of Mizrahi and Sephardi Jews

I want to offer an alternative narrative to the one so roughly outlined above: A Jewish community develops in Iraq after the destruction of the Temple and for thousands of years flourishes in the major metropolitan areas. Jewish Iraqis are found in nearly every sector of society, while maintaining a unique cultural and religious identity. They have deep cultural connections to other Jewish communities, notably in India and France. When the British colonize Iraq after World War I, anti-Jewish sentiment is imported along with a different set of colonial hierarchies.[4] In 1941, the Jews of Baghdad experience the *farhud,* an anti-Jewish riot that was, according to historian Orit Bashkin, a result of "German propaganda disseminated into the Iraqi print market," "an intense debate among intellectuals concerning Nazism and fascism," and the general conflation of Zionism with Judaism in a nationalist, postcolonial era of Iraqi politics.[5] After the State of Israel is established in 1948, a backdoor deal with the government of Iraq expels the Jews from Iraq, making them leave their possessions behind; they are then put in refugee camps (*ma'abarot*) and are marginalized as uncivilized, too close to the Arab neighbors of Israel in language, culture, and demeanor.[6] Israeli identity continually valorizes Western European Jewish culture in all segments of society, including the anti-occupation left.[7] The experiences of Iraqi Jews are unique, but they connect to the experiences of Jews from Yemen, Syria, Egypt, Iran, India, Morocco, and other Middle Eastern and North African countries in that they are continually marked as "other" in Israeli society. The term "Mizrahi" is symbolic of that otherness—a Hebrew term that translates literally to "eastern." While Mizrahi Jews constitute a majority of Jewish Israeli society, Ashkenazi Jewish culture and history dominates. Mizrahi Jews are told that the history of European Jews is the history of all Jews, everywhere.

Many scholars, most notably Ella Shohat, have remarked on the position of Mizrahi Jews within Israeli society: simultaneously included and excluded from the Israeli national collective, both a potential bridge between Jewish, Ashkenazi Israelis and Palestinians and more often, a fence that marks the Israeli collective's borders.[8]

The narrative above may be just as overly simplified as the one I began with, but I am using it to make the following point—that when talking about antisemitism, one cannot focus only on the experiences of white Ashkenazi Jews. To do so is to contribute to the ongoing erasure of Mizrahi Jews in Jewish communities in the United States and in Israel, and to perpetuate the idea that European Jewish history is the history of all Jews. At the same time, it is equally problematic to assume that antisemitism as it presented in Europe can be "found" in the histories of Mizrahi Jews.[9] In some cases, when we start with the assumption that antisemitism is a natural and eternal part of the Jewish condition, or the human condition, it can lead to orientalizing the Mizrahi experience, by attempting to "discover" the equivalent of a pogrom or a ghetto in Mizrahi history, essentially analyzing Mizrahi history through the lens of European history.[10] We assume that the status of Iraqi Jews in the early twentieth century must have been similar to those of Polish, German, or Bavarian Jews, when in fact, they were living in a totally different political context, and grappling with totally different histories. If one focuses only on antisemitism as the primary, or only, way Jews have been oppressed throughout time, and define antisemitism through the events of European exclusion and discrimination, then one is perpetuating a Eurocentric understanding of history and erasing the exploitation of Mizrahi Jews at the hands of Ashkenazi Jews.

In the United States, many Jewish historians lack an analysis of how antisemitism works alongside and intersects with other systems of oppression, like racism, sexism, and classism.[11] I saw a version of this history of antisemitism while at the Association for Jewish Studies' annual conference, at a panel discussing what kinds of pedagogical tools one can bring to a social justice–grounded Jewish Studies classroom. One panelist discussed how her Jewish American history class is often confronted by what she saw as the contradictions of US history: how did American Jews move so quickly from marginalization and discrimination to almost total acceptance, a journey so unlike that of other minority groups?

What was remarkable to me in her discussion of the ways labor, capitalism, and "up by the bootstraps" perseverance had transferred American Jews from margin to center was the complete absence of any acknowledgment that race may have played a role. Many people of color in the United States have probably heard the phrase "I'm not white, I'm Jewish" from white, Jewish US Americans. At the same time, many scholars have examined the social processes in the United States before World War II that established "Jewishness" as ethnically separate, while allowing (some) Jews full entrance into whiteness in the decades that followed.[12] Keith Feldman, in particular, has made a compelling case for looking at Israel and Palestine and the ongoing occupation as a series of events that deeply influenced the meaning and function of race in America.[13] Rather than focus on the Jewish involvement in the civil rights movement or simplistic understandings of "Black-Jewish relations," Feldman traces the rise of Zionism in US American Jewish institutions, the vexed relationship to Israel within Black liberation and Black power movements, and the impact of the events of 1967 on Arab communities in the United States, Israel, and beyond to explain not only how Jews became white, but how in the end Palestine became "America's last taboo."[14]

We cannot fully understand the experiences and histories of Mizrahi Jews unless we also confront the ways Zionism and the State of Israel contributed to—and in some cases, may be the source of—Mizrahi Jewish oppression. And in the United States, the cultural articulation that equates Jewishness with whiteness, without accounting for the impact of Zionism on Jewish racial identity, furthers and perpetuates white Ashkenazi dominance in Jewish spaces. The collective impact of this is to allow progressive white Jewish communities in the United States to avoid confronting racial oppression within the Jewish community, within the United States more broadly, and within Israel/Palestine.

Things Are Not Better on the Left—on Mizrahi Erasure in a Common Analysis of Antisemitism

Attempts to theorize antisemitism "from the left" equally ignore the impact of whiteness and white supremacy on Jewish communities. In the past few years, I've come across a common theory of antisemitism in leftist organizing that often perpetuates Mizrahi erasure and assumes that all Jewish people are white and of European descent. For the purposes of this essay, I'm going to focus on one iteration of this theory, April Rosenblum's 2007 zine, "The Past Didn't Go Anywhere: Making Resistance to Antisemitism a Part of All Our Movements."[15] I chose this zine because it is incredibly popular in leftist spaces, and precisely because it tries—and fails—to think about the experiences of Mizrahi Jews and Jews of color.

The zine treats antisemitism as equivalent to "anti-Jewish oppression." The core assumption in the zine is that antisemitism, or "anti-Jewish oppression," looks and works differently from other forms of oppression. As Rosenblum states, anti-Jewish oppression "can make its target look extremely powerful."[16] In other words, antisemitism makes the "ruling classes invisible" by "diverting anger at injustice toward Jews instead." According to this theory, Jewish people are a scapegoat for the rage produced by economic and racial injustice: "The point of anti-Jewish oppression is to keep a Jewish face in front, so that Jews, instead of ruling classes, become the target for peoples' rage." Therefore, "it works even more smoothly when Jews are allowed some success, and can be perceived as the ones 'in charge' by other oppressed groups."[17] My first problem with this analysis of antisemitism is a seemingly minor one—the passive voice used to describe the position of Jewish people. Jews "are allowed some success" rather than "achieving" success, therefore erasing the ways some Jewish communities actively participated in cultivating whiteness in the United States, not to mention the active participation in the European colonization of Palestine.[18] This analysis of antisemitism works as an explainer for the Jewish position in medieval Europe, but falls short in taking the current realities of race and ethnicity in the United States and Israel into account.

For example, Rosenblum's analysis of internalized oppression claims that

> on an individual level, Jewish people—especially men—often perceive themselves as physically weak. We were legally banned from being allowed to carry weapons for substantial periods under Christian and Muslim rule. European society excluded us from mainstream professions (e.g., farming) that strengthened the body. We were literally unable to protect ourselves and our families from mass violence and rape.[19]

This analysis, while factually suspect,[20] also lacks an acknowledgment of white Ashkenazi dominance—in that the value of a strong, masculine body is a European, Christian invention, directly tied to the emergence of nationalism.[21] It also completely ignores the ways Zionist masculinity developed as a direct response to this invention, with the settler-pioneer-farmer in the figure of the *sabra*, and that white Jewish belonging in the United States was contingent on participation in the same settler-colonial narratives.[22]

It also lacks an intersectional analysis of Jewish communities by collapsing all Jewish people together. Black and Latino Jewish men confront a totally different set of cultural scripts around masculinity. Rather than weakness, they contend with a racialized hypermasculinity that enables state violence against them, often by portraying them as those "we" must protect "ourselves" from. The fact that Jewish men of color experience such racism does not mean that they don't also experience antisemitism, but one would not know that from this analysis. For another example, Rosenblum claims that "Jewish people—especially women—often feel disgust about ourselves and our bodies, because, as the main racial 'Other' in Europe, European society and popular culture created its images of what was ugly and disgusting based on our Jewish faces, and its fantasies of what our bodies looked like."[23] This analysis assumes that all Jewish women are of European descent, that there is a particular kind of "Jewish look" that is shared among all Jews. This excludes converts, Mizrahi Jews, and other Jews of color.

My basic problem with this theory is that it lets white Jews off the hook— it excuses the ways racism, white supremacy, and classism manifest themselves within Jewish communities. It is one thing to say that Jewish power is a myth of antisemitism; it is something else entirely to say that powerful Jewish people are a symptom of antisemitism. For example, the idea that there is some kind of secret cabal of Jews that control the media or foreign policy is a deeply antisemitic trope that has contributed to violence against Jews in Europe and in the United States, among other places. But white people, including white Jews, can and do hold power in the United States, and Jewish institutions, by and large, do not work to combat the ways white supremacy and racism manifest themselves in Jewish communities. This theory claims that antisemitism "works more smoothly when it allows certain Jews success." I argue that it is whiteness, not antisemitism, that allows (some) white Jews success in the United States.

As a queer person, I see parallels in queer activism and communities, where a focus on white, male, upper-class gay issues contributes to the erasure of, and violence toward, working-class queers and queers of color. While the lack of marriage rights in the United States certainly contributed to queer oppression, the fight for same-sex marriage often railroaded the issues that had an impact on poor and working-class queer people and queers of color (homelessness and the disproportionate targeting of trans women of color by the policing and prison systems, for example).

The questions of racialization that come up when thinking about the history of Jewish identity in the United States are ever more fraught when thinking about Mizrahi Jews in this country. Sigal Samuel artfully thinks through the question of Mizrahim vis-à-vis race in the United States in an op-ed published in *The Forward* titled "I'm a Mizrahi Jew. Do I Count as a Person of Color?"[24] She takes multiple aspects of the question into account—her personal experiences, which includes racial profiling in airports; her family's heritage; the US Census, which as of this writing classifies Arab and Middle Eastern people as white; and academics, who are decidedly mixed in their interpretation of the location of Mizrahi Jews in the United States. She ends by claiming herself a "woman of color"—a politicized, coalitional term that comes to us via feminist thinking and activism.[25] But even that term can hold its own complexity, its own way of masking difference between those who inherited a racial category due to the settler-colonial violence in the United States, and those of us who come to our racialized identities due to historical events elsewhere.[26] Similarly, Keren Soffer-Sharon writes that "as Arab Jews, our very existence calls into question some of the most basic values that our mainstream Jewish community has tragically come to hold about the 'threat' that Palestinians and Arab Muslims in general pose to our collective safety."[27] While Mizrahi Jews are uniquely positioned to point to the damage done by assuming all Jews are European, or that Jews are somehow in opposition to Arabs, we are not immune to perpetuating and participating in racisms. There are many ways this can manifest, but for now, I would like to focus on a US-based organization, JIMENA: Jews Indigenous to the Middle East and North Africa.

JIMENA and the "New Antisemitism"

Since at least 2004, a group of pro-Israel advocates, notably Kenneth Marcus of the Louis D. Brandeis Center for Human Rights Under Law, have attempted to redefine antisemitism to include criticism of Israel. Such advocates have argued that when anti-occupation activists target Israel, they are singling it out as the only Jewish state, while other human rights abuses go unobserved. While this argument has very little merit—many anti-occupation activists come to their activism through a sense of moral outrage that is not limited to human rights abuses in Israel and Palestine, and we should stringently distinguish between antisemitism and anti-Zionism—these pro-Israel advocates nonetheless use false charges of antisemitism to target activism on behalf of Palestinian human rights, as noted elsewhere in this volume.

JIMENA is an organization that ostensibly works to educate US American Jewish communities about the histories and cultural practices of Mizrahi Jews. A project of the San Francisco Jewish Community Relations Council, it uses the claim of indigeneity via Mizrahi Jews to further the aims of the State of Israel, that is, to undermine the struggle for Palestinian human rights. The most explicit example of this is the fact that JIMENA currently uses the website "nakba.com" to redirect to its website.[28] In JIMENA's view, "Nakba" does not connote the Palestinian expulsion from Palestine in 1948, as the term is more commonly known, but rather what they refer to as the "expulsion" of Mizrahi Jews from other Middle Eastern countries (ostensibly to safety in Israel). On its website, JIMENA applies its interpretation of the "new antisemitism" to claim,

"Though veiled as political activism, BDS campaigns are in effect vehicles for anti-Semitism, as they target the world's only Jewish State, and lead to silencing and bullying of Jewish and pro-Israel students."[29] This blatant misinformation obscures the ways Palestinian human rights activism is often targeted on university campuses.[30] BDS, as a nonviolent set of tactics, is responding to a call by Palestinian civil society to enact boycott, divestment, and sanctions until Israel complies with international law. But JIMENA's purpose is to use Mizrahi identity to further silence such activism:

> BDS and anti-Israel activism relies on a false narrative which portrays Jews as white European colonialists who invaded a third-world country, displaced a significant portion of the indigenous Palestinian population, oppressed and segregated the remainder. As North America's primary organization representing Jewish refugees from the Middle East and North Africa, JIMENA is uniquely positioned to refute these myths by empowering students with the personal narratives of former Jewish refugees indigenous to Arab countries and Iran. We teach students that: 'Jews and Israelis are not white colonists, we are indigenous to the Middle East and North Africa. We speak Arabic. We have been made refugees from countries we lived in for over 2,500 year [*sic*]. In today's value, we had $6billion confiscated when we fled.' BDS messaging preys on college student's ideologies of empathy and support for the 'third-world victim' while singling out those with 'white privilege' as the oppressors. This has had a catastrophic effect on Jewish students [*sic*] confidence, willingness, and ability to support Israel. This damaging BDS messaging has effectively served to isolate, unaffiliate, and disempower many of our Jewish students and potential student supporters of Israel. There is no better counter defense to this propaganda than the story of Jewish refugees from Arab countries.[31]

Here, JIMENA is using a claim to indigeneity to further a settler-colonial project. "Jews are not white colonists, we are indigenous to the Middle East and North Africa" is a flipping of the centrality of white Ashkenazi experiences, but also does so to intentionally erase the participation of European (and non-European) Jews in the Nakba, the occupation, and the creation of the Palestinian refugee population. I am personally outraged by their use of my family's heritage to justify the continual dispossession of Palestinians, but it is it is essential that we understand Mizrahi positionality in all its complexity, including the potential to be used to further the aims of the Israeli government, or to continue the injustices of the occupation. JIMENA is, at its core, a "brownwashing" organization, albeit a sophisticated one—using the experiences of Jews of color and Mizrahi Jews in particular to justify the occupation. I'm using the term "brownwashing" as a derivative of the term "pinkwashing" to note the ways both cynically use marginalized identities—Arab and queer—to promote anti-Palestinian aims. To fully combat this use of Mizrahi history, progressive Mizrahi Jews and Jews of color must take collective action, and work to produce an analysis and a language to address our heritage, histories, and inheritance in ways that fight back against the exploitation of Palestinians.

Notes toward a Conclusion

What would an intersectional understanding of antisemitism look like? If we take the particularities of multiple Jewish histories in the United States into account, does that mean that we are left without a way to confront the legacies of violence against Jewish people, or an accounting of the ways Jews were seen as the "other" of Europe?

My answer, as is my answer to most things, is not an either/or formulation, but a both/and one. European antisemitism has had a real impact on American culture, and continues to proliferate as European nationalism enjoys a kind of resurgence.[32] At the same time, the current manifestations of antisemitism are not a recurrence of past forms of antisemitism, and we do ourselves a disservice if we think they are. We must contend with the ways some Jews have access to power and privilege, with the racial differences within the Jewish community, and, crucially, with the ways Muslims and Arabs have been targeted in the United States after 9/11. We must learn about our histories, and for those of us who fight for a better future, think carefully about what kinds of lessons we learn. As David Biale notes, "Traditional Jewish memory, with its emphasis on recurring persecutions, can only reinforce the traumas of recent Jewish history; history itself, in all its complexity, may provide the needed therapy."[33] My hope is that we can move into a future where the fight for justice—what Rabab Abdulhadi calls "the indivisibility of justice"—takes all of this into account.[34]

Part II:

Confronting Antisemitism and Islamophobia

Trump, the Alt-right, Antisemitism, and Zionism

Arthur Goldwag

On August 25, 2016, Hillary Clinton delivered a speech in Reno, Nevada, in which she warned of the de facto merger between the Donald Trump campaign and, via its campaign CEO Stephen Bannon and the Breitbart News Network (the right-wing website he formerly headed), the "alternative-right" or "alt-right." Quoting the *Wall Street Journal,* Clinton defined the alt-right as "a loose but organized movement, mostly online, that 'rejects mainstream conservatism, promotes nationalism, and views immigration and multiculturalism as threats to white identity.'" Trump's open trafficking in racist, sexist, and antisemitic appeals was unprecedented, she said.

"Of course, there has always been a paranoid fringe in our politics," she continued, "a lot of it rising from racial resentment. But it's never had the nominee of a major party stoking it, encouraging it, and giving it a national megaphone. Until now."[1] It was a powerful speech, but it was undercut by the off-the-cuff remarks she made at an LGBT fundraiser two weeks later about Trump's "basket of deplorables," in which she insinuated that as many as half of his supporters were irredeemably bigoted.[2] Though Breitbart's readership is very large (it claimed 31 million unique visitors in July 2016), most of its readers are of course a far cry from the programmatic haters that make up the alt-right, and countless Trump supporters had never heard of either Breitbart or the alt-right.[3] In implying otherwise, she further inflamed their sense of grievance and put herself back on the defensive. I will have much more to say about Steve Bannon and the Breitbart News Network, but first I want to dig a little deeper into the intellectual roots of the alt-right. If nothing else, its progenitors show that it's possible to hate Jews and Judaism while also wholeheartedly supporting the Jewish state, and to do so with intellectual consistency.

Richard Spencer is generally given the credit for introducing the term "alternative-right" to the American political lexicon. He first used the phrase in print in a survey of conservative book publishing in *Taki's Magazine* in 2008.[4] Then, in 2010, he launched his website AlternativeRight.com, which was underwritten by Peter Brimelow's anti-immigration VDare Foundation. Underestimating the staying power of the political brand he had unleashed, Spencer dismantled the site in 2013, redirecting traffic to his new *Radix Journal*.

The thirty-eight-year-old Spencer holds an MA in humanities from the University of Chicago and was briefly enrolled in a PhD program at Duke University. He cut his paleoconservative teeth as an assistant editor at Pat Buchanan's *American Conservative*, then came out as a full-blown white nationalist during his stint as executive editor of *Taki's Magazine*. Today he is the president and director of the National Policy Institute, a white nationalist think tank that was founded in 2005 by William Regnery, Sam Francis, and Louis R. Andrews. Styling himself a racial "identitarian" (as opposed to a "supremacist"), Spencer has referred to his mission as a "sort of white Zionism," claiming to desire nothing more than peaceful racial coexistence in separate, ethnically cleansed monocultures.[5] Back in 2010, Spencer wrote:

> It is, in my mind, still highly legitimate—and philosophically powerful, if not yet politically effective—to inform people like Abe Foxman, and others who are as fanatical in their Zionism as their anti-racism, that the Traditionalist Right and White Nationalists desire things that aren't unlike the stated goals of the Israeli government: an ethno-state for one's own, and respect for the aspirations of other nations.

He added, "I say all this not because I love Israel or Zionism (which I don't), or because I care about the fate of the Palestinians (which I don't). I say this because I love the West and the European race of man and desire that both survive."[6]

Spencer excludes Mizrahi and even Ashkenazi Jews from the European race of man, their pale skin notwithstanding. "Pigmentation really is 'just skin deep,'" he explains. "It's a significant, but by no means definitive, element of race. Identity is formed by a combination of race, culture, spirituality, and history. And Ashkenazi Jews have an identity apart from Europeans."[7] Spencer cites a *Times of Israel* op-ed by the Zionist Hila Hershkoviz to buttress his point: "Ashkenazi Jews are not genetically white," she wrote. "Whether the world likes it or not (and apparently it does not), [they] are direct descendants of the Tribes of Israel, as we know from history, culture, science and a little something I like to call reality. Those who wish to deny it for political or theological reasons, should try forming an alliance with Holocaust deniers because the two are no different."[8] The many Holocaust deniers who agree with her on the question of Jewish whiteness and the desirability of a Jewish state would no doubt be puzzled by her last turn of thought.

If the thought leadership of the alt-right has an *éminence grise*, it is Jared Taylor. Born to missionary parents in Japan in 1951, Taylor graduated from Yale with a degree in philosophy and received his MA in international economics from the Institut d''Études Politiques de Paris.[9] In his 1993 book *Paved with Good Intentions: The Failure of Race Relations in Contemporary America*, and a steady stream of articles in *American Renaissance*, the journal of the New Century Foundation think tank that he founded, Taylor propounds a philosophy that he calls "race realism." When it comes to Jews, Taylor is at odds with Spencer and, indeed, the rank and file of his movement. He not only admires the Israeli ethno-state as a model for a would-be white nation to emulate, but firmly rejects the notion that Jews are "enemies of the white race," or, for that matter, non-white. In 2012, when Israel began aggressively deporting refugees from South Sudan, Taylor took to the pages of *American Renaissance* to applaud the country's leadership. "With a boldness that every Western country should imitate," he wrote, "the Israelis have mandated expulsion for the explicit purpose of keeping their country Jewish—even for keeping it *white*.... The Israeli government is doing exactly what we would like our government to do. We should point to Israel as a model and encourage our rulers to copy it."[10]

Taylor's philosemitism carved a deep rift in his movement in 2006, when the former KKK Imperial Wizard, neo-Nazi, Holocaust denier, and frequent political candidate David Duke stood up at an American Renaissance Conference to deplore the silence in the room about the "power in the world that dominates our media, influences our government and that has led to the internal destruction of our will and spirit."[11] That power, of course, was the one Duke wrote about in his 2001 book *Jewish Supremacism: My Awakening to the Jewish Question*. Duke's comment prompted an angry retort from a Jewish attendee, who was loudly jeered by many in the crowd. Ten years later, hardcore neo-Nazi groups continue to berate Taylor as a Jew-lover and his partner, Evelyn Rich, as a crypto-Jew. In a recent interview, however, Taylor allowed that "a strong case can be made about the extent to which Jewish intellectuals have undermined white racial consciousness."[12] Clearly, he was nodding to Kevin MacDonald.

MacDonald has published in both Taylor's and Spencer's journals and participated in events they organized, and is widely respected throughout the alt-right. In "The Alt Right & the Jews," a September 2016 essay published on the *Counter-Currents* website, MacDonald, formerly a professor of psychology at California State University, describes the full scope of the "role of Jews in White dispossession, both historically and in the contemporary West."[13] In his Culture of Critique trilogy, consisting of *A People That Shall Dwell Alone* (1994), *Separation and Its Discontents* (1998), and *The Culture of Critique* (1998), MacDonald elaborated his theory that Jewish "parasitism" and subversion are key components of a group evolutionary strategy that is fueled by high ethnocentrism, high aggressiveness towards out-groups, high psychological intensity, and high intelligence.

Counter-Currents' publisher Greg Johnson's take on the Jewish Question is simple. While he believes that "Jews are not just *different* from whites, but powerful and malevolent enemies who bear significant responsibility for causing white decline and opposing white renewal," the mere fact of their difference suffices to define the solution: "Once one recognizes that Jews are a distinct people, the ethnonationalist solution to the Jewish question is Jewish nationalism, i.e., Zionism."[14]

Trump's ascension reminded America's fractious congeries of race theorists (who are no less schismatic than any other radical movement) of what they do hold in common. Much to Trump's embarrassment, who was forced to repudiate him, David Duke moved swiftly to endorse Trump, telling his radio audience that "voting against Donald Trump really is treason to your heritage."[15] Taylor enthusiastically endorsed Trump as well, as did Spencer and MacDonald. (Taylor and Duke were both prominently featured in a Clinton campaign commercial that was released around the time of her alt-right speech.)[16] MacDonald enjoyed the distinction of being retweeted by Donald Trump Jr.[17]

Trump himself, of course, drew headlines for retweeting @WhiteGenocideTM and other antisemites and white supremacists throughout his long campaign. The infamous image of Hillary Clinton, superimposed on a pile of money with "Most Corrupt Candidate Ever" emblazoned in a Star of David, that appeared on his Twitter feed originated on a white nationalist website.[18] Andrew Anglin, editor of the neo-Nazi website the Daily Stormer, did not believe that those retweets were inadvertent, as Trump's campaign insisted. "There is no way that this could be anything other than both a wink-wink-wink and a call for more publicity," he posted. "Today in America the air is cold and it tastes like victory."[19]

"Donald Trump may win or lose," Jared Taylor declared in September 2016, "but we will grow, with him or without him."[20] As fate would have it, Donald Trump did win, and when the National Policy Institute convened in Washington for its annual meeting on November 19, 2016, Spencer was ebullient. "It's been an awakening," he said. "This is what a successful movement looks like." Though he acknowledged that Trump had yet to sign on to the full scope of the think tank's racialist ideas, he held out hope that "moving forward, the alt-right as an intellectual vanguard can complete Trump. We can be the ones who are out front, who are thinking about things that he hasn't grasped yet." "In the long run," Taylor added, "people like Bannon and Trump will be open to the clarity of our ideas."[21]

For all the media attention that Taylor, Spencer, and MacDonald's endorsements of Donald Trump brought them (and Spencer gained even more notoriety when he was videotaped at an informal gathering after the NPI conference shouting "Hail Trump" and "Hail Victory" as members of the audience gave stiff-armed salutes, and musing about whether certain members of the "Luegenpresse" qualify as "people at all"), as theorists they occupy a fairly rarefied realm.[22] As it is represented in the articles, podcasts, comments, and social media of Steve Bannon's Breitbart News Network, the alt-right is significantly more raucous and diverse, and vastly larger and younger, bringing together anti-feminists and pickup artists, isolationists, neo-Nazis, pro-Russians, biological-determinists, gamers, Ron Paul libertarians, anarcho-capitalists, Alex Jones conspiracy theorists, and white tribalists of every stripe. Memes like Pepe the Frog and the insult "cuckservative," a portmanteau of "cuckold" and "conservative" that was ruthlessly hurled at mainstream figures like Jeb Bush, epitomized the aggressive and relentlessly ironic style of the alt-right's legions of Internet trolls. As Breitbart's Milo Yiannopoulos and Allum Bokhari put it in "An Establishment Conservative's Guide to the Alt-Right," alt-rightists are no more bigots "than death metal devotees in the 80s were actually Satanists. For them, it's simply a means to fluster their grandparents. . . . Young people perhaps aren't primarily attracted to the alt-right because they're instinctively drawn to its ideology: they're drawn to it because it seems fresh, daring and funny, while the doctrines of their parents and grandparents seem unexciting, overly controlling and overly serious."

Cracking jokes about the Holocaust? "It's just about having fun."[23] What about traditional *Protocols of the Elders of Zion*–style conspiracism—or straight-up Nazi calls for mass extermination? More lulz, the half-Jewish (and openly gay) Yiannopoulos told talk show host Dave Rubin:

Generation Trump, the alt right people . . . they're not anti-Semites. They don't care about Jews. I mean, they may have some assumptions about things, how the Jews run everything; well, we do. How the Jews run the banks; well, we do. How the Jews run the media; well, we do. They're right about all that stuff . . . It's a fact, this is not in debate. It's a statistical fact. . . . It's not anti-Semitic to point out statistics. . . . I want people to understand this because nobody seems to, when Jonah Goldberg of *National Review* is bombarded with these memes, and anti-Semitic "take a hike, kike" stuff, it's not because there's a spontaneous outpouring of anti-Semitism from 22-year-olds in this country. What it is is a mischievous, dissident, trolly generation who do it because it gets a reaction.[24]

It certainly is a fact that Jewish journalists, Never-Trump conservatives and progressives alike, were the objects of antisemitic vitriol and threats throughout Trump's campaign. Julia Ioffe shared some of the offensive messages that were sent to her with the *Guardian* after her profile of Melania Trump ran in *GQ*,[25] and the *Observer*'s Dana Schwartz sent an open letter to her employer, Jared Kushner (Trump's son-in-law and an orthodox Jew), after she was similarly deluged with hate mail after she made comments about Trump's Star of David tweet.[26] I experienced this in a small way myself after the *New York Times* ran an op-ed I wrote that was critical of Trump.[27]

Donald Trump's speech on October 13, 2016, in West Palm Beach, Florida, which was rumored to have been cowritten by Bannon, was replete with dark allusions to the cosmopolitan elites that pull the levers of world power.[28] The final commercial of his campaign used similar language while flashing sinister images of Lloyd Blankfein, the Jewish CEO of Goldman Sachs; Janet Yellin, the Jewish chair of the Federal Reserve; and the Jewish billionaire George Soros. "When I saw the ad," Senator Al Franken remarked, "I thought this was something of a German shepherd whistle, a dog whistle, to a certain group in the United States. I'm Jewish, so maybe I'm sensitive to it. It had an *Elders of Zion* feeling to it, an international banking conspiracy to it."[29]

After Hillary Clinton's alt-right speech, the Breitbart News Network and Bannon himself defended themselves against charges that they are antisemitic. They were especially adamant on the issue in the aftermath of Bannon's announced appointment as White House chief strategist and senior counselor to the president. During Bannon's 2007 court battle over the custody of his children, his ex-wife gave sworn testimony to the effect that when they were touring the Archer School for Girls, he remarked that "he doesn't like Jews and that he doesn't like the way they raise their kids to be 'whiney brats' and that he didn't want the girls going to school with Jews."[30]

"Breitbart is the most pro-Israel site in the United States of America," Bannon protested to the *Wall Street Journal*.

> I have Breitbart Jerusalem, which I have Aaron Klein run with about 10 reporters there. We've been leaders in stopping this BDS movement in the United States; we're a leader in the reporting of young Jewish students being harassed on American campuses; we've been a leader on reporting on the terrible plight of the Jews in Europe. . . . These claims of anti-Semitism just aren't serious. It's a joke.

While he concedes that the alt-right "includes some racial and anti-Semitic overtones," he claimed to have zero tolerance for them.[31]

Writing in the *Jewish Press*, Alan Dershowitz exonerated Bannon and Breitbart of antisemitism, but not of making "bigoted statements about Muslims, women and others, which I do not condone. That is why I do not support Bannon, even though I do not think he's an antisemite. Bigotry against any group should be disqualifying for high office." Dershowitz noted that his former research assistant Joel Pollak, "an Orthodox Jew who wears a kippah . . . assures me that he never heard a single antisemitic utterance or saw an antisemitic action in the four years he worked together with Bannon."[32] It's telling, however, that for all his high-mindedness about bigotry, Dershowitz did not see any reason to condemn Pollak for his comment in Breitbart News that "Palestinian nationalism is not actually a form of nationalism, properly speaking. It is a mass psychosis."[33]

Before he became a publisher and a kingmaker, Bannon was a dealmaker at Goldman Sachs and a banker and entrepreneur in Hollywood, where, irony of ironies, he secured a share of the royalties from *Seinfeld* for himself. In an interview with the *Hollywood Reporter*, he argued that "I'm not a white nationalist, I'm a nationalist. I'm an economic nationalist." But he also let slip a curious and telling boast.

> Like [Andrew] Jackson's populism, we're going to build an entirely new political movement. . . . It's everything related to jobs. The conservatives are going to go crazy. I'm the guy pushing a trillion-dollar infrastructure plan. With negative interest rates throughout the world, it's the greatest opportunity to rebuild everything. Shipyards, ironworks, get them all jacked up. We're just going to throw it up against the wall and see if it sticks. It will be as exciting as the 1930s, greater than the Reagan revolution—conservatives, plus populists, in an economic nationalist movement.[34]

As exciting as the 1930s? Exactly what country was he talking about? The 1930s were an epoch of secular stagnation in the United States. Hitler, however, presided over an economic miracle that was driven by massive public spending on infrastructure and rearmament. Shipyards and ironworks were humming in Germany, not over here.

The late Andrew Breitbart, it's worth remembering, was Jewish, and the Breitbart News Network was conceived in Israel, according to its cofounder (and Breitbart's coreligionist) Larry Solov. "It was the summer of 2007, and Andrew had been invited to tour Israel as part of a media junket. I agreed to tag along as his lawyer and best friend," Solov relates. "One night in Jerusalem, when we were getting ready for dinner, Andrew turned to me and asked if I would de-partner from the 800-person law firm where I was practicing and become business partners with him. He said he needed my help to 'change the world.' Perhaps it was because we were in such an historic place, or because I was energized by the courage of the Jewish people in the Holy Land, or maybe it was the alcohol at cocktail hour, but I said 'yes.'"[35]

The most disturbing thing about Bannon and the alt-right might not be what they think or say about Jews. It's what they expose about the ultra-nationalist, racialist roots of Zionism—and of some extreme Zionists' willingness to collaborate with their fiercest enemies.

"Our Liberation Is Intertwined"

An Interview with Linda Sarsour

The fight against antisemitism is intimately linked to the fight against Islamophobia and anti-Arab racism, and Linda Sarsour's work on the streets, online, and in the media exemplifies these connections. JVP's executive director, Rebecca Vilkomerson, interviewed Linda via email. The responses were lightly edited for clarity.

Can you say a little about yourself and the work you do?

My name is Linda Sarsour and I am a Palestinian Muslim American born and raised in Brooklyn, New York. My parents immigrated to the United States from El Bireh in the West Bank.

I have dedicated the past fifteen years to advocating on behalf of Arab Americans, Muslim Americans, and communities of color. My work focuses on national security reform, police accountability, immigrant rights, and combating hate and racism. I have been at the forefront of major civil rights campaigns including the incorporation of Muslim school holidays into the New York public school system and creating the first-ever inspector general for the New York Police Department by passing landmark legislation, the Community Safety Act. I am the cofounder of the first Muslim online organizing platform, MPOWER Change. MPOWER Change is a grassroots movement rooted in diverse Muslim communities throughout the United States who are working together to build social, spiritual, racial, and economic justice for all people.

I will never forget the day of 9/11 when I walked home from my college campus to my community in Bay Ridge and it was a ghost town. The businesses were closed, the mosque door was bolted—people were afraid. A few weeks later I came to volunteer at the Arab American Association of New York to serve the community I was born and raised in. The community was heavily targeted by law enforcement in the months after 9/11 where men were picked up from their homes and disappeared for days, weeks, and months at a time.

My work focused on working with women and families to locate loved ones and connect them to legal services. I was Arab American, Muslim American, spoke Arabic fluently, and felt the responsibility to use my skills to advocate for those in my community who felt marginalized and targeted.

How would you define Islamophobia?

I prefer the Center for American Progress's definition of Islamophobia, which states that it is an exaggerated fear, hatred, and hostility toward Islam and Muslims that is perpetuated by negative stereotypes resulting in bias, discrimination, and the marginalization and exclusion of Muslims from America's social, political, and civic life.

What is the impact of Islamophobia on the work you do? What are some of the ways you see Islamophobia in our present culture?

Islamophobia has taken a toll on the already-daunting work and has created even more obstacles to achieving civil rights wins. Our community is in constant reactionary mode responding to anti-Muslim policies, programs that target Muslims and those perceived to be Muslims, media narratives that misinform people about Islam and label one group suspect. Arab American, Muslim American organizations are under continuous attacks by right-wing white supremacist groups and right-wing Zionists and their media channels.

Oftentimes people believe Islamophobia to be a climate of irrational fear of Muslims and those perceived to be Muslim. Islamophobia should be called what it is, and that's anti-Muslim racism and is also institutionalized. We see Islamophobia manifested through government policies and programs, media narratives, and through individual acts of hate and harassment. The Islamophobia industry in the US is backed by hundreds of millions of dollars and has been very effective.

Bigotry, racism against Arab Americans and Muslim Americans is generally accepted in our present culture. There are no major consequences for leaders, elected officials, media personalities or pundits who engage in racist, hateful rhetoric against Muslims. The lack of consequences sends a message to ordinary citizens that it's acceptable. Islamophobia has become an institutionalized form of bigotry against one segment of the US population. Clear examples of this are bloated no-fly lists and unmanaged and unaccountable watch lists, unwarranted surveillance of Muslims by multiple levels of law enforcement, mandatory secondary screenings for women in hijab and Sikh men, anti-sharia legislation in numerous states, anti-BDS legislation, and executive orders that infringe on freedom of speech, intimidation, and harassment of Palestinian rights organizations and groups on college campuses, and the list goes on.

What is the role of progressive Jewish activists in combating Islamophobia? What is the work we can do as allies?
The Jewish community has had a long history of marginalization, exclusion, and [being] targeted for one's religious beliefs. They fundamentally understand the struggles of American Muslims and have showed solidarity on numerous fronts. While Jewish Americans continue to face antisemitism, it is now a more unacceptable form of bigotry in most spaces—both private and public sectors. The progressive Jewish communities of the United States can continue to use their voices, platforms, and positions to defend and advocate for the inclusion and respect of Muslim communities and their religious practices. The most powerful work has been when Muslims and Jews have come together to stand up for immigrant rights and Black lives. Using our religious traditions as drivers for justice silences the religious right and the opposition; together we send a strong message that Judaism and Islam are rooted in justice for all people. We should be writing together, speaking on panels together, organizing direct action and civil disobedience together. Our visible unity is a threat to the opposition who plays on the assumption that we do not work together and that our differences are too great of an obstacle, when in fact we have seen the exact opposite.

How is the fight against Islamophobia connected to other movements for justice? Is there a relationship between Islamophobia and antisemitism? What is that relationship?
Islamophobia is one branch on the tree of racism. Islamophobia, homophobia, anti-Black racism, and antisemitism are all connected and we cannot dismantle one without the other. Our liberation is intertwined, our stories are intertwined, our identities are intertwined. Our opposition is united, so we too must be united.

Islamophobia and antisemitism are connected. Most often the same groups who are anti-Muslim/anti-Islam are also antisemitic. Oftentimes the opposition uses our communities and our traditions to pin us up against each other. We must defeat Islamophobia while we monitor and defeat antisemitism.

How do you see the fight against Islamophobia connected to the fight for Palestinian liberation?
Right-wing Zionist groups and hardline pro-Israel politicians have labeled

the fight for Palestinian liberation as antisemitic when many of those at the forefront of Palestinian liberation are Jewish Americans. They have worked tirelessly to defame, shame, and silence pro-Palestinian activism by claiming it is antisemitic. We saw this recently with NY Governor Cuomo's signing of an executive order against BDS. We have also seen the vilification and defamation of student leaders and professors who have strong pro-Palestinian views. We have to be firm and stand together and send a clear message led by our Jewish sisters and brothers that says being pro-Palestinian and pro-justice is foundational to the tradition of Judaism. That wanting freedom and justice for Palestinians is not antisemitic; in fact, it reflects the teachings of Judaism, which focuses on uplifting the oppressed.

Centering Our Work
on Challenging Islamophobia

Donna Nevel

As those of us who are part of Jewish organizations or communities working for justice in Palestine reflect upon the issues we address, are passionate about, and are committed to acting upon, I come back to the importance of keeping our work and heart centered on challenging Islamophobia. I see this as integral and necessary to how we, as members of Jewish Voice for Peace and other Jewish groups and communities, frame and move forward with our work as partners in the movement for justice in Palestine, for racial justice, and for ending all forms of oppression.

Many of us enter this work against Islamophobia rooted in our own histories as Jews living in the United States, coming from different communities and parts of the world, with our varied experiences and relationships to being Jewish and to struggles for justice. For some of us, our families' and communities' histories of antisemitism and oppression demand that we stand with all communities facing grave injustice. For others of us, we particularly stress the importance of having Jewish voices speaking out against Islamophobia as a means of holding our own communities accountable, particularly Jewish organizations that speak out against antisemitism and bigotry but then hypocritically promote Islamophobia and an anti-Muslim narrative in their work. And still many others of us want to be part of a Jewish voice for justice that stands together with the broader movement, with all those impacted by Islamophobia, and all those fighting multiple forms of oppression. Of course, many of us relate to some or all of these entry points or locate our work through a different lens altogether. But the unifying thread, I think, is the commitment to standing against Islamophobia at a time when it is rampant.

The impact of Islamophobia on those experiencing and targeted by it cannot be underestimated. Violence explicitly and interchangeably targeted at

South Asian, Muslim, and Arab communities, as well as those perceived to be Arab or Muslim, has intensified globally as well as in the United States, where we have seen a proliferation of hate crimes and violence together with relentless anti-Muslim propaganda.

I'd like to focus on an examination of Islamophobia within a context of imperialism, the US so-called "war on terror," and US and Israeli state violence that both feed and rely on Islamophobia.

A very carefully orchestrated anti-Muslim propaganda campaign seeks to equate Islam and Muslims with violence. In our work and organizing, we speak of the importance of resisting and reframing this kind of propaganda. But I do think that we need to examine whether there are ways we unwittingly end up taking it in and even perpetuating it. How many of us, in a quiet, internal moment, have read something in the paper and wondered for more than a fleeting moment if Islam promotes violence more than other religions? The conflation of violence with Islam and with Muslims is so all-encompassing that I do not think it is farfetched to suggest that many of us can easily get trapped in a narrative that is rooted in Islamophobic assumptions and propaganda.

Religious scholars can provide evidence until they are blue in the face that every religion preaches both violence and peace and that every religion has individuals committing acts of violence in its name. But we don't have a propaganda machine that is dedicated to the demonization of Christians or Jews, just to name two religions that are not immune from extreme acts of violence committed in their names.

I know that sometimes conversations about violence perpetrated by Muslims take place with good intentions—trying to show a *reason* for violence that isn't about Islam as a religion—that is, explaining that the violence is an understandable outgrowth of US or Israeli policy. I don't mean to suggest that this reasoning—this pointing to a larger context—does not have some validity, particularly when it is contextualized for the express purpose of challenging the Islamophobic narrative. However, what I find problematic is that it is still often based on Islamophobic assumptions about *whose* violence is the worst and needs to be "explained," which also perpetuates a false narrative about "Muslim violence" and covers up the larger truth that the greatest violence being carried out globally is by the US government and its allies.

In my view, if we are thinking about or discussing violence, we should focus on the massive levels of violence perpetrated by the US government (which includes helping to make possible the violence perpetrated by Israel as an occupying power). This is not to "explain" why Muslims engage in violence—rather, it is to re-center the conversation about violence where it belongs. The United States has wreaked havoc on, and continues to do irreparable damage to, countries and societies and peoples across the globe. Further, within the United States, violence and systemic racism are rooted in policies and practices that make necessary the prison abolition movement, the Black Lives Matter movement, and the struggles for an end to massive inequality, just to name a few. If we want to have conversations about violence, that's where I would begin.

Islamophobic acts—from bigoted subway ads, to murders, and other acts of violence—take place in the context of the ongoing, state-sponsored Islamophobia of the US government, whose foreign policy relies on Islamophobic premises as it has set out to bomb countries with large Muslim populations, and by an Israeli government whose apartheid polices interact with, and are buttressed by, its equation of Islam with evil. Human rights lawyer and activist Bina Ahmad has written, "Islamophobia necessitates convincing people that there's a war at home and abroad," and that this messaging "pushes through a brutal agenda and also allows our government to mask its true agenda."[1] In its war on Muslims abroad, Islamophobia at home becomes amplified, and intentionally so. The government's focus is on alleged violence of Muslims rather than on the pervasive violence of imperialism and occupation.

Professor and activist Deepa Kumar, author of *Islamophobia and the Politics of Empire*, has written about the centrality of empire in fostering and sustaining Islamophobia. She has written, "At its core, liberal Islamophobia flows from the logic of liberal imperialism. As several scholars have argued, liberal imperialism is based upon using liberal ideas to justify empire, and spans the gamut from the narrative about rescuing women and children from brutal dictators to fostering democracy. Liberal Islamophobia flows from this logic."[2] Therefore, Islamophobia, US imperialism, and the "war on terror" must be understood to be inseparable and an integral part of our analysis and organizing for justice in Palestine and worldwide.

How do those of us who are part of Jewish organizations and communities interact with this work? Where do we enter? What is the "right" way to do it?

While Islamophobia has a long and ugly history beginning way before 9/11, I think for many of us from outside the Muslim community, our activism and awareness about what Islamophobia is and how it manifests itself is relatively recent. For me, it was my involvement several years ago with a Muslim principal of an Arabic dual-language public school who lost her position because of a sustained Islamophobic campaign—directly related to Israel politics—that brought this issue to my attention. I had never seen or understood the many dimensions of Islamophobia so starkly as I did with this campaign. And while the rabid Islamophobes did their damage, the real damage was done by the mayor's office of New York City and the Department of Education—government institutions—that capitulated to the demands of the Islamophobes who demanded the principal's resignation. Similarly, it is the Islamaphobes again who have stirred up fears of Muslim violence in New York, but it was the mayor who endorsed police surveillance of the city's entire Muslim community.

There has been, and continues to be, significant organizing happening to challenge Islamophobia, inspired by the leadership of those most impacted by its injustices. There is meaningful, ongoing organizing within Muslim communities and among communities that are working together on issues challenging Islamophobia, racism, and other forms of oppression. Intersections and connections are being made that strengthen the distinct yet overlapping struggles for justice.

To work within our communities and to be a partner in this work, we created JVP's Network Against Islamophobia. We share resource and curriculum materials, develop organizing ideas, and initiate actions with JVP chapters across the country, and participate as partners within the broader movement. Several principles help guide and frame our analysis and our work, which we articulate in the following way:

1. Those of us within the Jewish community doing this work want to be as visible as we possibly can in our opposition to Islamophobia and anti-Arab racism, particularly within our communities. Our goal is to stand together, as principled, respectful partners, with the Muslim community and all those impacted by Islamophobia.

2. While we don't minimize individual acts of Islamophobia—they are reprehensible—we also want to stress the damage and extent of structural and state-sponsored Islamophobia, which often does not get addressed in the broader society, including within the mainstream Jewish community. So, for example, while an organization may oppose hate crimes against Muslims, that same organization might not oppose state-sponsored surveillance of the Muslim community. We are committed to opposing *all* forms of Islamophobia.

3. We believe identifying the relationship and connections among

Islamophobia, politics connected to Israeli and US domestic and foreign policies, and the "war on terror" are critical to an analysis of how Islamophobia works and flourishes.

4. Another critical dimension of Islamophobia that we strongly oppose in our work and that relates to Israel politics is the "good Muslim/bad Muslim" paradigm, introduced by Mahmood Mamdani. We oppose the ways in which mainstream Jewish and other groups apply an Israel-related litmus test to Muslim or Arab American groups or individuals in an attempt to identify the "good" Muslims or Arabs with whom they consider it "acceptable" to work. The central message behind this thinking is that "unless proved to be 'good,' every Muslim is presumed to be 'bad.'"

5. As has become increasingly clear—and the powerful organizing going on across so many communities reflects this reality—the struggles against Islamophobia, racism, and other forms of oppression are deeply connected. Our work to challenge Islamophobia is part of the broader movement and ongoing organizing for justice and integrity for all communities.

This past Chanukah, in the midst of virulent anti-Muslim propaganda and violence, hundreds of JVP members in sixteen cities across the United States joined Jews Against Islamophobia, a coalition of Jewish Voice for Peace–NY and Jews Say No!, and the Network Against Islamophobia in organizing actions rededicating ourselves to challenging Islamophobia and racism. Our goal was to be as clear and visible as we possibly could in our opposition to Islamophobia and racism and in articulating our recommitment to challenging them in *all* their forms and manifestations. Holding signs in the shape of a menorah, participants read aloud commitments in public spaces that conveyed the following messages:

1. We will not be silent about anti-Muslim and racist hate speech and hate crimes;

2. We condemn state surveillance of the Muslim, Arab, and South Asian communities;

3. We challenge, through our words and actions, institutionalized racism and state-sanctioned anti-Black violence;

4. We protest the use of Islamophobia and anti-Arab racism to justify and perpetuate Israel's repressive policies against Palestinians;

5. We fight anti-Muslim profiling and racial profiling in all its forms;

6. We call for an end to racist policing—#SayHerName, #Black-LivesMatter, #BlackTransLivesMatter;
7. We stand against US policies driven by the "war on terror" that demonize Islam and devalue, target, and kill Muslims; and
8. We stand strong for immigrants' rights and refugee rights.

While the signs were central to each action, in each of the sixteen cities, the events took shape growing out of their own locations, experiences as a community, histories, and relationships. Passersby received handouts that described why we were standing together and the sentiments behind each of the signs.

Building upon these highly visible events (media coverage was extensive), we also began a process of community education so that our organizing could be as principled and effective as possible. We began to create curricula and share resources on Islamophobia, detailing how Islamophobia manifests itself; the differences among and multiple manifestations of Islamophobic acts, both state-sponsored and those committed by individuals; the relationship among Islamophobia, Israeli politics, and US policies; and how we can organize within our communities and as part of the broader movement for justice.

We also created posters so that we could canvass our neighborhoods and communities. One of the posters, which says "Refugees Are Welcome Here" and was created by Micah Bazant, a member of JVP's Artists and Cultural Workers Council, is a powerful visual expression of solidarity with the refugee community. The second poster says "Stop Profiling Muslims," written in large white block letters on a black background. The latter mirrors a T-shirt we created in response to a time of increased surveillance of Muslims in airports and elsewhere. The canvassing campaign began in January 2016, when a number of JVP chapters, often together with other groups, went to businesses, other storefronts, and malls to encourage storeowners and managers to display these signs. The JVP-Bay Area chapter also made its own poster that says, "We Support Our Muslim Neighbors." In addition to having great visibility, this campaign has led to meaningful conversations with community members in different neighborhoods across the country about anti-Muslim and anti-refugee attitudes, hate crimes, and government policies, as well as to relationship-building and thoughtful coalition work.

We know that for Muslims and those perceived as Muslims, there is no need to describe the seriousness of Islamophobia. And those who, for example, were targeted by NYPD's stop-and-frisk policies, also don't need to understand what it is to be targeted. They experience it daily. But for those of us whose communities are not experiencing Islamophobia, I believe we must be certain not to minimize in any way what it means to be targeted and surveilled by the government; what it means to have one's children see the venom that shows up on subways and in our streets; what it means to have one's house of worship opposed and considered as a threat; what it means to live in a society in which you are treated with suspicion, deported for no reason, degraded in the media, by politicians, and in public spaces; and what it means to have daily acts of bigotry and violence committed against your community.

As we engage in our work to challenge Islamophobia, I believe our role as members of Jewish communities standing for justice is to continue to speak out in our opposition to Islamophobia, including from our different locations and identities and within our communities; to continue in our work to expose the underlying issues and links related to Islamophobia and the politics of both Israel and the United States; and to be principled, consistent, responsive, and responsible partners in this work.

[The above remarks above are largely drawn from my presentation in the opening panel at the JVP National Membership Meeting, held on March 13, 2015, entitled "We're Not Waiting"—other presenters included Rebecca Vilkomerson, Amer Shurrab, Eran Efrati, and Rev. Dr. Heber Brown III. I would like to acknowledge the many groups and individuals who have profoundly shaped my thinking for this piece, and for my work. I can't mention them all but would like to acknowledge my dear friend and comrade Bina Ahmad for her thinking and organizing rooted in justice and in love, which I have had the honor of experiencing firsthand. Special thanks also to Elly Bulkin, coauthor in writing about Islamophobia, and co-convener, together with many others, of Jews Against Islamophobia and the Network Against Islamophobia.—D.N.]

Who Am I to Speak?

Aurora Levins Morales

I am a child of two oppressed peoples, a New York Puerto Rican mother, raised Catholic, and a New York Ukrainian Ashkenazi Jew, raised communist. I was born and grew up in rural Puerto Rico, where during the McCarthy years of blacklisting my radical parents survived by farming. I have relatives in mass graves on three continents, and the African and Indigenous dead of my family weigh as heavily as the Jewish dead.

Who am I to speak? A colonial subject, a woman of color, an immigrant, disabled and chronically ill, of mixed class, with personal experience of both poverty and middle class privilege, and a Jew. I am targeted by many oppressions, which has taught me to sift and compare them.

My father's family lived in a small southern Ukrainian village where each spring, the Easter sermons sent their neighbors rampaging against the Jewish farmers and craftspeople who lived among them. For centuries, Jews had been forbidden to own land, but in the early 1800s as the Russian Empire was pushing up against the Ottoman Turks, it started settling Jews, and other people it didn't mind sacrificing, on the newly conquered lands of southern Ukraine as a kind of buffer. In 1807 my family climbed onto a wagon and drove south to become part of that buffer in the brand new agricultural settlement of Israelovka (Jew Town). They were given farms, seeds, tools, and draft exemption, and ordered to grow wheat, which had to be sent to northern bakeries to provide bread. Jewish farmers could not travel without permission, or pursue any other occupation until they had farmed for twenty years and gotten written permission from the authorities.

By the time my great-grandparents were born, the draft exemption had been canceled, and Jews did other kinds of work. My great-grandfather Abraham, known as Pop, had to bribe a guard at a checkpoint every day to get to his job in a town where Jews were not allowed. When war broke out with Japan in 1904, he left for the United States to avoid military conscription. Two years later his wife and my young grandmother followed with other relatives, so they were not in Israelovka when the Nazis murdered several hundred Jews, including Pop's sister and brother, their spouses, and their children, on a single day in May 1942.

I say all this because in the public discourses of antisemitism, having lost relatives to the Nazis is often wielded as a source of moral authority, exempting us from the challenge to think critically. I have been accused of betraying the Jews who died at the hands of the Nazis because, like the last six generations of my family, I believe our safety lies in the solidarity of working people, and not in a Zionist state. I have been accused of being a retroactive Nazi collaborator by people who claim that dead children also accuse me. I am at peace with my ghosts. In none of my lineages do my ancestors demand that I build gated homelands. They tell me to protect the people, protect the land, that everyone must be equally free.

I am also saying that Jewish oppression is real, that it goes underground and emerges again like an indestructible weed, that this is its nature, to lie dormant, its roots intact beneath the ground, and when conditions are ripe, it bursts up through the well-manicured lawns and does its job. That it does not need to be a rampantly flaming flower to be a threat. That my father was fearless as a communist and frightened as a Jew because he knew what antisemitism is for, that its purpose is to protect the Christian elites from the outrage of the oppressed by throwing Jews under the bus, by redirecting their rage toward Jews, and that you never know when it will come in handy to someone. As it did for the Republicans in the New York State Senate who proposed cutting $500 million from the budget of City University of New York, slashing at the educational resources of working-class students who are overwhelmingly people of color, because this is what Republicans do, but using a series of antisemitic incidents to justify the move, claiming it was a response to Jewish upset over antisemitism.

What Are We Talking About?

The oppression of Jews as Jews, as a racialized people believed to possess inheritable inferior or immoral traits that justify our mistreatment, is a thoroughly European Christian phenomenon, and as such, has been carried throughout the world as part of the conquering ideology of European colonialism. It arrived in Puerto Rico with the Spanish, and a woman of my name was burned at the stake in 1520 under suspicion of being a secret Jew and desecrating a crucifix. It arrived in New York City long before my great-grandparents did. It arrived in North Africa and the Middle East with the British, French, German, and Spanish colonizers and landed on people who had suffered Ottoman despotism and discrimination as non-Muslims, but by and large had not been systematically singled out for persecution as Jews. It arrived as part of an arsenal of domination, because it was every bit as useful as racism, but a lot sneakier.

Because I have sifted and compared my own experiences as a mixed heritage Jew of color, it's more than an intellectual exercise for me when I hold racism and anti-Jewish oppression, one in each hand, and weigh them, when I watch them move through the world, distorting the air around them, when I recognize their behaviors, their camouflages. Racism is like a millstone, a crushing weight that relentlessly presses down on people intended to be a permanent underclass. Its purpose is to press profit from us, right to the edge of extermination and beyond. The oppression of Jews is a shunt that redirects the rage of working people away from the 1%, a hidden mechanism that works through misdirection, that uses privilege to hide the gears.

Unlike as with racism, at least some of the targets of antisemitism must be seen to prosper, must be well paid and highly visible. The goal is not to crush us, it's to have us available for crushing. The white, male Christian rulers use us to administer their power and set us up in the window displays of capitalism for the next time the poor pick up stones to throw. What is hard for the angry multitudes to see is that Jews don't succeed *in spite* of our oppression, but as part of it. We are kept insecure by our history of sudden assaults, and as a strategy of survival, some of us accept the bribes of privilege and protection offered to us. Bestowing privilege on a visible segment of us is the only way to make the system work. Then, when the wrath of the most oppressed, whether Russian peasants starving on potatoes or urban US people of color pressed to the wall, reaches boiling point, there we are: the Tsar's tax collector, the shopkeeper and the pawnbroker, the landlord and lawyer, social worker and school administrator. And whether it's a Polish aristocrat watching the torches go by on pogrom or the Episcopalian banker discreetly out of sight while working class people tell each other that Jews control the economy, the trick works. Agent of the rulers, scapegoat for their crimes. This was our history in Europe.

When European Jews began arriving in the United States in large numbers, none of us were considered white. We were poor tenement dwellers, and the demagogues of the day said we brought disease, immorality, crime, and sedition in our tattered pockets. But after World War II, the GI Bill, and the slow end to quotas and redlining, we got some traction and began climbing right back into those middle-agent roles, moving to suburbs and renting our old homes to people arriving by way of the Great Migration and the Guagua Aerea, the Black and Puerto Rican migrants filling the cities we also landed in. My Puerto Rican grandmother moved into the garment work my Jewish great-grandmother was just leaving.

And in order to be middle agents again, in order to be buffers between the ruling class and the poor and working class in which most people of color were concentrated, those Jews who could do so had to take on white identity. It was part of the job description. The ones who could were offered the same old deal. The ones who could not, the ones who were too dark and foreign, became unimaginable as Jews and weren't offered anything. In the United States, the Jews in the display window are light of skin, assimilated, and have money.

What I Know

I am not a student of Zionist history, not a scholar of Middle East colonialism, or the Nakba, or the evolution of the State of Israel, but I am an anti-imperialist Latin American, a colonial subject who understands what happened when the British decided that breaking up the Ottoman Empire would help them defeat the Germans in their bloody competition to own more of the world, when arrogant British officials put themselves in charge of those lands, and then promised them to Arab nationalists seeking independence, Zionist Jews seeking a territory, and the French seeking control.

I am a native of an occupied colony being systematically stripped of everything that supports life, and I know exactly what I am looking at in Palestine. I too am a thirsty resident in a land of privatized water, of massive land grabs and toxic waste disposal, a majority of my people unable to live in my country. I am a citizen of a continent famous for invasions, occupations, death squads. I am familiar with the pornographic distortions of marketing through which oppression is sanitized, with shiny brochures that proclaim Puerto Rico to be paradise and Israel the home and hearth of freedom. I wrote: "I am a colonial subject with a stone in my hand when I watch the news. I am a fierce Puerto Rican Jew holding out a rose to Palestine."[1]

I am also a Jew who knows the deadliness of that middle-agent role, who recognizes empire's habit of using proxies, who understands and is enraged by the setup in which imperial backing is bestowed on oppressed and fearful colonizers with racist entitlement. The Jews who came from Europe could have built something quite different in a place that enjoyed centuries of co-existence; they could have come as respectful migrants, to be neighbors, not conquerors, but whatever it could have been, what we have now is this. I am a Latin American, and when I see soldiers shooting children and calling *them* terrorists, I know what that is.

Arguments among Jews

In my grandmother's village there was a three-cornered argument about what, if anything, would save the Jews: The Orthodox said it was in God's hands. The Zionists said only Jews could be counted on to stand by Jews, and we needed a defensible territory of our own where we called the shots. The communists and socialists and anarchists said only an alliance of all the working people can dismantle our oppression and everyone else's. As a boy, my father took part in that same ongoing debate on the boardwalk in Brooklyn. But after the Holocaust, after the Nazis destroyed so much of the world of European Jews, after the solidarity that existed was not enough, and the old Russian antisemitism that had been punished as a crime against socialism became a part of Soviet policy, after all that, the three-cornered debate turned lopsided under the weight of despair, and the Zionist minority of my father's childhood has grown to dominate all debate, aggressively silencing dissent.

The Jews who write to tell me that I should have died in a Nazi concentration camp before living to denounce the crimes of Israel believe with all their hearts that their only possible safety in the world is a state where Jews dominate society and have protected privileges. They believe this is so essential to our survival as a people that we can't afford to consider the most basic human rights of Muslim and Christian Palestinians. They think that requiring accountability is an injustice to Jews, that it threatens our existence, that if we stop for a moment, the Holocaust will catch up with us and that therefore any means toward total control are justified, and anyone who disagrees wants us dead.

Some of the Jews who think this openly justify the horrific abuses required to hold such absolute power, and with extreme racism, utterly dehumanize non-Jewish Palestinians and call for their expulsion and slaughter. Some say violence has been forced on Jews by violence, that resistance is aggression, that the anger of dispossessed Palestine is rooted not in rage over colonialism, but in hatred of Jews, and that all the armed paraphernalia of a brutal and brutalizing Israeli state is the necessary self-defense of innocent people simply occupying their ordinary privileges. That there was no Nakba, just voluntary departure by people who didn't happen to want to live in those villages under continual assault. They dig in stubbornly, claiming the right to an unthreatened existence they believe they have earned through suffering, while those they have displaced have not. It's the common narrative of people determined to do the wrong thing because they think anything else will kill them.

Many more are in denial about the human cost of an exclusively Jewish homeland, claiming that it's not as bad as people say, that as usual, everyone is picking on the Jews, that other countries in the region treat people worse, that all countries start with invasions and slaughters and expropriated lands and it's unfair to criticize Israel for what everybody does, citing Native genocide in North America as if Native people were not still here, still fighting back, as if one bad history licenses another. Many are deeply uneasy but believe the suppression of Palestinian society is an unfortunate necessity, or tell themselves, as many white people in the United States do, that atrocities are committed by a few bad apples in a basically sound barrel. They don't write to wish me dead, but they don't want me to speak. They think I have betrayed them, that a Jewish-dominated Israeli state is our best and only shot at long-term survival, and any protest, criticism, or challenge to that state, if not an outright act of attempted genocide, gives aid to our enemies, who are always waiting to fall upon us once more. These are the people who shout "antisemitism" at any whisper of dissent. It's not exactly crying wolf, because unlike the fabled shepherd they really do believe the wolf is there in the underbrush, but they cry it so often that when the real scapegoating nastiness takes place, no one believes them.

What I Want

I said I was not a student of Zionism, but I am a student of historical trauma, and I know that the cyclical nature of anti-Jewish oppression has proven over and over that the violent scapegoating of Jews can erupt in the midst of the most apparent security (Spain in the 1400s, Germany in the 1920s, that this fear is not unjustified, that it is not paranoid to think it could all happen again. But I am also a student of how such trauma is recycled and reenacted, how the determination to prevent what has already happened—to never again be victims—justifies everything from domestic violence to wholesale slaughter. The oppression of Jews, imperialist manipulation, and profound racism have all enmeshed to create this nightmare, and I want all my peoples to be free of it. In the face of a widespread belief that domination is the most trustworthy answer to fear, I am fighting for both the freedom of Palestine and the souls of Jews.

I am a child of two traumatized tribes and when I fight for justice in Palestine, when I reject the premise that criticism of Israeli crimes is anti-Semitic, I am not supporting a faraway people out of an abstract and benevolent idea of doing the right thing for someone else.

I am fighting for myself. For an end to this recycling of pain. I am fighting for my deepest source of hope, the belief in human solidarity, in our ability to decide that we will expand our hearts and our sense of kinship to include each other and resist the urge to contract in fear, to huddle and bare our teeth and lash out. When I speak out for the humanity of Palestine I am defending the humanity of everyone, including all Jews. When I stand firmly against the hidden reservoirs of antisemitism that bubble up when the ruling class needs them to, when I tell my gentile friends not to get distracted from resisting the real power of the white Christian male 1%, to stay the course and stay clear-headed, I am standing for accuracy, for clarity, for revealing the structures of domination that crush our world, including the people of Palestine.

When I keep saying that Israel's war against Palestinians only multiplies danger and pain for all of us, when I denounce and chant and recite and sing against this injustice, when I say I will have no part of it and I am accused of denying Jews a future, I know that I am fighting for the only real future there is.

When I insist that we can be on each other's sides, that we can make sure everyone has enough allies to be safe, that this is the only work that matters, I am pushing back against despair, lifting my corner of that three-sided fight toward a justice big and beautiful enough for us all.

Captured Narratives

Rev. Graylan Hagler

I am writing out of the North American context, and the ways that these Black eyes have perceived the issues of race and power. As this book explores antisemitism I am compelled to explore it as an outsider, as a Black person who has experienced the effects of racism and power. My understanding and historical perspective inform me that there is a vast difference between biases or prejudices and racism. We often confuse biased judgment with racism, but I contend that if it has the power to alter one's ability to exist, if in its formality or informality it is an immutable reality, and if it is implemented and enforced by laws and/or systems of power and therefore institutionalized, it meets the definition of racism and not that of simply biased prejudice. Many immigrant groups were met with stares, harshness, and the hostilities of nativism upon arriving on the shores of North America, but within a generation or two were singing "God Bless America" with the gusto of other assimilated and accept- ed white ethnic groups. My issue and discomfort with exploring the subject of antisemitism is to assume that we are speaking in terms similar to that of racism, where power dynamics and institutions have the force of rule and the ability to distort lives. Indeed, whenever the charge of antisemitism is leveled, it is expressed in much the same ways that we express charges of racism in this culture. In this case the charge is of being anti-Jewish. But it is difficult for this Black person to see or understand the charge of antisemitism in the same ways that I understand racism and its implementation against Blacks or any other permanent group of color. In North America, the Jewish establishment and in general the Jewish community currently exist endowed with white privilege. This is not the same for all Jews, like Jews of color, for example; but for the vast majority the Jewish narrative in North America is clothed in white privilege, which brings with it attitudes of entitlement and belonging. It is not to say that there are not persons and groups that hate Jews for being

Jews—certainly there are. Yet we see great power and influence exerted onto the national and even the international scene that is not proportionate to the numbers of Jews in the country or world. This power does not exist for those attempting to defend themselves from the many scourges of racism, but it is normative for those in seats of power and in the networks of influence that guide the overall society and culture.

In September 2015 I went to Rochester, New York, to speak on Israel/Palestine and was met with a chorus of hostile voices that accused me of being antisemitic, and I received a death threat from someone identifying themselves as Christians United for Israel, not only accusing me of being an antisemite, but also threatening to kill me in the name of Christ! My experience with the charge of antisemitism is that it is used as a tool to limit discussion; to thwart debate and silence anyone that differs from the "established Jewish" perspective. But how did generalized and accepted perspective on Israel find itself as the established norm? Why can't Israel and its policies be discussed? How is the narrative controlled? How was a central narrative established and for anyone to question to run the risk of being charged and shunned as an antisemite? Part of the answer to that question for me comes out of the lessons of Hebrew scripture and history, where there were diverse tribes that made up what became the coalition of tribes and groups constituting the biblical Israel. But part of the cohesiveness of that unity came from individual clans and groups buying into an overarching narrative of slavery in Egypt and the power of God in their liberation. In other words, tribes and people bought into the narrative, and even if they did not personally experience Egypt or the saga of enslavement, it became one of the foundational narratives resulting in a certain cohesiveness. Hence when people gather around the table for Pesach and reenact the Haggadah, it is reaffirming the centrality of the narrative for future generations.

The Holocaust of Jews during the Nazi era is one of those cohesive marks in the narrative. As the significance and severity of that era is recognized, re-told, and recounted, even people who were not directly affected are affected, as we should be, and the narrative not only creates cohesiveness but a sense of cultural nationalism. The cultural nationalism of the Zionist movement is linked with some real history of genocidal pogroms culminating in massacres and expulsions offering examples of realized fears and proven with extreme clarity under the Nazi machinery moving against Jews, Gypsies, the disabled, and other cultural minorities. The experience of these histories and the narratives that come out of these experiences has created a cohesiveness of perspective and also of perceived dangers. This has rendered terms like "antisemite" to be perceived and heard in much the same way that the term "terrorist" or "terrorism" is heard. The charge of antisemitism causes ears to no longer hear or for people to no longer be rational in discourse. It conjures up fears, real or imagined, and it creates almost insurmountable obstacles for people to be heard or grievances to find the light of day. For people like me, I am charged with being antisemitic when I speak of Israel/Palestine, but to a Jew critical of the so-called "established cohesive" Jewish point of view, it is possibly even more devastating when they are dismissed as a self-loathing Jew. In either case it brings the hellish hounds of history against you, where in the mists weeping and wailing can be heard, and the chant of "Never Again" rises toward a crescendo. I understand the emotionalism, but I also know how emotionalism can easily produce a mob mentality where themes of justice, fairness, rationality, and mercy are lost in the heat of the masses fed on a constant diet of fear.

I am fascinated by narratives. Narratives define how we view ourselves, what histories we stress; and help to define our importance and purpose in the context in which we live. A narrative can be factual or fictitious or something in between. Usually we find that narratives are often always somewhere between factual and fictional. Narratives create cohesiveness, and those individuals that question the veracity of the narrative are considered traitors or the enemy. In order to understand racism in the United States you have to demythologize the country's narrative of "goodness" and "opportunity," unearthing the aspects that usually are not raised up, such as a legacy of chattel slavery for over four hundred years. With the term "antisemitism" there is a narrative that is presupposed, and to run against that narrative is to bear the charge of being an antisemite, or of being a self-loathing Jew.

It seems to me that the established Jewish narrative has constructed a perplexing and often contradictory narrative, whereby in the North American context it can claim oppression while maintaining the ability to wield power and influence greater than its demographic numbers would suggest it has. Narratives are formed to serve one sociopolitical perspective or another; to create national or nationalistic identity and fervor; to create a framework for the status quo and to maintain that status quo; and to maintain a collective memory through an established and agreed upon set of perceived historical events. A narrative is generally written or spoken; it is used to frame political thought or social connections and generates particular attitudes and political outcomes that challenge, affirm, or advance the status quo. There can be more than one narrative at a time and sometimes those competing narratives struggle with each other to win the mantle of truth. Narratives often compete for the same space and for dominance in officialdom. The narratives that win out are usually those that are accepted and sanctioned by the dominant culture because they advance the ends of that dominant culture and are affirmed by those who are engaged in a conspiracy of shared dominance. Each narrative has the potential for misuse, and though each narrative claims objectivity in its telling, each is subjective and therefore molded and framed for particular sociopolitical outcomes. The truth of one narrative challenges the truth of the competing narrative, and yet each side of the telling claims its own veracity and objectivity. All narratives are developed from some modicum of truth, but development and embellishment can divorce that truth from pure veracity.

As the European settlers advanced across the United States in the sixteenth, seventeenth, and eighteenth centuries, there were already indigenous people settled on the land, and they would need to be displaced if room was going to be made for those settlers, and landholding was going to be proven profitable. The narratives operating from a background of truth were of competing interest. The European interest and the Native American interest were divergent, but the European settlers' interest had the power of guns, the apparatus of government, instruments of communication, and the so-called rule of law on its side. The narrative was altered so that Native Americans were depicted as crazed savages killing and scalping white settlers for no other reason than to impede progress and to quench their own bloodthirstiness. This narrative was used for the removal and genocide of entire Native nations while avoiding any pangs of conscience by the dominant chorus. The realities were quite different in history with white settlers taking land, initiating and relying upon violence, and where the bloodthirstiness of government and settlers was the norm, and Native people mostly operated to defend themselves from genocide. A narrative can be easily altered by the will of those in power. The victim can look like the aggressor and the aggressor can be portrayed as the victim, depending upon who wields power on the emerging narrative and controls it. Language and the use of words can create an atmosphere of justification for murder, genocide, exploitation, and discrimination.

In 1915 a silent movie, *Birth of a Nation*, hit the movie houses from coast to coast. It was even shown in the White House by President Woodrow Wilson. It was a revisionist and triumphalist history of how the Ku Klux Klan saved America from the Black savages of Reconstruction, and redeemed the government from being controlled by Blacks. Following the release of the movie, the country experienced increased Klan membership; the East Saint Louis white riots of 1917; the Red Summer of 1919; and in 1921, attacks by white mobs on the Black residents of Tulsa, Oklahoma, that left the community destroyed and ravished.

The propagation of racism in our culture and the world has been advanced and defended by the narration of events and the assertions of people's impressions of those events. I have existed all my life in a world that has presented its impressions of Coloreds, Negroes, Blacks, and African Americans. The narrative has been of slave, ghetto thug, drug addict, whore, absentee dad, fatherless child, and in most cases the portrayal of a Black person's reliance upon the generosity of a benevolent white person. I have lived all my life in a country and a world that has been anti-Colored, anti-Negro, anti-Black, and for some, anti–African American. I have also witnessed the proliferation of anti-Latino feelings particularly in light of the immigration issue. I have experienced the anti-LGBTQ sentiment that exists as part of the culture wars. I have been challenged by the charge of antisemitism. We continue to deal with anti-Islamic passions and rhetoric. All of these "anti-" feelings and sentiments demonstrate how strained and broken we are as a society. Although the "anti-" feelings of society and culture are disheartening and troubling, for some groups in the United States there have been grace and openings in time to escape the limiting hostilities of the "anti-" feelings and join with the dominant culture in its politics, narrative, acceptability, and privilege. But not all groups are afforded this mobility.

I am using the word "'anti-' feeling" and not "racism" because if a group eventually overcomes the biased prejudice against it, then that prejudice is not a fixed and immutable reality but a historically temporal one, and thus the "anti-" feeling did not amount to the severity of racism and the harsh realities of it. Racism is a paradigm of institution, policy, and power used against people to deny humanity, place, self-directed purpose, and overall potential and possibilities. When an "anti-" feeling is not immutable or clothed in power, it is simply a bias or prejudice that can be short-lived and overcome. Many groups who can testify to their hardships of entering the United States can also testify that it ultimately became a land of opportunity as they became white and part of the dominant structure.

People often try to draw parallels to Black people's plight by citing how the Irish, Italians, Poles, Jews and other racial and ethnic groups met the challenges of being different and overcame. Thus the problem with Black people in overcoming, the narrative of the larger culture would suggest, is that Black people will not give up their victimization and join the dominant strain. But there is a mobility that is afforded lighter peoples after a period of time to become white and celebrated as part of the rich fabric of the country. Groups use the challenges of their ethnic history to "sing an American tune" (to quote singer/songwriter Paul Simon), while merging their difference into the common thread of whiteness.

Let me make it plain: the Irish were the victims of "anti-" feelings but were able to accept the dominant narrative and merge their narrative with it to become white. Italians have done the same. In general the Jewish community in the United States has become white, with the exception of those darker-complected Jews who because of melanin will never cross the color line of acceptability—at least not in the near future. But the lighter-skinned Jewish community in general has accepted the narrative of the dominant culture and has merged their own unique narrative into the overall narrative, thereby gaining power, voice, and influence. Black and darker people will never be afforded this acceptance or merger of narrative because of the melanin in our skin, the history of enslavement, and the nation's unresolved issues with color that makes darker-skinned peoples' experiences radically different than others in the United States.

This brings me to the conclusion that antisemitism—though existent before, during, and shortly after World War II, as evidenced by housing and other postwar covenants—has all but ceased to exist in North America as a paradigm of racism in the postmodern era. If we agree that racism is defined by institution, power, and policy, then we have to refer to antisemitism as an "anti-" feeling in the ways that it is currently defined and experienced in the overall culture. The Jewish immigrants I met, for example, in the 1950s and '60s growing up in Baltimore, Maryland, were "other," and definitely not white, but their children merged into the assumptions and attitudes of the dominant culture even while holding onto their own particularities of culture and narrative. They began to merge and sing an American tune. In the United States, those lighter-complected Jews became white. It is like the whiteness of a Ted Cruz or Marco Rubio, individuals of Cuban descent who have merged completely and thoroughly into the dominant culture, even as that culture subjugates scores of the population who have been here longer, served in its military, paid taxes, and yet remain as second- and third-class citizens. Antisemitism no longer exists as a racist paradigm propagated by the core institutions and frameworks of official power in the United States. It exists as "anti-" feelings, as bias and prejudices, but it doesn't hinder the Jewish establishment from attaining the mantle of power and dominance in a culture that once viewed it as "the other." It seems to me that after the death camps of Europe, Jews began to use their victimization and cohesiveness, particularly in the West and certainly in the United States, to garner sympathy, influence, and power. In my view, there is nothing wrong with Jewish organizations laboring to keep the crime of the world's apathy before the world, particularly in regard to the Jewish Holocaust. But the difference is that when one talks about racism against Black and Brown people, it is considered race-baiting by the dominant culture, or of playing the race card, and the history of chattel or economic slavery does not draw the same kind of empathy, if it is acknowledged at all.

It seems to me, that at least in the United States, the narrative of the Jewish community, even as it holds onto being oppressed and a victim, still mirrors the dominant culture in its ability to control, define, and redefine the narrative. The origins of the word "semite" and how it has been used in history illustrates my point. The word "semite," or the accusation of "being an antisemite," actually comes out of the oppression of Jews in Europe, which owed to hatred fueled by white European Christian supremacy. The term "antisemitism" was coined in the nineteenth century in Europe in an effort to define the anti-Jewish campaigns being carried out at that time in central Europe. But in typical European fashion, it fails to recognize who else is encapsulated by the term "semite," because the term actually denotes a language group and not a race, and there are other languages that are part of this lingual group. The Semitic languages are derived from an Afro-Asiatic group of languages. Semitic languages are spoken by more than 300 million in Asia, North Africa, and the Horn of Africa. Known languages that we classify as Semitic are Arabic (some 300 million Arabic speakers); Amharic (some 22 million speakers), Tigrinya (some 7 million speakers), and Hebrew (some 5 million speakers). So why is it that being antisemitic is defined as anti-Jewish in the narrative and not anti-Muslim, anti-Arab, anti-Ethiopian, or anti-Eritrean? Though Jews may not have coined the term, the application of the word, in typical Eurocentric fashion, denies non-Europeans inclusion. The word has been effectively co-opted to focus on one people instead of all the rest that are covered in the classification. This would suggest a new power dynamic after World War II, one infusing a narrative into the overall narrative with such finesse, purpose, and power that it negates or lessens the narratives of other peoples.

There is also the importance of the term "the Holocaust," defining a uniquely Jewish experience in Europe during World War II. And there is no room here for anyone to doubt the devastation or the horror of the Nazi Holocaust. To deny the existence of a Holocaust is a preposterous position that refutes evidence; but again, I want to point out the holocaust in Europe during World War II was no more genocidal and destructive than the holocaust of the Middle Passage, or the holocaust of brutal chattel enslavement in the Americas, or the genocide carried out against Native peoples in the New World, just to name a few. So why do hearts and minds turn solely toward the death camps of Europe and the plight of Jews when "holocaust" is mentioned? Why does it always have "the" in front of it? It would seem that the narrative is claiming there is nothing more devastating, genocidal, and destructive than what happened to this particular group during World War II. What I am saying is that numbers of peoples have had a holocaust, so why is the narrative exclusive to the Jewish European experience—why is it "the Holocaust," thus lessening the brutality, pain, and realness experienced by others? It seems that when held up to the light, these experiences on European soil, carried out with the conspiracy and complacency of European nations, shames the narrative of "European civilization" carried out against other Europeans. It also shames the European church, who allowed its theology to spew hatred that reached the level of genocide and ethnic cleansing. But again I must point out that there was no such shame when Europeans made billions off the slave trade, killed scores of Black and Red peoples, colonized Africa and robbed African riches and history, often in the name of Christianity. There is no such shame or repentance even to this day. In the United States Black people are still awaiting reparations. In Washington, DC, the first emancipated jurisdiction in the country, the slave master was compensated by the government for the loss of his property—his slaves—and the slaves even received a "thank you" for the liberty and wages stolen from them.

Certainly, there is a holocaust that is part of the Jewish narrative, but that narrative has also tampered discussion and debate, and also justified acts of aggression and oppression for the sake of safety and security. The capturing of the narratives illustrates how generally Jews have moved from powerlessness—being victims, suffering and surviving one pogrom after another—to total control over the narrative, now defining and redefining how it is to be used, and its meaning. This demonstrates a unique power as a group brings influence to already existing systems of power, exclusivism, and influence.

Art has particular influence in changing and altering the perspective of a culture and nation and influencing the narrative of that culture (may I remind you of the 1915 movie *Birth of a Nation*?). Another movie that illustrated a landscape shift was *Gentleman's Agreement*. When I re-watched this movie, my Baltimore reared-and-raised ears heard the word "antisemitism" for the very first time. Starring Gregory Peck and Dorothy McGuire, the movie came out shortly after the close of World War II in 1947, and explores how antisemitism inflicts people both externally and internally.

I remember being moved by the story line, which centers on a man who pretends to be Jewish in order to expose antisemitism. The question the story line answers is, will he be accepted into the white WASP society of Darien, Connecticut, and therefore the culture of white America, and after the European Holocaust, will the American dream, and the hope that comes with it, be afforded to American Jews? It illustrated for me a social issue that I experienced for the first time through film, as I am sure this was case for many others who have seen the movie. However gracefully the theme unfolded, or the stars played their roles and engaged their respective love interests, it prompted people to begin to ponder something called "antisemitism" and begin to make the assertion that Jews are just like white people. The main character, a man only pretending to be a Jew, can not be distinguished from a real Jew, and overall whiteness is affirmed in WASP and Jew alike.

But even though there is the potential for acceptance in American culture, it is also clear that there is a paranoia that comes from an experience like the European Holocaust. When Black people come together, race and racism are so powerfully a part of the discourse. You cannot have a history of four hundred years of enslavement and one hundred years of de facto enslavement and not have race and racism be topics of regular interactions. I can imagine that it is the same way with the Jewish narrative: you cannot have noted that a holocaust is part of your common identity and not manifest its effects upon your psyche. Again, the narrative of the Nazi Holocaust is one of those points on the story line just as slavery in Egypt under the Pharaoh is one of those points. It is a narrative that all Jews experience physically or emotionally, and it becomes part of the collective psyche. The State of Israel was established in part out of that effect upon the psyche. The need to be tough as a state comes out of the narrative of "never again a victim." But it is also this kind of effect upon the psyche that blurs the vision and allows for a people to justify the oppression of others—in this case the oppression of Palestinians—and transform the prospect of coexistence, equality, and mutual trust into an overwhelming, fear-inducing plan of imminent destruction.

It is the backdrop of a holocaust and a narrative of cohesion that disallows criticism of Israel or Zionism. Even those who are Jewish can suffer the wrath of being labeled self-loathing Jews if they raise ethical issues about the State of Israel's actions in the world, or how Zionist organizations interact, engage others, and apply undue influence using its narrative. Immediately, a person is saddled with the accusation of being antisemitic if they question Israel, equate it with the apartheid state of South Africa, or advocate for the BDS movement. Antisemitism is thrown around so easily, and the design is not only to control the narrative but to define and redefine it according to systems of power. Antisemitism exists only if systems of power, governments, and policies are structured against Jews or the State of Israel because of its Jewishness. But in the contemporary state of affairs, it is Israeli, Jewish, and Zionist establishment organizations that seem to be a part of networks of influence and systems of power—not those who are currently questioning the policies of Israel or the Zionist organizations—that support Israel no matter what. So antisemitism becomes a charge that is harder to sustain given the fact that the people and organizations that it is leveled against have little or no power or influence over the existing networks of dominance.

Antisemitism doesn't exist within the defined framework of racism within the United States. Jews are not the tenants filling the for-profit jails in the United States, nor were their neighborhoods devastated by the crack epidemic of the '80s or the mortgage meltdown of the 2000s. Antisemitism does exist as an "anti-" feeling that is part of the balkanized fabric of nation, state, and religion. European Jews who were victims of antisemitism-as-racism before and during World War II in Europe, and in the former Soviet Union under Communism, as well as their descendants find that within the American culture of race and racism, being of European origin affords acceptability, privilege, and white power. In general, Jews have become white. I realize that there are other nationalities that also define themselves as Jewish but are not white; however, the bulk of people's experience with Judaism in the United States has been largely with those who are European and of European descent and orientation. It is inescapable: America's sin is racism, its apathy to deal with it, and its blindness to see it. But the uniquely tailored narrative in the United States of Jews as victims camouflages their newfound first-world status, and it portrays Jews simply as a people fiercely guarding themselves against a world of antisemites, Muslims, and people seeking to take away Israel, which, according to the narrative, is the only bastion of protection for Jews in the world!

But as I stated earlier, there are competing narratives, even within Judaism. I have worked often with Jewish Voice for Peace, which embraces movements and other people with grace and solidarity. This organization questions the narrative of the Jewish establishment and attempts to lift up qualities that they define as Jewish—showing hospitality, healing the creation, loving one's neighbor, and doing justice. Yet the Jewish establishment continues to malign groups like this as being "not Jewish" or as self-loathing. But I say, thank the Creator for narratives that challenge the dominant narrative, and I believe that with much work and effort a narrative of justice will become manifest in our world, and we might truly heal our souls, the world, and even the United States of America, which so sorely needs to be healed from its history—its past as well as its present.

"We're Here Because You Were There": Refugee Rights Advocacy and Antisemitism

Rachel Ida Buff

We're here because of you.
We're here because you were there.
We've arrived from every corner of the planet to this nation
to seek the fulfillment of a promise of America.

—Immortal Technique, "Open Your Eyes"

This essay focuses on the politics of immigrant and refugee rights advocacy in Jewish communities. It emerges from the intersections of my scholarly research on the history of immigrant rights in the United States; from my participation in immigrant rights and Palestine solidarity efforts; and from my engagement with Jewish communities, including Jewish Voice for Peace (JVP), in my hometown of Milwaukee, Wisconsin. These intersections have been generative and sometimes explosive. I want to explore their possibilities and perils in context of the contemporary crises around the figure of the refugee.

Articulated most recently by extremist politicians such as Donald Trump and widely circulated by mass media, concerns that Muslim refugees in particular may harbor terrorists among them point to a cycle of colonialism and catastrophe that continuously displaces thousands around the world. Attending the historical roots of this cycle redirects immigrant and refugee rights advocacy toward a broader politics of solidarity.

History creates refugees, as people flee the violence caused by wars and natural disasters. Contemporary refugee cohorts are no exception. Impelled by decades of conflict in their homelands, refugees from Central America and the Middle East cross oceans and borders, seeking the shelter of asylum. Europe and the United States are at once destinations that refugees desire and powerful agents of displacement. Current crises evolve out of decades of war and violence sponsored largely by the United States and its European allies.

Jews figure importantly in the history of refugee policy. While the phenomenon of having to flee a homeland is ancient and ongoing, the World War II Holocaust and subsequent crisis of displaced persons (DPs) impelled the creation of international protocols for refugee relief. Although thousands of non-Jews were displaced after the war, the figure of the newly liberated Jewish Holocaust survivor, emaciated and stateless, animated the international conversation that led to the formation of the United Nations High Commission on Refugees (UNHCR). Of course, that same figure similarly inspired the founding of the State of Israel in 1948 with the resulting displacement of Palestinians in the Nakba (Arabic for "disaster").

The coming of the Jewish state meant the creation of hundreds of thousands of refugees. The founding of a homeland for the "saving remnant" of European Jewry directly contributed to the creation of refugee camps in Gaza, the West Bank, Syria, Lebanon, and Jordan, and the displacement of thousands more who left the area entirely. The disastrous consequences of antisemitism, then, have been foundational to both the international recognition of the need for refuge for displaced and persecuted people, and to the creation of more refugees.

International political acknowledgment of refugees took place at the same time as the founding of the State of Israel. The United Nations Relief and Works Agency for Palestinian Refugees in the Near East was founded in 1949 to provide temporary assistance to displaced Palestinians in the present-day occupied territories and neighboring nations; it celebrated its sixtieth anniversary in 2009. The founding Convention of the UNHCR in 1951 recognized basic rights for those seeking asylum in other countries, including access to courts, to education, and to necessary travel documents, including passports. The Convention recognized that the seeking of asylum would inevitably incur the breaking of national immigration regulations, but it also forbade the expulsion or return of refugees against their will. Most UN refugee policy dealt primarily with European DPs, expanding in the early 1960s to contend with refugee crises in Africa, Asia, and Latin America.[1]

International military engagements such as the 1980s Dirty Wars in Central America, ventures in Iraq and Afghanistan, and ongoing support for brutal Israeli occupation in Gaza and the West Bank create refugees. The upheaval created by these interventions returns to Europe and the United States in the form of transnational criminal and terrorist activity. Fear of imported violence, in turn, leads to state regimes of securitization and the spread of nativist suspicions. Refugees from the Middle East have been particularly targeted by this cycle, because they hail from what Moustafa Bayoumi calls "geographies of suspicion." Central American refugees are often not recognized as such, and are often categorized as "illegal" because of anti-Latinx racism. Refugee crises, then, comprise part of an ongoing cycle of catastrophe.[2]

Refugee questions link the experiences of migration and displacement to diplomatic and trade policy; to climate change, war, and global wealth distribution. Viewed systemically, the study of migration cannot be limited to the story of one ethnic group's migration from one country to another. Refugees are created by world events: refugee questions are international questions.

Advocacy for refugee relief and for immigrant rights takes place in context of this global cycle of catastrophe. Confronting the challenging local contexts that result from securitization, racism, and nativism, immigrant and refugee advocates are sometimes forced to limit struggles for refugee rights in context of national citizenship. This strategic move can conceal the transnational causes of migration. The simultaneous inscription of the refugee into international human rights policy and creation of refugees in Palestine underlies a deep contradiction in the policies and practices of refugee relief. Given the rifts existing in Jewish communities over US foreign policy in the Middle East, this contradiction is particularly pronounced in context of Jewish advocacy for refugee rights.

In the United States, mainstream Jewish advocacy for immigrant rights draws on a social justice tradition that combines Torah, historical Jewish American involvement in civil rights struggles, and an implicit parallel between the experiences of antisemitism and racial oppression. Both Jewish history and Talmudic tradition dictate a deep commitment to social justice. At the same time, over the course of the twentieth century, Ashkenazi Jews in this country have had increasing access to the power and privileges of white identity. Particularly after World War II, many Jews have counted as white people in a highly segregated society, with all the access—to housing, education, employment, freedom from fear of the police—that comes with that designation. This whiteness has complicated some prior political alliances.

Historically, Jews in the United States have been involved in civil rights organizing. Well-known examples include Jewish American legal and financial involvement with the NAACP through the mid-twentieth century, and the involvement of leaders such as Abraham Joshua Heschel with Dr. Martin Luther King and the organizers of the 1963 March on Washington. While it is often remembered as emerging from an ethical imperative, Jewish civil rights activism originated in a period when most Jews were not decisively included in the privileges of whiteness, and often faced discrimination in housing, employment, and education.

Historical memory of this alliance has been clouded further by the postwar legacy of anti-Communism: Jewish engagement with multiracial freedom struggles throughout the twentieth century often took place in context of Old Left organizations such as labor unions and political parties sympathetic to Communism. Because a virulent anti-Communism still contours our historical imagination, much of this vital history has been neglected or forgotten.

In my forthcoming book, *Against the Deportation Terror*, I uncover a twentieth-century history of immigrant rights advocacy by tracing the story of the American Committee for the Protection of the Foreign Born (ACP-FB). Along with immigrants from Europe, Asia, and Latin America, Jewish ACPFB activists like Abner Green and Rose Chernin were prominent in struggling for racial equality and immigrant rights in the 1940s and 1950s. Historian George Sanchez has written about the ways that struggles of this period concerning local politics and civil and immigrant rights brought Jews into multiracial social justice work with their predominantly Mexican American neighbors in Boyle Heights, Los Angeles.[3]

The ACPFB understood immigration in context of global politics. They criticized colonialism and opposed Cold War military ventures. Eventually, this anti-imperialist, multiracial organizing came under fire during the post–World War II Red Scare. Abner Green spent time in jail, and there was a long, ultimately unsuccessful campaign to denaturalize Chernin, who had fled Russia with her family when she was a child.

The government's case against Chernin turned on the accusation of her "willful misrepresentation" of her purpose in entering the United States because she later joined the Communist Party. The Justice Department claimed that Chernin's "lie" invalidated her oath of loyalty, and that, as a Communist, she was clearly only loyal to Russia. Sixty-four years later, in 2014, the Immigration and Customs Enforcement Agency (ICE) pursued a similar course of denaturalization in the case of Palestinian American immigrant rights activist Rasmea Odeh.[4]

The multiracial, internationalist work of organizations like the ACPFB has largely been forgotten. In her acclaimed book, *Eyes off the Prize: The United Nations and the African American Struggle for Human Rights, 1944–1955*, historian Carol Anderson traces the ways that anti-Communists cast opponents of segregation as subversive. In order to survive in this climate, rights advocacy organizations were forced to adopt a civil rights, rather than a human rights, framework, de-emphasizing their transnational, anti-colonial alliances. The chilling effects of this historical transition linger, affecting the field of possibilities for contemporary activist work. Further, the Israeli conquest of Gaza and the West Bank in the Six-Day War in 1967 complicated Jewish alliances with communities of color, many of whom increasingly identified with Palestinians against the Israeli occupation.[5]

Historically, the politics of international alliances have complicated mainstream Jewish American engagement in domestic freedom struggles. Recently, as the global BDS movement has gained traction in the wake of Israel's illegal occupation of Gaza and the West Bank, the contradiction between welcoming refugees and defending the "Jewish homeland" has become more pronounced. In a dangerous world wracked by racism, terrorism, and antisemitism, many Jewish people see Israel as a lone refuge for Jews. Because of a perceived need to defend Israel against its enemies, any criticism of Israel is taken to be criticism of Jews in general. Reflexive defense of Israel occasions support for both global and domestic securitization and militarization. Mainstream Jewish immigrant rights advocacy is impelled to resist these imperatives.

In Milwaukee, I have participated in founding a group called MIKLAT! A Jewish Response to Displacement. MIKLAT! has established a Jewish presence in the predominantly Latinx immigrant rights organization called Voces de la Frontera. A workers' center, Voces de la Frontera organizes Latinx immigrants in Milwaukee around civil rights as well as labor equity. Founded in 2001, the organization provides legal clinics as well as English and citizenship classes. Voces, as it is known locally, advocates for people facing deportation. The organization holds a march for immigrant rights every year on May Day, and organizes around key issues confronting immigrant communities, such as state-issued identity cards, in-state tuition for undocumented students, and the ways that increased securitization negatively affects daily life.

As is true in many cities, most Jewish congregations are located in the affluent suburbs, which in Milwaukee's case are on the north side. The center of Latinx life in the city is on the south side, a traditional destination for new and less-affluent arrivals. To say that these two worlds rarely meet in a city that is consistently ranked one of the most segregated in the nation is a considerable understatement. MIKLAT! has created moments that bring these two very different communities together in solidarity.

In the past two years, MIKLAT! has been housed in the Social Action Committee of Congregation Sinai, a liberal Reform community. The congregation held what it called "Immigrant Freedom Seders" in collaboration with

Voces de la Frontera in 2012 and 2015. In 2014 Sinai became the first and only Jewish congregation in the area to join the New Sanctuary Movement (NSM), the arm of Voces de la Frontera that mobilizes diverse faith communities to support those faced with deportation, whether for themselves or a family member. Subsequently, Sinai became the first Jewish congregation to host the monthly prayer vigil for people facing deportation. A small cadre of Sinai Social Action members has attended the annual May Day march. Members of Sinai's Social Action Committee frequently show up at monthly NSM rallies outside of the ICE office and temporary holding center in downtown Milwaukee.

Miklat is the Hebrew word for "refuge." Drawing on the Talmudic tradition of social justice, the idea behind MIKLAT! is that Jews have a particular role to play in advocating for immigrant rights; that we are all too familiar with the experiences of displacement and alienation. There is an abundant ethical imperative in the Torah to "welcome the stranger": the phrase is used thirty-six separate times in the five Books of Moses, the Jewish Torah. The history of experiencing nativism as "strangers in the land," to borrow a phrase from historian John Higham, creates a particularly Jewish approach to social justice: sympathy for, and alliance with, the stranger—those who are expelled from or excluded by society.[6]

Speaking at a June 2015 rally against Milwaukee County Sheriff Dave Clark's brutal collusion with ICE, Rabbi David Cohen of Sinai asserted: "Had a Jewish prophet never spoken, Jewish history itself would teach us what happens when the rights of the stranger are trampled." Importantly, Cohen draws on Jewish ethical tradition to oppose the securitization efforts represented by the "Secure Communities" program that enabled Sheriff Clark's forces to arrest and detain immigrants at the courthouse. Further, he contextualizes defenses of law and order in light of Jewish history by repeatedly reminding the audience that "we"—Jews—have heard such defenses before; it's an implicit reference to antisemitic uses of state power in the past. This invocation draws effectively on the power of the Torah, as well as suggesting parallels between Jewish experiences of antisemitism and the encounters of contemporary migrants with nativism and exclusion.[7]

MIKLAT!'s vocal opposition to the repression of immigrant rights by state and federal forces has created some key spaces for solidarity and organizing. MIIKLAT!'s work has established connections, potentially clearing way for further collaboration between the predominantly suburbanized Ashkenazi Jewish community and Latinx immigrant communities. Organized by a Sinai member who worked briefly as NSM coordinator, the NSM monthly vigil in January 2016 featured speakers from Milwaukee's Hmong and Muslim communities, opposing the recent raids and deportations of Central American refugees. Our local JVP chapter was represented, along with Sinai/MIKLAT! members. As with any crisis, the current moment offers powerful possibilities for solidarity and opposition.

And yet, attending to the cycle of catastrophe also points to some road blocks ahead. Mainstream commentators were baffled at the appearance of thousands of minor children from Central America at the US-Mexico border during the summer of 2014. Public discourse about this crisis almost completely neglected a history of US involvement in the region, including CIA-backed coups against progressive regimes like that of Jacobo Arbenz in Guatemala in 1954, support for right-wing death squads during the Dirty Wars of the 1980s and ongoing funding of terror under the War on Drugs and counter-insurgency initiatives. This history contributed to the contemporary violence in the region and helped Central American cities such as Tegucigalpa become the murder capitals of the hemisphere. Central American children fled the direct consequences of violence in their homelands, caused by the very country in which they sought and were largely denied refuge.

Similarly, the recent mass displacements in the Middle East have been triggered by decades of warfare waged by the United States and its allies in the Middle East. This includes support for the Israeli occupation of Palestinian territories. As journalist Max Blumenthal points out, one of the few ways to escape constant war and terror in occupied Gaza is to join the refugee stream and take passage across the Mediterranean.[8]

Just as civil rights advocates during the Cold War were compelled by anti-Communist repression to operate in a national rather than a global frame, the insistence of most mainstream Jewish organizations on "standing with" Israel limits refugee and immigrant rights advocacy in the name of opposing anti-semitism. During the Cold War, multiracial alliances were viewed as suspect if they had worked alongside Communists. Similarly, expressions of solidarity with Palestine or Palestinians in the Middle East as well as in the United States and Europe are widely viewed by mainstream Jewish organizations as treasonous. For instance, outside of JVP, no Jewish organizations came forward to support Rasmea Odeh's fight against deportation.

Has Zionism once and for all drained the power of the parallel between Jewish experiences of antisemitism and other forms of racial oppression? The founding of Israel was a consequence of a refugee crisis at the same time it created more refugees. The Nakba, then, is a Jewish issue. Jewish and Palestinian destinies and homelands are entwined: of course the displacement of

Palestinians is and should be significant for all Jews. Surely there is room in the historical and ethical lexicon of our oppression for this fact.

Our current historical moment is bleak. A cycle of securitization, exclusion, and militarism, if it remains unabated, will continue to create refugees and then imprison, detain, and deport them. There will be no civil rights, no human rights. The one bright possibility, the one bell-clear option is solidarity.

European Antisemitism: Is It "Happening Again"?

Rabbi Brant Rosen

January 2006: A twenty-three-year-old Jewish man is kidnapped, tortured, and left for dead in Paris by a gang who later confess they did it "because he was a Jew, so his family would have money."[1]

March 2012: A gunman enters the Ozar Hatorah School in Toulouse, France, and kills three children and an adult, including a rabbi and his two children.[2]

May 2014: A gunman murders four people in front of the Jewish Museum in Brussels.[3]

January 2015: Two days after the Charlie Hebdo murders in Paris, a gunman takes hostages in a Jewish supermarket, killing four.[4]

February 2015: After murdering one person at a Copenhagen cafe, a gunman walks to a synagogue and opens fire, killing one.[5]

We cannot dismiss or rationalize it away—the rise of antisemitic violence in Europe is undeniable, increasingly traumatizing European Jewish communities and unsettling Jews the world over. Beyond the violence, we are also witnessing the dramatic rise of far-right nationalist political parties throughout Europe (i.e., the Jobbik party in Hungary, the Sweden Democrats, the Golden Dawn party in Greece, and the Freedom Party in Austria) led by demagogic politicians who unabashedly express antisemitic and xenophobic attitudes in their campaigns.

And so the inevitable questions are being asked out loud: Is it happening again? Are Jews truly safe in Europe? Are we witnessing the nascent stirrings of another Jewish nightmare in that part of the world?

Questions such as these have been asked and parsed repeatedly by the mainstream media over the past several years, displaying portentous headlines such as: "Exodus: Why Europe's Jews Are Fleeing Once Again,"[6] "Is It Time for the Jews to Leave Europe?,"[7] "Antisemitism on the Rise across Europe 'in Worst Times since the Nazis.'"[8]

The "it's happening again" meme is also being promoted, not unsurprisingly, by Israeli politicians openly urging European Jews to flee their countries and immigrate to Israel. Following the Paris market tragedy, Prime Minister Benjamin Netanyahu pointedly proclaimed: "To all the Jews of France, all the Jews of Europe, I would like to say that Israel is not just the place in whose direction you pray, the State of Israel is your home. . . . This week, a special team of ministers will convene to advance steps to increase immigration from France and other countries in Europe that are suffering from terrible antisemitism."[9] He offered similar words after the Copenhagen synagogue attack: "Jews were killed on European land just because they were Jewish. This wave of attacks will continue. I say to the Jews of Europe—Israel is your home."[10]

By all accounts the Jews of Europe aren't heeding the call. In May 2015 it was reported that there had indeed been a 40 percent rise in European Jewish immigration to Israel.[11] The majority of these immigrants, however, came from Russia and Ukraine rather than Western Europe—and most cited the economy and political unrest in the Ukraine as their primary reasons for moving. There was a rise in French immigration by the end of 2015,[12] but according to an Israeli journalist, this was "actually in line with the gradual increase in immigration from France over the past four years and (was) largely attributed to economic hardship."[13] In the end, the segment of French Jewish immigrants into Israel in 2015 was 1.6 percent of France's total Jewish population, which though not insignificant, is far short of an "exodus."

Many European Jews in fact, are publicly expressing their desire to remain in their home communities—and resent the suggestion that they should respond to antisemitism by fleeing to Israel. One particularly dramatic instance occurred when Netanyahu visited France following the Jewish market attack. After he delivered his message in a Paris synagogue, the congregation rose to their feet and burst into the French national anthem as he awkwardly stood by.[14] Rabbi Menachem Margolin, director of the European Jewish Association, later commented: "Every such Israeli campaign severely weakens and damages the Jewish communities that have the right to live securely wherever they are. The reality is that a large majority of European Jews do not plan to emigrate to Israel. The Israeli government must recognize this reality . . . and cease this Pavlovian reaction every time Jews in Europe are attacked."[15] Similarly, after the Copenhagen attack, Denmark's chief rabbi Jair Melchior said he was "disappointed" in Netanyahu's remarks, adding, "Terror is not a reason to move to Israel."[16]

It is also notable that in the aftermath of these attacks, the liberal leaders of these European nations have responded by voicing firm solidarity with their Jewish communities. French prime minister Manuel Valls: "A Jew who leaves France is a piece of France that is gone."[17] Danish prime minister Helle Thorning-Schmidt: "I want to make very clear that the Jewish community has been in this country for centuries. They belong in Denmark. They're part of the Danish community and we wouldn't be the same without the Jewish community."[18]

It would seem that comparisons of contemporary European antisemitism to the antisemitism of Nazi Germany are motivated more by an overzealous media and an Israeli political agenda than honest political analysis. Perhaps the most important point to make in this regard is that European antisemitism of the 1930s and '40s was state-sponsored, institutional oppression against Jews and other minorities. By contrast, these recent attacks have been committed by individual Muslims motivated by extremist ideologies.

While these are not isolated incidents to be sure, they are not part of a uniform movement that the political right routinely refers to as "radical Islam," "Islamism," or "Islamofascism." These problematic terms actually refer to a wide-ranging spectrum of groups,[19] not all of which share the same ideologies and some of which (most notably al-Qaeda and ISIS) are at odds with each other.[20] Moreover, reputable political experts agree that however dangerous these groups might be, they do not pose an existential threat to Europe or the United States.[21]

This is not to dismiss the reality—and dangers—of Muslim antisemitism. While a comprehensive analysis of antisemitism in the Muslim world is beyond the scope of this essay, one crucial point bears noting: historically, Islam has not demonized the Jews—it was Christian theology that introduced antisemitism to the world. As Professor David Greenberg has noted, "Unlike in Europe, Jews in Islamic lands were not expelled or forced to convert or, with a few exceptions, consigned to ghettos."[22]

This changed in the nineteenth century for two essential reasons: the arrival of European colonists who brought Christian-style antisemitism into the Muslim world; and the growth of political Zionism and the colonization of Palestine, which seemed to "prove" the Christian antisemitic canard that Jews are conspiratorial and bent on world domination.[23]

Many are suggesting that the antisemitism of Muslims in Europe today has been inflamed by traditional European-style antisemitism as well. In the *Atlantic* article quoted above, journalist Jeffrey Goldberg explained it this way:

> That the chief propagators of contemporary European antisemitism may be found in the Continent's large and disenfranchised Muslim immigrant communities—communities that are themselves harassed and assaulted by hooligans associated with Europe's surging right—is flummoxing to, among others, Europe's elites. Muslims in Europe are in many ways a powerless minority. The failure of Europe to integrate Muslim immigrants has contributed to their exploitation by antisemitic propagandists and by recruiters for such radical projects as the Islamic State, or ISIS. Yet the new antisemitism flourishing in corners of the European Muslim community would be impoverished without the incorporation of European fascist tropes.[24]

If we truly want to identify the reasons behind the rise of European antisemitism then, we cannot begin and end with so-called "radical Islam." The attitudes of many European Muslims toward Jews are disturbing to be sure, but they are being incubated within the larger context of traditional European Jew-hatred. In order to better understand our current situation, it would be far more appropriate to focus our concern on the rising popularity of far-right political parties throughout Europe, whose racism is directed at Muslims and Jews alike.

Tellingly, a 2015 report by Tel Aviv University's Kantor Center for the Study of Contemporary European Jewry indicated that "a record influx of Muslim refugees [in 2015] coincided with a sharp decline in the number of violent antisemitic incidents in major European countries, many of which bore the brunt of the refugee crisis." These findings "clearly show that as the refugees started coming in by the tens of thousands per day starting about a year ago, Europe became a safer place to be Jewish."[25]

Meanwhile, as journalist Paul Hockenos has observed, "The same tools and tropes that were once used to create fear of and resentment toward Jews have been turned against Muslims. They claim that Muslims are swamping their countries and diluting their national cultures—claims once made against Jews. Whereas Jews were claimed to partake in blood rituals, Islam is cast as an inherently violent religion and all Muslims as threats to European security and identity."[26]

European Islamophobia was a significant problem well before the 2015 Syrian refugee crisis, but this new influx of refugees into Europe indicates that Muslims have become the current "scapegoat du jour." In 2016 the first annual European Islamophobia Report, presented at the EU parliament, revealed that "since the attacks on Charlie Hebdo, anti-Muslim attacks increased in France more than 500 percent ... 75 percent of the victims [were] women," who on account of their head scarves were easier to identify as Muslim than men were. In addition, "According to a recent poll by the Bertelsmann Foundation, 61 percent of Germans believe that Islam does not fit in the West."[27]

It has also been reported that "far-right parties in some European countries are winning over Jewish voters by exploiting fears about militant Islamists." After Austria's 2016 elections, Rabbi Pinchas Goldschmidt, the head of the Conference of European Rabbis, expressed concern that "a not insignificant part of the [Jewish] community here voted for [Norbert] Hofer for the presidency."[28] (Hofer is a leader in the far-right Freedom Party that demonizes Muslim immigrants and has a history of antisemitic innuendo.)[29]

Although the Europe's far right nationalists would love nothing better than to set the Jewish and Muslim communities against each other, the most appropriate response is, as ever, solidarity. Thankfully, there are indications that in some corners of Europe, Jews and Muslims are indeed finding common cause. Following the Copenhagen synagogue shooting, for instance, the Muslim community in Oslo organized a peace vigil and formed a symbolic circle around a synagogue while elderly Jewish congregants filed out of Shabbat services.[30] In Malmö, Sweden, a city that has seen its share of antisemitic incidents in recent years, Malmö's Network for Faith and Understanding held a solidarity vigil following a 2012 synagogue attack. Leaders of several Christian churches, two Muslim groups, and other spiritual and social organizations came together and offered public speeches of support and solidarity.[31]

In 2014, during rising tensions over Israel's military attack on Gaza, Malmö resident Rabbi Rebecca Lillian reported that the Malmö interfaith group met to speak "candidly about the need to work together to fight any kind of hate crime." According to Rabbi Lillian: "At a panel discussion, I spoke as a Jew for humanitarian aid to Gaza and for an end to the killing and injuring of civilians. The Imam on the Board spoke about the need for Muslim youth to not attack people and property. We all spoke of co-existence ... and the good news is that is indeed happening."[32]

Beyond local efforts at solidarity and understanding, however, we must confront the larger context in which this unrest is occurring. In this regard, Goldberg's fleeting reference to "flummoxed European elites" is critical. If we are to compare today's European antisemitism to that of the 1930s and '40s, we would do well to consider the circumstances that led to fall of the Weimar Republic: the failed policies of the Western elites that created a profound economic depression, which in turn led to sociopolitical instability that eventually led to the rise of fascism.

While the circumstances today are obviously different, it is worth noting that we currently live in an era in which the liberal Western elites have exploited a newly globalized world by enacting draconian neoliberal policies—which have in turn caused markets to crash, widened the gap between rich and poor, and created a class of disenfranchised, frustrated masses who rightly believe that these elites have amassed power at their expense.

The role of a Western military hegemony has been key to this process as well. As Glenn Greenwald has observed:

> In 2011, NATO bombed Libya by pretending it was motivated by humanitarianism, only to ignore that country once the fun military triumph was celebrated, thus leaving a vacuum of anarchy and militia rule for years that spread instability through the region and fueled the refugee crisis. The US and its European allies continue to invade, occupy, and bomb predominantly Muslim countries while propping up their most brutal tyrants, then feign befuddlement about why anyone would want to attack them back, justifying erosions of basic liberties and more bombing campaigns and ratcheting up fear levels each time someone does. The rise of ISIS and the foothold it seized in Iraq and Libya were the direct byproducts of the West's military actions. . . . Western societies continue to divert massive resources into military weaponry and prisons for their citizens, enriching the most powerful factions in the process, all while imposing harsh austerity on already suffering masses. *In sum, Western elites thrive while everyone else loses hope* (emphasis mine).[33]

It must be stated here that Israel is an intrinsic and critical player in this Western hegemony. Economically speaking, Israel was an active participant in the neoliberal transitions of the 1980s and '90s[34] and today is a crucial driver of the twenty-first–century "global war economy."[35] As the most militarized nation in the world, Israel routinely markets its weapons as "battle tested" on human subjects and is the top exporter of security systems and crowd control/surveillance techniques to Western nations. It is also geographically situated in a part of the world that makes it an important strategic ally to the West, enjoying a "special relationship" with the world's only superpower.

It is understandable that a people who have been maligned for centuries as a powerful cabal that seeks to dominate the world might be sensitive to the suggestion that Israel is now complicit in the imperial designs of the West. Nevertheless, Israel is a powerful nation that commits human rights abuse at home and exports it abroad—and it is not antisemitic to say so. Through the creation of the State of Israel, it might well be said that the

Jewish people has made a Faustian bargain with power and empire. Zionism, whose raison d'être was to make the Jews *ke'chol hagoyim* (like all the nations) has helped to create a Jewish nation-state that is now an active player in the Western imperial elite.

Israel is not, as some might argue, merely a pawn in the designs of US-led empire, but neither is it somehow manipulating the world's largest superpower to pursue policies that are counter to its own national interest. It is deeply problematic to claim, as some in the Palestine solidarity movement do, that Israel's oppressive behavior and policies are "against the United States' interest." In the end, we cannot divorce Israel's interests from the interests of larger hegemony of which it is a part. (Given the devastation wrought by Western militarism, we would do better to ask whether or not these hegemonic actions are in the *world's* best interest.)

Though it might seem strange to refer to a Middle Eastern country as part of a "Western hegemony," Israel is at heart a European nation. The roots of political Zionism are buried firmly in the soil of nineteenth-century European nationalism and colonialism. Zionist figures from Theodor Herzl (whose novel *Altnueland* imagined the Jewish state in Palestine à la nineteenth-century Vienna) to former prime minister Ehud Barak, who infamously described Israel as "a villa in the jungle,"[36] have fancied the country as a European-style nation-state outpost in an otherwise uncivil Middle East.

Israel has been also proving its European bona fides through the nationalist racism that plagues its civic life. Indeed, the rise of xenophobic nationalism in Israel mirrors similar trends in Europe: from European-style racist soccer clubs,[37] to Israeli street hooligans who wear T-shirts with neo-Nazi insignias,[38] to the increasing number of xenophobic far-right nationalist members of the government (one of whom, who currently serves as minister of justice, has openly called for the genocide of Palestinians).[39]

Given this parallel, it is not surprising that Israeli politicians are finding common cause with European far-right political parties. In 2016, for instance, Heinz-Christian Strache, party chief of the far-right Austrian Freedom Party was invited to Israel by the Likud party to meet with high-ranking Israeli officials. Strache was likely invited because of his strong nativist positions against Muslim immigrants, even though, ironically enough, he himself has a history of antisemitic behavior.[40]

So to return to our original question, "Is it happening again?" Perhaps the answer is both no—and yes. No, we are not witnessing the prelude to a "second Holocaust." Though many Jews may be unwilling to admit it, we currently live in an age of unprecedented Jewish power. The American Jewish communal establishment has become a genuine political force to be reckoned with. Israel is a heavily militarized nation, firmly embedded within a powerful Western hegemony.

European Jewish communities are certainly more vulnerable—but while contemporary European antisemitism is intolerable and abhorrent, it is not the kind of state-sanctioned antisemitism that existed in the days of the Third Reich. In the end, the violent xenophobia currently directed at European Jews—and European Muslims—is the inevitable blowback upon institutions that claim to cherish liberalism and democracy just as they enable systems of racism, oppression, and white supremacy.

Then again, maybe it is happening again, but not in the way most people would ordinarily assume. Although Jewish communities are no longer collectively targeted by state-sanctioned antisemitism, institutionalized racism is very much alive and well in the world. So we might well say it *is*, in fact, happening again. It is happening again in the streets of Baltimore and Chicago and in US prisons and immigrant detention systems. It is happening again in the checkpoints of the West Bank and the besieged Gaza Strip. It is happening again in Syrian refugee camps and in the bombed-out ruins of Iraq, Yemen, and Libya.

If we agree that it is indeed happening again, we must then confront a far more difficult question: how will we dismantle these systems of oppression once and for all?

Part III:

Fighting False Charges
of Antisemitism

Two Degrees of Separation:
Israel, Its Palestinian Victims,
and the Fraudulent Use of Antisemitism

Omar Barghouti

"A conquest may be fraught either with evil or with good for mankind, according to the comparative worth of the conquering and conquered peoples," wrote Theodore Roosevelt.[1] From the onset of Zionist colonization of Palestine, the conquering European settlers saw the place as a "land without a people,"[2] reducing the indigenous Arab population of Palestine to what I call "relative humans"[3] who are not worthy of equal rights, those accorded to "full" humans.

That degree of separation between the colonizers and the indigenous people of any colonized territory was the norm. Zionism, however, took it to the next level. By presenting Jews as superhumans, "the Chosen people," it has added a second degree of separation, so there is now one between Jews and the rest of the human species and another between that and the "relative humans."

Since the Nazi genocide in the 1940s of millions of Jews, among other human groups that were seen by Germans at the time as relative humans, the Zionist movement and, later, Israel have used the charge of antisemitism in many ways that are not related to actual anti-Jewish racism or discrimination.

With time, Israel focused on abusing the uniqueness of the Holocaust and using the charge of antisemitism to establish a doctrine of exceptionalism, which not only justifies and normalizes the Zionist ethnic cleansing of the indigenous Palestinians and the settler-colonial project in Palestine, but also shields Israel's regime of occupation, settler colonialism, and apartheid from accountability before international law.[4] With this exceptionalism, Israel has become a state above the law, placed "on a pedestal," as Archbishop Emeritus Desmond Tutu once said, above all other states.[5]

With the 2015 election of its "most racist government" ever, Israel has effectively dropped its already-thin mask of "democracy" and "enlightenment" and descended into a deeper-than-ever racist abyss.[6] This and the rise of worldwide grassroots support for the Palestinian-led Boycott, Divestment and Sanctions (BDS) movement have exposed Israel's system of injustice and reasserted Palestinian rights, encouraging much more ethically consistent, courageous critiques and a steady erosion in its world stature.[7] A BBC poll in 2014, for instance, showed Israel competing with North Korea in popularity around the world, including among Europe's largest nations.[8]

Israel's failure in the last decade to stop the accelerating loss of its international grassroots support base has prompted it to defiantly pump more money into re-branding and expensive propaganda campaigns aimed at whitewashing those policies and structures.[9]

When this strategy proved to be futile, Israel resorted to its weapon of choice—trying to bully dissenters, opponents of its grave human rights violations, and people of conscience who stand in solidarity with Palestinian rights by labeling them as "antisemites." The formula is simple: to maintain Israel's impunity and exceptionalism, those who dare to question must be bullied into silence, and there is no better "silencer" than the epithet of antisemitism.

Unprecedented criticism of Israel's regime and society, however, has started to come from unexpected corners of late. Ehud Barak, a former prime minister and highly decorated general, lamented that Israel has been "infected with the seeds of fascism," while Israel's current deputy chief of staff, Major General Yair Golan, has compared "revolting trends" in Israeli society to pre-Holocaust Germany.[10]

Apart from the Israel "choir," including politicians whose devotion is "bought and paid for by the Israel lobby," according to Thomas Friedman,[11] hardly anyone is taking Israel seriously when it tries to stick the antisemitism label on anyone who dares to question its exceptionalism by suggesting that international law should be applied to it as to any other state committing comparable crimes.

But in Israel's twisted logic, if a label does not fit, it must be redefined in order to fit.

Is the "New Antisemitism" Antisemitic?

Israel, its lobby groups, and the international Zionist movement have been aggressively trying to normalize and impose a new definition of antisemitism[12] that encompasses anti-Zionism, criticism of Israel's policies or laws, and advocacy of effective measures to hold it accountable to international law, especially through the BDS movement for Palestinian rights.[13]

Ethical principles aside, this attempted distortion of the concept of anti-Jewish racism to protect Israel from censure and accountability dehumanizes Palestinians by portraying our struggle against Israel's regime of oppression as if fueled by a visceral "hatred" toward Jews, not a genuinely human pursuit of freedom, justice, and equality.

This fraudulent "new antisemitism" dogma presents a substantial danger to people of conscience everywhere, including those of the Jewish faith, standing in solidarity with the Palestinian struggle for rights, as it seeks to delegitimize human rights campaigning against Israel's system of injustice or even its specific policies.

Conflating opposition to the State of Israel with antisemitism is also perilous to Jewish communities the world over as it dilutes the notion of anti-Jewish racism beyond recognition and, arguably, nourishes real anti-Jewish bigotry by indirectly implicating Jewish communities at large in Israel's egregious crimes against the Palestinians and others. Zionism, after all, has always thrived on *real* antisemitism, including during the rise of Nazi anti-Jewish legislation in Germany in the 1930s, viewed by the Zionist movement at the time as a victory against the worst enemy of Zionism—assimilation.[14]

Even today, Israel's right and far-right parties maintain what has been termed a "holy alliance" with Europe's far-right antisemites based on shared Islamophobia.[15] Israel's regime is more than ever unabashedly allying itself with explicitly antisemitic forces in the United States as well. Aside from its tight partnership with anti-Jewish Christian fundamentalists, Israel's far-right government and political leadership have applauded the election of Donald Trump to the American presidency on a platform of Islamophobia, extreme nationalism, and hard-right support for Israeli occupation and apartheid. Far-right pro-Israel voices and groups in America, meanwhile, have denied or downplayed the rise of antisemitism connected to Trump's campaign, with the Zionist Organization of America courting alliances with Steve Bannon, a leading figure in the white nationalist and antisemitic "alt-right" movement and now chief strategist to Trump.

Israel's War on BDS: Stigmatizing the Struggle for Palestinian Rights

Since it was launched in 2005 by the absolute majority in Palestinian civil society, BDS has never targeted Jews or Israelis as Jews; it has sought to end an unjust regime that enslaves our people with occupation, apartheid, and denial of the refugees' UN-stipulated rights. BDS targets complicity, not identity.

Anchored in the Universal Declaration of Human Rights, the BDS movement is an inclusive, nonviolent, non-sectarian movement that rejects all forms of racism, including Islamophobia, antisemitism, and Israel's tens of racist laws.[16] It calls for equal rights for all humans, irrespective of identity. It targets Israel and entities that are complicit in its regime of oppression, not on the basis of on any real or claimed identity, whether religious, ethnic, or otherwise, but on the basis that this regime of oppression denies Palestinians our UN-stipulated rights under international law.

An often-overlooked aspect of the BDS Call is its direct appeal to conscientious Israelis "to support this Call, for the sake of justice and genuine peace." Indeed, there are Jewish Israeli partners in the BDS movement that play a significant role in exposing Israel's regime of oppression and advocating for isolating it, and a significantly high number of Jewish activists have joined the BDS movement.[17] The fast growth of membership in Jewish Voice for Peace, a key partner in the BDS network, is an indicator of this inspiring phenomenon.

Israel and its well-oiled propaganda machine immediately accuse any supporter of BDS of antisemitism as a form of bullying and shutting down all dissent. This smear tactic is particularly used against Europeans and Americans who support the boycott. The strategy exploits the guilt over the Holocaust and Israel's relative success for decades in channeling that guilt into silence toward or complicity in its regime of oppression against the Palestinians. But this antisemitism smear tactic does not work with Palestinians, the victims of Zionism and its settler-colonial project who played no role in the Holocaust and should not be made to pay for it in our rights.

Calling for equality in rights, as the BDS movement does, addresses everyone's rights. It is crucial for the US public, conscientious Jewish Americans included, to approach BDS and the struggle for Palestinian rights in a way that thinks *out of the Jewish box*. There is nothing Jewish about Israel's apartheid and colonial oppression; there is nothing inherently anti-Jewish, then, about a nonviolent, morally consistent struggle against this oppression.

Anti-Palestinian voices have raised many arguments in their incessant attempts to undermine the struggle for Palestinian rights, including by associating almost all criticism of and opposition to Israel with anti-Jewish hatred. The following are some of the most frequently used.

"If Israel = All Jews, Then BDS = Antisemitism"

A boycott of Israel, according to one argument, is *inherently* anti-Jewish since

Israel is synonymous or coextensive with "all Jews." This argument is deeply problematic, ethically speaking, because it is premised on *essentializing* and *homogenizing* all Jewish persons.

Placing all Jews into a single category—as Israel does—is to suggest that group is intrinsically different in nature from all other humans, and is thus a case of essentializing and exceptionalizing them. Claiming that Israel is coextensive with all Jews strips them of human diversity and reduces them to a monolithic or homogeneous sum. *That* is truly antisemitic.

It is precisely because BDS has consistently refused not to essentialize or homogenize Jewish persons and communities that Israel's smearing of the movement and its charges of anti-Jewish racism is akin to the Ku Klux Klan accusing Martin Luther King and Rosa Parks of racism!

A purportedly more "rational" variation on this argument claims that Israel may not be synonymous with all Jews but it surely represents them all, being the only "Jewish state," and therefore a boycott against it is necessarily antisemitic.

This is logically false. Even if A entirely represents B, a call for boycotting A is *not* necessarily the same as a call for boycotting B or proof that it is racist against B. This is so because A, by definition, has attributes that are not shared by the full set of B, even though it represents it. Representation never entails a complete overlap.

Even in the case of the Vatican, an entity that exclusively and legitimately represents Catholics worldwide, anti-Catholic bigotry cannot be inferred from a hypothetical call for boycotting the Vatican, say, over its anti-gay policy. Only if an anti-Vatican boycott is called explicitly on the basis of some anti-Catholic premise (as in arguments that essentialize Catholics) can it be accused of being motivated by bigotry or discrimination against Catholics.

The US government, like any other ostensibly "democratic" and "freely elected" government, arguably represents all Americans. Yet one can call for a boycott or sanctions against the United States without being anti-American, as the establishment has attributes that are not shared with all Americans but that may trigger a call for boycott (I am sure many readers can think of quite a few).

Similarly, even if the overwhelming majority of the world's Jews were to freely decide that Israel represents them, a call for boycotting Israel would still not be necessarily an attack on them or triggered by racism against Jews. It all depends on the purpose of the boycott and its goals.

The antisemitism charge must be proven by revealing anti-Jewish discriminatory behavior or expression. Just as Islamophobia cannot be inferred from, say, an anti-Saudi boycott that targets its regime's war crimes in Yemen or its misogynistic laws, anti-Jewish racism cannot be inferred from a boycott that targets Israel's denial of Palestinian rights.

A boycott against Saudi Arabia, though, that is based on, say, a premise that Muslims are "backward" or "violent" would clearly be Islamophobic, regardless of any policy, law, or violation that the Saudi regime may be accused of.

By the same token, a boycott against Israel may indeed be anti-Jewish if it targets Israel not because of its regime of oppression or policies of injustice, but because of its embodiment of attributes assumed or perceived to be associated with Judaism or Jews. A boycott of Israel, say, that is based on the premise that "those people crucified Christ," or "those people control the banks," would be not just anti-Israeli but also anti-Jewish.

The argument of representation, even if Israel truly represents all Jews, is never sufficient to prove antisemitism. What matters is the underlying basis of the boycott, what its goals are and, crucially, whether or not the boycott focuses on or targets an attribute perceived to be "shared" by most or all Jews.

"Use of Stereotypical Anti-Jewish Language in Criticizing Israel Is Antisemitic"

Criticism of Israel can be considered antisemitic, some argue, if it uses stereotypical anti-Jewish language to describe Israel, such as labeling an Israeli leader as a "child killer," or characterizing Israel's influence in the media, Hollywood, or Congress as excessive. It is worth mentioning that according to a poll in 2015, "three quarters of highly educated, high income, publicly active US Democrats—the so-called 'opinion elites'—believe Israel has too much influence on US foreign policy."[18]

This is tricky. There is no uniform tool that can be used to assess all such cases. Sometimes associating Israel with stereotypical attributes that are associated with Jews is antisemitic. Sometimes it may not be. Regardless, and given the hurt that verging on antisemitic language causes to Jewish communities, we who advocate for Palestinian rights must be quite vigilant about using such language and must try our best to adhere to the most accurate, non-emotive description of the facts as possible.

But even then, just stating the facts, as accurately as humanly possible, may sometimes solicit accusations of evoking antisemitic stereotypes. Consider the following cases, out of a thousand others:

In 2002, at al-Amari refugee camp, during a mass roundup of Palestinian males, teenagers and elderly included, Israeli troops inscribed identification numbers on the foreheads and forearms of Palestinian detainees awaiting interrogation.[19] Raising this fact triggered accusations of "antisemitism" simply because it evoked an obvious, albeit implicit, Nazi practice.

Israel's chief rabbi for the Sephardic community has recently called for the ethnic cleansing of all "non-Jews" from "the land of Israel."[20] Again, highlighting this is often met with charges of antisemitism as if all Jews are indirectly implicated in this criminal call.

A Jewish settler leader has called Palestinian and other Christians "blood sucking vampires" who should be "expelled" from Israel.[21] He called for torching even more Palestinian churches,[22] after many Palestinian churches and mosques have indeed been torched by far-right settlers, and the assailants in those attacks were protected, and therefore supported, by the Israeli military, security forces, and judiciary.[23]

Settlers who have burned to death Palestinian toddler Ali Dawabsheh and his parents last year and later celebrated their gruesome acts of terror have yet to be sentenced for the murders.[24]

In its assault on Gaza in 2014 Israel killed more than 500 Palestinian children, mainly because of targeting residential neighborhoods and schools where there is a disproportionately high percentage of children.

When UN officials recommended adding the Israeli occupation army (known as the Israeli Defense Forces, or IDF) to the list of armed forces that violate children's rights, some shouted "antisemitism," saying that this amounts to accusing the Israeli army of being a child-killer, a typical antisemitic charge against Jews. But consider that the Israeli army has in fact killed thousands of Arab children by deliberately targeting civilian neighborhoods in Beirut and Gaza, adopting a shoot-to-kill policy against Palestinian children who are throwing stones at Israeli military vehicles in the occupied Palestinian territory during the First and Second Intifadas. It has also poisoned Palestinians, including many children, by deliberately polluting Gaza's water supply and soil, causing disproportionate suffering for Palestinian children and the incidence of new, extremely rare diseases associated with pollutants such as methemoglobinemia. These practices make it a serial violator of children's rights par excellence.[25]

All the above is accurate. All of it indicates extreme racism, criminality, total disregard for Palestinian lives, and sometimes fanatic Jewish fundamentalism. Is pointing this out antisemitic?[26] Absolutely not. If by speaking truth to power the oppressed may offend the oppressor, clearly this is the problem of the latter, not the former.

Israel's attempt to deny us not just our freedom, our land, our human rights, and our dignity but also our very right to assert rights and to scream when injured, when killed and, yes, when massacred is beyond unethical. It may shed light on why such "revolting trends" remind Israel's deputy chief of staff of 1930s pre-Holocaust Germany.

"Denying Israel's Right to Exist as a Jewish State [in Palestine] Is Antisemitic"

Whether or not Jews around the world constitute a nation or not is up to Jewish communities themselves, first and foremost, to decide. It is worth remembering that during the eighteenth and nineteenth centuries, the period of Jewish emancipation in Europe, those claiming that Jews were a separate nation were called antisemites for arguing that Jews could not be citizens of the countries where they lived.[27]

But the question is whether a *Jewish people*, if a definition is agreed upon by most Jewish communities, has the right to a "Jewish state" in British Mandate Palestine—at the expense of the indigenous population of the land—and whether denying this right is antisemitic.

Professor Joseph Levine of the University of Massachusetts writes in the *New York Times*:

> The very idea of a Jewish state is undemocratic, a violation of the self-determination rights of its non-Jewish citizens, and therefore morally problematic. But the harm doesn't stop with the inherently undemocratic character of the state. For if an ethnic national state is established in a territory that contains a significant number of non-members of that ethnic group, it will inevitably face resistance from the land's other inhabitants. This will force the ethnic nation controlling the state to resort to further undemocratic means to maintain their hegemony . . . [in the case of the Zionist movement, this meant] expulsion in 1948 (and, to a lesser extent, in 1967), occupation of the territories conquered in 1967 and institution of a complex web of laws that prevent Israel's Palestinian citizens from mounting an internal challenge to the Jewish character of the state.[28]

Indeed, Palestinian civil society and all Palestinian political parties, including those with representation in the Israeli parliament, do not and cannot accept the exclusionary, supremacist notion of Israel as a "Jewish state" or the "state of the Jewish people" in historic Palestine. The overwhelming majority of Palestinians would not accept an Islamic state, a Christian state, or any exclusionary state in historic Palestine either.

Even the terribly compromised and visionless Palestinian "leadership" rejects the "Jewish state" notion, and so does the most "moderate" Palestinian member of the Knesset.[29] A democratic "state of all its citizens" is what Palestinian political parties in present-day Israel call for instead.

Levine concurs: "There is an unavoidable conflict between being a Jewish state and a democratic state. I want to emphasize that there's nothing antisemitic in pointing this out, and it's time the question was discussed openly on its merits, without the charge of antisemitism hovering in the background."[30]

It would take a long process of Israeli colonization of Palestinian minds and a subsequent steep sense of self-deprecation for a colonized people to accept its colonial masters' "right" to maintain this *inherently* unjust and racist order.

"BDS Calls for Delegitimizing/Destroying the Jewish State"

There are a number of variations on this theme. Three of these are detailed below.

First, boycotts targeting Israel, not "the occupation," by definition "delegitimize" Israel's very existence as a Jewish state and are therefore antisemitic.

BDS addresses comprehensive Palestinian rights, not simply ending the Israeli occupation of some densely populated Palestinian territory in order to save Israel as a "purer" apartheid.[31] Under international law, Israel is the state that bears responsibility for the occupation and injustice against the Palestinians. The BDS movement calls for boycotting Israel, not just the settlements, just as South Africa was the target of boycotts protesting its apartheid regime and Sudan protesting its crimes in Darfur, despite the obvious differences among these cases.[32]

If our call for equal rights and freedom is regarded as a threat to Israel's "existence," what does that say about Israel?[33]

But BDS is not a one-size-fits-all type of movement. As a decentralized human rights movement, it has its rights-based platform that all its partners agree on, but beyond that, when it comes to tactics and targeting, it adopts the principle of "context sensitivity." This means that activists anywhere decide what to target, how to target it, and what kind of coalition they will build to achieve their goals. We defer to our partners' decisions in this respect and we rely on their moral consistency and unbound creativity. Many partners choose to boycott only settlement products, and that is perfectly fine as a major step toward fully isolating the entire regime of oppression.

Second, boycotting Israel until it recognizes the right of Palestinian refugees to return to their homes of origin is antisemitic because it aims to end Israel's existence as a Jewish state by "flooding the country with non-Jews."

We are struggling to achieve our basic rights in accordance with international law, including the most important right—the right of return for our refugees, who constitute a solid majority of our people. If the exercise of an inalienable right causes the colonial community to lose its colonial privileges, why is that problematic?

During the 2000 "peace negotiations," Human Rights Watch reminded Ehud Barak, Bill Clinton, and Yasser Arafat of their legal obligations toward respecting the right of return for Palestinian refugees. It stated, "The options of local integration and third-country resettlement should not extinguish the right of return [of Palestinian refugees]. Rather, they should enhance the choices facing individual refugees. All three options should be available. [The right of return] is a right that persists even when sovereignty over the territory is contested, or has changed hands."[34]

The Zionist fear—which stems from the realization that if Palestinian refugees exercise their inherent and UN-stipulated right of return to their homeland, Jewish Israelis would become a minority—is racist and irrational. It is also common among colonial communities. Colonizers always fear that the colonized will one day rise against them and do to them what they have been doing to the colonized.

In terms of Palestine and the Arab region, this Israeli fear of Jews becoming a minority again, as they were prior to the systematic ethnic cleansing of the indigenous Palestinian Muslim and Christian population, is racist because it privileges the "right" to maintain a supremacist, exclusionary Jewish state over the rights of the refugees.

It also imposes a patently European history of anti-Jewish racism, pogroms, and eventually genocide on an Arab reality that does not share such a history. Non-Muslim Arabs may have experienced inequality in the Arab region, but that bears no comparison to the pogroms, ethnic cleansing, and massacres that took place in Christian Europe. Jewish culture thrived in Andalusia (Spain) under Arab Islamic rule. Prior to Zionist colonization of Palestine, anti-Jewish racism—let alone violence against Jews—was not a phenomenon in Arab history, with some rare exceptions. Jews have for centuries been part of the mix that made up Arab culture and Arab civilization. They were—and still are in some cases—indigenous in Arab communities, including in Nablus, in the occupied Palestinian territory.

Also, one cannot but ask: Where are Jewish communities thriving the most? In the United States and Western Europe, where they are tiny minorities and where they live in relatively secular states that largely respect the separation of state from church and have democratic values and laws to protect them.

Is Israel today, with its Jewish majority, the safest place for Jews to live? Absolutely not. Because the state is founded on injustice, and Jewish Israelis have to live "by the sword," as colonial masters oppressing another people— the Palestinians.[35] When Israel built its illegal wall in the occupied Palestinian territory, some wondered whether it was walling the Palestinians in a ghetto or walling itself into a new ghetto.

Third, by insisting on equality in Israel between Jews and non-Jews, BDS aims to destroy Israel's unique character as the world's only Jewish state, and is therefore antisemitic.

This is an argument that is premised on the exceptionalism doctrine that grants Israel, of all states, the *right* to maintain a system of apartheid. Attempts by some anti-Palestinian "liberal Zionists" to claim the mantle of victimhood and, as a result, to naggingly demand that the actual victims of Israel's oppressive regime must first commit to preserving Israeli apartheid and colonial rule before their UN-stipulated rights are granted are ludicrous and intellectually dishonest, at best. At worst, these attempts betray a deeply colonial and racist mentality that has marked political Zionism since its inception in the womb of European racist and colonial ideologies in the nineteenth century.

The BDS movement's call for full equality in law and policies for the Palestinian citizens of Israel is particularly troubling for Israel because it raises questions about its self-definition as an exclusionary Jewish state. Israel considers any challenge to what even the US Department of State has criticized as its system of "institutional, legal, and societal discrimination"[36] against its Palestinian citizens as an "existential threat," partially because of the apartheid reality that this challenge reveals.[37]

Tellingly, a recent attempt by Israeli liberals to have their civic national identity as "Israelis" recognized by the state was squarely rejected by Israel's Supreme Court on the grounds that it posed a serious threat to Israel's founding principle: to be a Jewish state for the Jewish people.[38]

Israel remains arguably the only country on earth that does not recognize its own nationality, as that would theoretically avail equal rights to all its citizens, undermining its "ethnocratic" identity.[39] The claim that BDS, a nonviolent movement anchored in universal principles of human rights, aims to "destroy" Israel must be understood in this context.

Did equality destroy the American South? Or South Africa? Equality and justice only negate inequality and injustice.

"BDS Is Antisemitic Because It Singles Out Israel"

Accusing the oppressed of singling out the oppressor with their resistance is beyond hypocritical and intellectually insincere; it is entirely nonsensical.

When Rosa Parks triggered the boycott campaign against the Montgomery Bus company over its racial discrimination policies, was the civil rights movement's singling out of that company hypocritical, given the presence of far more atrocious companies operating in Africa or in Mexico?

As Desmond Tutu once said, South African apartheid was not the most egregious form of human rights violations if compared to wide-scale genocide elsewhere around the world. But should South Africans have struggled against all worse forms of abuse before fighting apartheid in their homeland?

Our direct oppressor is Israel and its complicit institutions. If we were to call for boycotting all the partners in Israel's regime of occupation and apartheid—the United States being the most important of those—we would end up falling into armchair gesturing, which in situations of dire and intensifying oppression is not just a luxurious privilege but is outright unethical. As human rights defenders and activists, we have limited resources; we have to invest them strategically to achieve maximum impact in the pursuit of our inalienable rights under international law.

BDS, after all is not an academic exercise; it is a deeply ethical praxis aimed at realizing our freedom, justice, and equality.

Morality aside, and as Naomi Klein once argued, a boycott of the United States is patently dreamy, as it cannot possibly work, given the state's hegemony and its superpower status.

Finally, those in the West who support BDS do so out of a profound moral obligation to offset the damage that their tax money is doing to Palestinian lives and livelihood. Because their quasi-democratically elected governments are deeply involved in maintaining Israel's regime of occupation, settler colonialism, and apartheid, BDS supporters have an ethical responsibility to end this complicity. Many BDS supporters are also active in other racial, gender, social, economic, and climate justice movements.

Western governments are not shoring up the Sudanese regime in its crimes against Darfur nor the North Korean regime in its appalling denial of human rights. But they have singled out Israel as a key partner, establishing a very special, privileged, and hypocritical relationship that sustains a system of occupation and apartheid and protects the state from accountability.

Conclusion

Israel's exceptionalism must be challenged, not only by its main victims, the Palestinians, but by all people of conscience, including Jewish intellectuals and activists, as its model of brutal racial oppression, securitization, and militarism is being exported around the world with devastating consequences, from Ferguson to Sao Paulo and from Paris to Delhi. As part of that challenge, we must reject the abuse of anti-Jewish racism, along with the way charges of anti-Jewish racism are used to justify colonialism and apartheid, and we must reject the privileging of any racial/ethnic/religious group above any other.

Antisemitism has no place in the worldwide Palestine solidarity movement, including BDS. This is a principled position and there can be no compromise over it. But in fighting antisemitism, we should never accept placing it, as Israel is placed, on a pedestal, above all other racisms, including the centuries-old anti-Blackness and arguably the most prevalent racism in the West today—that directed against Arabs and Muslims.

Privileging one racism over others assumes a ranking of the "comparative worth"—as Roosevelt would put it—of the human groups that are targeted by these different racisms. Such ranking of racisms is not only patently racist, it also perpetuates the "privileged" racism. This is precisely why Israel and the international Zionist movement obsessively advocate it.

The nineteenth-century notions of superhumans and subhumans must be confronted head on, to do away with the two degrees of separation between Israel and its Palestinians victims. Only then can Israel be treated like all other offenders committing similar crimes, not better and not worse. Only thus can freedom, justice, peace, and equal rights prevail.

A Double-Edged Sword:
Palestine Activism and Antisemitism
on College Campuses

Kelsey Waxman

During the first few weeks of my freshman year at UC Berkeley in 2012, several swastikas appeared on a bulletin board hanging outside of a student's bedroom in my dorm complex. Every resident promptly received an email about it the next day, a strongly worded pledge that this type of hateful action, or any other like it, would not be tolerated in student housing, or anywhere else on the Berkeley campus.

I don't remember thinking much of it. I had seen a fair share of swastikas before. I went to elementary school in a neighborhood on the north side of Chicago that had a large Orthodox Jewish population, as well as an active neo-Nazi cell. I remember arriving on the playground one morning to seeing the side of the school covered in graffiti, images of broken Stars of David and swastikas looming over the kickball court. In middle school, a student in my math class was suspended after drawing the symbol all over desks and chairs. I listened to punk bands growing up whose album covers (and body art) sometimes included swastikas. The symbol had appeared in so many innocuous situations that it quickly lost its historical significance for me.

Perhaps it was hard for me to fully digest these symbols of antisemitism because I grew up in a diverse, mixed-income neighborhood where I never really felt that my Jewish identity earned me any "exceptions." Sure, I missed a few days of public school a year to go to synagogue and couldn't eat peanut butter and jelly sandwiches during Passover, but at the end of the day I understood the immense privilege that came with my white skin and "gifted" education. To the extent that I internalized a sense of belonging to an "other" community, this idea was chiefly manifested in a sense of belonging to overcoming centuries of oppression. While I accepted that, sure, sometime, way far back in the history of my "people," we were oppressed, there were people around me who suffered every day in ways I could not fathom. Swastikas drawn on the side of a school did not seem like a genuine threat, whereas in my city, a bullet in the chest of a twelve-year-old boy of color with whom I rode the bus was a well-known and all-too-real possibility.

Yet, my whole life, mainstream Judaism has taught me and my peers that as American Jews we are entitled to an "exceptionalism" that other assimilated religious and ethnic minorities may or may not enjoy. This came into conflict with my earliest encounters of conversations about Israel and Palestine. Like many Jewish students at my public high school, I joined the Jewish Student Union and participated in community service projects to benefit underserved communities around Chicago in the name of *tikkun olam*, the Jewish principle of "repairing the world." But when it came to the State of Israel, the underserved Palestinian communities who suffered under Israeli occupation were deemed "terrorists" unworthy of our compassion, and those committed to fighting those inequalities were labeled as a threat to Judaism itself.

It was this self-contradictory viewpoint, this epidemic of "progressivism EXCEPT Palestine," that led me to Palestine solidarity organizing in my teens. If Jews were gifted with this ability to overcome tragedy, why shouldn't they help others who suffer the same under different oppressive hands? I began to explore this question through collaborations with Arab and Muslim students to educate our peers on antisemitism, anti-Arabism, and Islamophobia in our community. After traveling to Jordan to study Arabic before my senior year of high school, I met many students my age whose families had relocated to the country after the Nakba, the mass expulsion of Palestinians living in the newly established State of Israel in 1948. Revealing my Jewish identity to those I met in Jordan was not always easy, but most people I met were willing to engage with me in conversations about our histories, but more importantly, it did not affect the way they perceived me as a friend. I wish I could say the same for many Jewish peers I met in high school, many of whom had written me off by the time we graduated, confused as to why I was so committed to "fraternizing with terrorists," as one former classmate put it.

In reflection, I can understand my peers' resistance to recognize the problematic nature of this narrative because they had been socialized in traditional Jewish educational institutions, but I did not anticipate such a blind spot upon enrolling at UC Berkeley, known for its students' long-standing commitment to civil liberties and free speech. I was excited to continue my Arabic and Hebrew language-learning in college and meet other like-minded individuals, Jewish or not, who were committed to the same causes that I was.

I also assumed I would find a warm welcome to the West Coast at our university's Hillel Center, which had always been billed to me as a home away from home for Jewish college students. In my first few weeks of school, I attended High Holy Day services at the Center, feeling out of place and missing my family during my first Rosh Hashanah away from home.

In the midst of praying and reflecting on the previous year, against a backdrop of one of the most historically liberal university campuses in the nation, I was confused when the rabbi delivered a *d'var Torah* on the necessity to support and pray for Israel in the face of the growing Boycott, Divestment and Sanctions campaign gaining traction throughout the campus community. When I looked for Hebrew classes or Torah study programs through the Hillel Center, I found neither but was directed to myriad Israeli cultural groups and political Zionist entities, which operated out of Hillel's building. The students I met at Hillel were future lawyers, doctors, and aid workers committed to restoring justice in underserved communities. Not only did that compassion and commitment not extend to the Palestinian community; those who showed interest in Palestinian rights were quickly deemed as acting against the Jewish community. There was no middle ground.

While I struggled to find a Jewish community in Berkeley that felt like home, I quickly developed friendships with many Palestinians in my classes through my course of study. Many seem to find it hard to believe that in my four years in the Arabic Department at UC Berkeley, I have never heard an antisemitic comment directed toward me or anyone else. I have never felt uncomfortable as a Jewish student in any of my classes with Arab or Muslim professors. I have studied under the guidance of professors deemed "terrorists" by Zionist entities such as Canary Mission, a website that releases personal information of pro-Palestinian activists, and these professors have approached me with nothing but kindness and professionalism.

I spent most of my first three years of college listening to the stories of my Palestinian peers, professors, and their families. I studied the political, economic, social, and environmental histories of the Palestinian people with them. It was difficult to reconcile the knowledge I was gaining about the realities of Israeli oppression of Palestine with my search for Jewish community on campus. The few Jewish students I met who were not completely apolitical or wholeheartedly committed to the Zionist project directed me toward student organizations focused on "mutual understanding" and "non-partisan education," where critical discussion was often foregone for the sake of promoting a haphazard peace-building curriculum. I realize now that those organizations often do more harm than good in their contributions to discussions surrounding Israel and Palestine on our campuses, but at the time, they were the only political and emotional outlets I felt I really had.

I began actively working for Palestinian liberation on my campus after spending the summer of 2015 in the West Bank, teaching English in Aida Refugee Camp. Having received a grant from the UC Berkeley Center for Jewish Studies, I split my time between the refugee camp near Bethlehem and a Hebrew-intensive program at the University of Haifa. During my time in both cities, the stories of my Jewish and Palestinian peers weighed heavy on my conscience, and I realized that the injustices of the physical and political occupation perpetuated by the Israeli government were too great for someone like me, with immense privilege, to stay silent.

Since returning to campus, I have begun to speak out publicly against the people and policies in our Berkeley community that work to sustain the Israeli occupation of Palestinian land and the subjugation of Palestinian people. I have received an astounding amount of backlash, much of it seeking to delegitimize my Jewish identity. The Zionist opposition at UC Berkeley, like that of other American institutions of higher learning, wields accusations of antisemitism and terrorism at me and other colleagues involved in similar activism; the tactics that they employ against us, in any other context, would be considered antisemitic harassment. This is a form of harassment that goes largely unnoticed. It is born within our own community.

In the beginning, the incidents were minor—negative comments from community members on articles I had been quoted in for the school newspaper. Students I knew to frequent Hillel began to refer to me as one of those sad, confused "self-hating Jews." A good friend on campus told me she could no longer speak to me because my decision to go to Palestine and teach English to teenagers in a refugee camp was "an act of terrorism." Then, while speaking at a Day of Action for Palestine at UC Berkeley, another Jewish student representing a campus Zionist group made a sexually lewd gesture at me. The social media accounts for our campus organizers were soon flooded with hateful, antisemitic rhetoric by anonymous Zionist entities.

The backlash began to span beyond my fellow students. Last semester, a professor at UC Berkeley, a visiting lecturer from Israel who was supposed to serve as my thesis advisor, singled me out in a lecture because he was aware of my campus activism. When I pointed out that on no academic grounds could he prove that the recent surge of violence in Jerusalem was perpetrated by "young, bored Muslims," he suggested that I knew nothing and should "just stay quiet." Days later, in a meeting with a leader of our campus Hillel, I was told that if my relationship with my father had been stronger when I was younger that I would have more "sense" in regard to my support for Israel. While my personal experiences of having my identity criticized by Berkeley's Zionist constituency have been disheartening, I fear much more for the possible legal legitimization of the types of tactics that have been used against me and other activists to silence our critiques. Recently, the University of California Board of Regents almost adopted the State Department definition of antisemitism as official institutional policy. The State Department's definition of antisemitism, which some "pro-Israel advocates" were hoping to incorporate into a university-wide Principles Against Intolerance charter, dangerously conflates genuine antisemitic acts with political criticism of the modern State of Israel. If adopted, this definition would have reinforced the silencing of political criticism of the policies of the State of Israel rather than protecting students from legitimate acts of hate. The Regents of the University of California may believe they are acting in the "best interests" of students, but if they chose to enact a policy that will be used to delegitimize Jews like me, whose interest does that serve?*

I know that we are not alone in our experiences in the University of California community. According to *Stifling Dissent,* a report published by Jewish Voice for Peace in 2015, "being a full-fledged member of the organized Jewish community now entails passing a political litmus test, due to the guidelines that Hillel imposes with regard to Israel engagement on campuses, as well as threats and intimidation of Israel critics and Palestine rights supporters." The redefinition of antisemitism by Zionist campus groups is spreading quickly across campuses in an attempt to delegitimize students' commitments to social justice. The *Stifling Dissent* report notes that some Zionist organizations employ "Office of Civil Rights regulations to claim that criticism of Israel perpetuates a 'hostile environment' for Jewish students on campus, threats against administrators and faculty, [and] attempts to codify a particular definition of anti-Semitism to encompass criticism of Israel and activism for Palestinian rights . . ." These are the kinds of threats we are currently facing at the University of California.

As I prepare to graduate from Berkeley in the months to come, my outlook on the protection of free speech on our campus is grim. I believe that the Zionist establishment will continue to threaten solidarity activists, particularly

---

* In spring 2016, after the writing of this article, the UC Regents released their Principles Against Intolerance. Though the Principles did not use the State Department definition of anti-Semitism, they did condemn vague and undefined "anti-Semitic forms of anti-Zionism," and scarcely mentioned Islamophobia and other forms of racism on UC campuses. See the essay "This Campus Will Divest!" for more on the Regents.—Ed.

Jewish activists, with tactics that are directly related to our Jewish identities. I believe that Hillel and other mainstream Jewish establishments will continue to preach of Jewish "exceptionalism," which manifests itself in a culture of victimization and fearmongering. This spring, during Palestine Awareness Week events on college campuses across the country, Hillel Centers will be transformed into "refuges" for students who feel "unsafe" and "targeted" for their Jewish identities, while many acts of violence against students of color will go completely unreported. The saddest part of this manipulation of conversations about antisemitism is that not only does it completely delegitimize actual incidents of hate crimes against Jewish people, but it discounts so much of the progress that the resilient Jewish civilization has made over the past century by playing into the rhetoric of victimization.

While many Jewish students and organizations on American campuses claim to be at the forefront of progressive politics, no person on the right side of history condones hate crimes targeting specific ethnic, religious, or racial groups. Manipulation of antisemitic rhetoric in campus propaganda discredits the incredible work that has been done by the Jewish community for its own liberation—a struggle that defined our collective narrative for centuries.

It is this resilience and this commitment to the ethics of human liberation inscribed into Jewish doctrine and into my own personal Jewish experience that keeps me committed to Palestinian solidarity activism. I work in the name of Jewish activists who lost their lives to systematic antisemitism. It's for the young teens I met in Aida Refugee Camp last summer who had never met a Jewish person who was not holding a machine gun. It's for my freshman-year neighbor with the swastika drawn on their bulletin board. It's for those who have endured the collective struggle and continue to actively work for liberation; it is our responsibility as a liberated community to support the liberation of others. I do not think there is a more Jewish sentiment than that.

This Campus Will Divest!
The Specter of Antisemitism
and the Stifling of Dissent
on College Campuses

Ben Lorber

As student activists across the country turn the college campus into a vibrant front of the growing Boycott, Divestment and Sanctions (BDS) movement for Palestinian rights, pro-Israel opposition groups are spending hundreds of millions in a desperate attempt to stifle the grassroots movement. While campus chapters of Students for Justice in Palestine (SJP), Jewish Voice for Peace, and similar groups raise awareness of Israeli apartheid and pressure their universities to divest from occupation profiteers, Israel-aligned groups like the AMCHA Initiative and StandWithUs have resolved to derail the BDS movement by falsely smearing it as antisemitic. As they manufacture the myth that campuses are hostile spaces for Jewish students, these anti-BDS backlash groups in fact help foster an increasingly unsafe campus climate for Palestinian, Arab, and Muslim students across the country. As xenophobia and nationalism move mainstream, these organizations, far from fighting bigotry, are helping make Islamophobia and anti-Arab racism an acceptable and permanent part of American campus life.

The Campus Movement for Palestinian Rights

The first SJP chapter formed in 2003, and the first divestment resolution passed in 2010. Today, well over one hundred chapters of SJP and similar groups are active across the country, and over thirty student governments have passed resolutions demanding their university divest from corporations complicit in human rights violations in Israel/Palestine.[1] On campus after campus, student activists pursue divestment resolutions and referenda, and launch other BDS campaigns to remove Sabra hummus from dining halls, ban Caterpillar equipment on campus, implement the academic and cultural boycott of Israel, and more. The bold work of students has set the tone for Palestine organizing across the country, triggered a seismic shift in consciousness, and propelled the demand for justice in Palestine into national discourse.

As Israeli policy shifts ever further to the right, the momentum for BDS on campus is building—and the opposition is scared. Day after day, Israeli news headlines nervously report the results of divestment campaigns unfolding on campuses thousands of miles away. In America, elected officials on both sides of the aisle, hoping to win the support of powerful pro-Israel mega-donors, promise to make the fight against BDS on campus a central focus of their agenda while in office.

Meanwhile, the institutional leadership of the American Jewish community has decided not to voice the growing concerns held by many American Jews over Israeli policy, but to circle the wagons and defend Israel, at all costs, from mounting criticism. Trumpeted from the *bima* (pulpit) of our synagogues, splashed across the pages of our publications, and repeated throughout the fundraising appeals of our communal institutions, the mantra that American college campuses have become "new hotbeds of the age-old antisemitism" is accepted as self-evident and enshrined as dogma.

Riding this wave of fear, a plethora of anti-BDS organizations have emerged in the last decade, each eager to convince private donors, foundations, Jewish communal institutions, and other funders that they are best positioned to turn the campus tide. For this assemblage of opposition groups—which I call the "backlash machine"—college campuses are a laboratory where new strategies are deployed, tactics are tested, and talking points are perfected for the larger *hasbara* (pro-Israel public relations) movement. A close examination of the shifting frontiers and mobile battle lines of the campus war for BDS, then, helps us see the larger ways in which false antisemitism charges and other weapons are mobilized to muffle criticism of Israel outside the campus walls.

The Backlash Machine

As detailed by JVP in its 2015 report *Stifling Dissent*, today's pro-Israel opposition has flooded American universities with an army of consultants, researchers, organizers, and other professionals, a network of on-and-off campus institutions and organizations that works to re-brand Israel's image, quash BDS, and suppress student activism for Palestinian rights.[2] Across the country, Israel advocates coordinate *hasbara* programming inside Jewish student centers like Hillel, train students to derail SJP's talking points, and bring to campus an endless array of Israeli speakers, films, cultural events, and more. While SJP students have managed to build their grassroots movement on a shoestring budget, this backlash machine has raised hundreds of millions from institutions like the Jewish National Fund and individual donors like Sheldon Adelson to mount a "grasstops" counterattack that works frantically, and so far unsuccessfully, to stymie the rising tide.

To shore up lines of defense on campuses where the student movement is powerful, opposition groups mobilize networks of anti-BDS faculty, parents, alumni, and donors to apply private pressure and public outrage against SJP. They build close relationships with campus administrators, and fly student government representatives, many of whom hope to pursue a career in politics, to DC for an American Israel Public Affairs Committee networking event or to Israel for a propaganda trip. In at least one case, outside groups have offered student representatives re-election campaign contributions in exchange for a promised vote against divestment.[3]

When a divestment win appears likely, opposition groups mobilize state representatives, members of Congress, and local elected officials to write public letters to undergraduate student representatives, asking for a vote against the "divisive" and "antisemitic" BDS movement. Where these publicity campaigns fall short, elected officials craft repressive legislation to punish students for exercising the right to boycott. In early 2016, as the far-right Zionist Organization of America pressured the City University of New York (CUNY) system to ban SJP from its twenty-three campuses, members of the New York City Council drafted legislation requiring CUNY to report any "potentially anti-Semitic" SJP activity directly to the council.[4] Meanwhile, state legislators attempted to use the "crisis of antisemitism" as a pretext to push through $500 million in budget cuts to the CUNY system. Later that year, after Governor Cuomo signed an unconstitutional executive order creating a blacklist of entities that support BDS, New York senators sought to amend education law to defund pro-BDS student groups across the state.[5] At the time of writing, the outcome of much of this legislation remains uncertain.

The Specter of Antisemitism

As student activists awaken their generation to the reality of Israeli apartheid, the opposition has long since accepted that they cannot defend Israel's policies through politically sound arguments grounded in fact, history, or human rights principles, and that bringing live camels to "Israel block parties" on the campus quad, padding the campaign coffers of supportive student senators, or summoning the wrath of the state apparatus can only do so much to muffle the mounting campus cries against Israel's human rights abuses. To slow BDS, the accusation of antisemitism—a charge that, in the decades since the Holocaust, still carries a deep and arresting resonance in the imaginary of the American public—has risen to the top of the opposition's arsenal.

In 2014 and 2015 alone, over half of the almost three hundred incidents tracked by Palestine Legal, a legal support and advocacy organization, "involved accusations of antisemitism based solely on speech critical of Israeli policy."[6] On campus after campus, a vocal minority of trained pro-Israel students repeat the tired mantra that activism for Palestinian rights singles out, targets, and endangers Jewish students on campus. Before student government, on the pages of the campus newspaper, and in closed-door meetings with university administrators, these students assert that Israel is central to their Jewish identity, and that Israeli Apartheid Week, divestment, and other SJP campaigns make them feel harassed, threatened, or unsafe as Jewish students. Opposition groups help students frame their support for Israel, not as a personal political preference, but as the collective will of the Jewish campus community, compelling administrators to treat their anti-BDS demands as they would the demands of any other group for gender-neutral bathrooms, diversity and inclusion, cultural studies departments, and the like.

Opposition groups collect the testimony of this vocal minority of students and thrust it before the eyes of elected officials, media outlets, and university administrators, building the national narrative that a viral wave of antisemitism grips college campuses and endangers Jewish students everywhere. When an isolated incident of real anti-Jewish oppression does occur on a college campus—when, for example, a swastika is found scrawled on the wall of a Jewish fraternity, or a student makes a derogatory comment about Jews on an anonymous social media app like Yik Yak—pundits rush to blame SJP for the hate crime, insisting that divestment campaigns have turned the campus into a hotbed of anti-Jewish hatred. Not only does this move unfairly tarnish the reputation of a student movement for human rights and equality, it lets actual antisemites off the hook for their real attacks on Jewish students.

After establishing the narrative that Jewish students are endangered by nonviolent campaigns to promote freedom and dignity for Palestinians, opposition groups insist that administration must protect Jewish students by forcefully suppressing BDS activism on campus. "Lawfare" groups, such as the Tel Aviv–based Shurat HaDin–Israel Law Center, routinely pressure administrators by threatening to file civil rights complaints against universities for allegedly failing to adequately protect Jewish students from a hostile campus climate. Though the few complaints actually filed have been thrown out by judges, the mere threat of such a lawsuit is often enough to scare administrators into restricting the range of permissible activities for SJP on campus.

The Role of Repression

While the national discourse wrings its hands over the "unsafe campus climate" faced by Jewish students, it is actually the largely Palestinian, Arab, Muslim, and other students of color on the front lines of SJP who face increasing hostility, threats to safety, restrictions on freedom of speech, and outright repression on campuses every day. SJP chapters are routinely monitored by administration, forced to pay for extra security for events, and burdened with disproportionate bureaucratic hurdles and roadblocks whenever they want to receive a permit for an event, secure a meeting room on campus, and function otherwise as a normal student group. They are regularly suspended or denied funding after being accused of "threatening" Jewish students for installing a mock Israeli apartheid wall in the center of campus, slipping mock eviction notices under dormitory doors, setting up a mock checkpoint on the quad, holding a die-in, and engaging in other creative protest and nonviolent direct action. They are often unable to even secure a meeting with administrators, who are desperate to minimize controversy and avoid being seen as "insensitive to the concerns of Jewish students." Given that on most campuses, by contrast, Hillel and the pro-Israel student groups under its wing enjoy ready access to resources and a close relationship with administration, the claim that Jewish pro-Israel students suffer a hostile campus climate turns reality cruelly on its head.

Faculty, too, can be targeted with a smear campaign for serving as the advisor to an SJP chapter, reprimanded for teaching the Palestinian narrative in a way that makes Jewish students "uncomfortable," or even, in the well-known case of Steven Salaita, fired for tweeting about Israeli war crimes in a manner deemed "uncivil." In an industry where the promise of tenure has all but disappeared and pervasive job insecurity has become the norm, this McCarthyist atmosphere serves to bully adjuncts and other precariously employed faculty into silence. For both students and faculty, the effects of an orchestrated backlash campaign can cripple activism, threaten livelihoods, paralyze dissent, and have a chilling effect on free speech.

The claims that SJP is antisemitic, or that Jewish students face an unsafe campus climate because of BDS, are completely unfounded. Student activists for Palestinian rights rigorously distinguish between criticism of the policies of

Israel as a nation-state, on the one hand, and hate speech targeting Jews as a religious or ethnic group, on the other. Dedicated to the principle and practice of antiracism, SJP chapters work hard to build movements free from antisemitism and all other forms of oppression. And in spite of all the hype generated by the backlash machine, Jewish students consistently report high levels of safety and comfort on campuses across the country.[7] While some take a public stand on the Israel/Palestine conflict—and more, when they do, are joining chapters of SJP, JVP, or other left-leaning groups like J Street U—the majority, driven by a combination of indifference, apathy, confusion, and frustration, stay out of it entirely. Even if they sometimes experience discomfort when they encounter vocal pro-Palestine organizing on campus, most Jewish students recognize this discomfort as an integral part of a robust college experience, one in which political assumptions should be interrogated, personal beliefs should be questioned, and preconceived notions should be challenged.

New Definitions of Antisemitism

Increasingly, opposition groups are no longer using false accusations of antisemitism merely to slander BDS supporters and derail debate. Within and beyond the walls of college campuses, they're attempting to codify new definitions of antisemitism into public policy, definitions that, if adopted as law, could shut down debate before it even begins. In 2015, the AMCHA Initiative, a nonprofit dedicated to "protecting Jewish students" by "combating antisemitism at institutions of higher education in North America," began a campaign to pressure the University of California's Board of Regents to include a special definition of antisemitism in their soon-to-be-released anti-discrimination policy for UC campuses. According to the outdated and largely discredited three Ds definition of antisemitism proposed by AMCHA, speech can be considered antisemitic if it "demonizes," "delegitimizes," or "applies a double standard'" to Israel.

For UC student and faculty activists, AMCHA's moves were all too familiar. In 2012, then UC president Mark Yudof commissioned a team of fact finders, including the education chair of the Anti-Defamation League (ADL), to issue a report on the Jewish student climate around the UC system. The report stressed the "significant and difficult climate issues" faced by Jewish students as a result of Israel/Palestine organizing on campus, and urged the Regents to sanction such activities on the basis of the three Ds definition of antisemitism. Though the ADL's efforts were thwarted by a grassroots campaign—during which the findings of their report were publicly contested by a coalition of hundreds of Jewish UC students, faculty, and alumni—that summer, the California State Assembly passed H.R. 35, a nonbinding resolution calling on the

UC administration to do more to "confront antisemitism on its campuses" and to pass the ADL's proposed antisemitism definition.

In both cases, it was clear from the beginning that the ADL and AM-CHA's pressure campaigns were never about protecting Jewish students, but were meant rather to redraw the national battle lines against BDS on campus. Had the UC Regents followed AMCHA's recommendations and adopted the three Ds as policy, they would have set a dangerous precedent, giving themselves the broad power to outlaw divestment campaigns, apartheid walls, mock eviction notices, and virtually any campus action in support of Palestinian rights under the vague and slippery pretext that they could "single out" or "delegitimize" Israel. Emboldened by this victory, opposition groups would have repeated the strategy at universities around the country.

In early 2016, after sustained pressure from a coalition of student groups, graduate student unions, faculty, and organizations including JVP and Palestine Legal, the UC Regents dropped the three Ds definition from consideration. They proposed instead, however, to include the term "anti-Zionism" in their definition of antisemitism, a move that proved just as troubling. For a growing number of student activists within and beyond SJP, anti-Zionism is antiracism, plain and simple, because the logic of Zionism—long defined as the project to actualize a "Jewish state" in historic Palestine—compels Israel to enforce an apartheid legal system, maintain a Jewish demographic majority, and relegate Palestinians and other non-Jews to the status of second-class citizens.

Undeterred by their loss of the three Ds, AMCHA Initiative regrouped around "anti-Zionism" as their rallying cry for a new, Israel-friendly definition of antisemitism. Long before AMCHA, opposition groups had sought to prevent any serious discussion of democracy, civil rights, or the other issues raised by Palestinian rights advocates by framing "Zionism" and "Judaism" as practically interchangeable terms, and insisting that the attempt, by the BDS movement, to deny the Jewish people their natural "right to self-determination" was a thinly veiled form of modern antisemitism. In a similar vein, StandWithUs helps students write and present "Jewish students" rights' resolutions to student government before or during divestment campaigns. By insisting that student senators recognize and protect the Jewish people's "right to self-determination," the resolutions serve to re-center the conversation on Israel's abstract "right to exist," erase real Palestinians from consideration, and shield real rights violators from accountability.

In March 2016, over two hundred UC faculty members wrote an open letter to the Regents, insisting that "criticism of Zionism, a political set of beliefs and national ideology, has a complex history that has developed for over a century, and it is not to be conflated with antisemitism . . . Jewish criticisms of Zionism have been actively debated within the Jewish community since the time of Herzl . . . how would students gain an informed understanding of this issue of great public interest if we were not permitted to have all sides of that debate represented and scrutinized?"[8] When the UC Regents finally released their Principles Against Intolerance later that month, the document struck an uneasy compromise, affirming free speech but condemning "anti-Semitic forms of anti-Zionism," a term which was not further defined and thus left open to interpretation.[9] Though the Principles were purportedly designed to combat all forms of discrimination on UC campuses, the text focused mostly on the "unsafe campus climate" faced by Jewish students, and scarcely mentioned Islamophobia, anti-Arab racism, anti-Black racism, and the many other pressing forms of discrimination faced by marginalized UC student populations.

It remains to be seen whether the Principles will be truly used to safeguard student speech and protect marginalized students, or whether administration will stretch the label of "anti-Semitic forms of anti-Zionism" to smother divestment campaigns, apartheid walls, and other bold and principled student activism. Meanwhile, opposition groups continue to push the three Ds definition in policy arenas across the country, furthering a campaign that Palestine Legal attorney Liz Jackson, in the 2012 battle over H.R. 35, called "an anti-democratic attempt to intimidate and silence students from expressing pro-Palestinian views. . . . To argue that such speech should be restricted . . . is to decimate the principle of free speech and it is plainly unconstitutional."[10]

Islamophobia and Anti-Arab Racism

In a post–9/11 era marked by increasing Islamophobia and anti-Arab racism, Muslim and Arab students face real dangers on American college campuses. Across the country, Muslim and Arab students are heckled in the hallway, slandered on social media, called "terrorists" on posters or by speakers around campus, and physically attacked for wearing traditional Islamic clothing. According to a 2012 Muslim Public Affairs Council survey, 76 percent of Muslim and Arab students on UC campuses had seen or observed intimidation on campus, and 71 percent felt the UC system didn't do enough to protect their communities.[11] Many cited an email sent by UC president Mark Yudof to the entire student body expressing a zero-tolerance policy toward antisemitism, and the lack of any such email regarding Islamophobia or anti-Arab racism, as evidence of a double standard.

Other times, Muslim and Arab students are directly attacked by administration and the state. In the early 2000s, as the US government stepped up its "war on terror" at home and abroad, Muslim students in New York, New Jersey, and Pennsylvania were monitored by police and the FBI for years, and spaces like the Muslim Students Association (MSA) were infiltrated by agents intent on "fighting terrorism." In 2011, ten Muslim student activists at UC Irvine were handed misdemeanor convictions by the Orange County District Attorney's office for briefly performing nonviolent civil disobedience at a speech given by Israeli ambassador Michael Oren.[12] The "Irvine 11" case, as it came to be called, reeked of Islamophobia, and was trumpeted by the opposition as a warning to the many Palestinian, Arab, and Muslim students then organizing for divestment across the UC system.

On and off campuses, the "war on BDS" and the "war on terror" work hand in hand to stigmatize Muslims and Arabs. When campuses become battlegrounds for divestment, the opposition works to portray Israel as an outpost of "Western" values of democracy and tolerance, and to label Palestinians—and, by extension, their supporters on campus—as radical, extremist, and antisemitic. At times, the opposition's use of Islamophobia steps out from behind its use of dog whistles and coded language and into the light of day. In 2015 and 2016, the far-right David Horowitz Freedom Center plastered campuses in California with graphic posters likening SJP, MSA, and individually named Arab and Muslim student activists to Islamic fundamentalists and "genocidal Jew-haters." The Freedom Center drew its inspiration, and lists of students' names, from Canary Mission, a shadowy website formed in the summer of 2015 to "document the people and groups that are promoting hatred of the USA, Israel and Jews on college campuses in North America." Featuring an online catalogue with detailed profiles of hundreds of mostly brown and Black student and faculty activists, Canary Mission seeks to bully its targets into silence by defaming them as terrorists and antisemites, exposing them to harassment by pro-Israel trolls on social media, harming their job prospects, and more.

Beyond their encounters with explicit hate speech or implicit stigmatization, Palestinian, Arab, and Muslim students face structural discrimination in their daily struggle to make their voices heard. The bureaucratic roadblocks, sanctions, and other concrete repression disproportionately faced every day by SJP chapters constitute a full-frontal attack against what, on many campuses, is the sole or most prominent space for Palestinian, Arab, and Muslim students to gather and act politically. Time and again, Palestinian student activists are accused by campus administrators of "making Jewish students feel uncomfortable" for dancing *dabke* on the campus quad, narrating their family's experiences during the Nakba in class, or detailing Israel's war crimes at campus divestment hearings.

In addition, while an administration will cancel a course on Palestinian history and culture if a Jewish student, backed by a pressure group, claims it makes them feel unsafe, Muslim students are routinely ignored when they report that their hijab was torn off, that they were called a terrorist, or that they faced other very real threats or physical violence. By privileging the desires of Jewish students to avoid seeing SJP protests on the quad over the desires of Palestinian students to avoid seeing their tuition dollars fund the bombs that fall on their families, university administrators are silencing the voices of already-marginalized students and replicating the very racist and colonialist power dynamics in dire need of dismantling in Israel/Palestine.

The cruel and tragic irony of the situation is clear—in conjuring the specter of antisemitism, opposition groups weaponize the real and painful legacy of anti-Jewish persecution, and use it to bludgeon into submission the struggles of marginalized communities in our own time. This cynically exploits not only the memories of the real victims of anti-Jewish oppression throughout history but also the identities and fears of Jewish students today. It can also have a dangerous "boy who cries wolf" effect, desensitizing the ears of university administrators, and the broader public, to any real anti-Jewish persecution that may arise.

Jewish Students Fight Back

Faced with a backlash machine that maintains a stranglehold on Jewish identity, Jewish students who support Palestinian rights must carve out a new Jewish voice, space, and movement on campus. Across the country, both within SJP chapters and in their own JVP student groups, Jewish students who oppose the occupation and apartheid committed in their name hold Palestine solidarity Shabbat dinners and Passover Seders, host pro-BDS rabbis and other Jewish speakers, and launch campaigns that challenge the coercive limits of dissent imposed by the pro-Israel consensus. Striking at the root of the opposition's narrative, they challenge the Islamophobia and anti-Arab racism fostered within their own communities, and build new Jewish identities founded not upon red lines and specters, but upon justice and liberation for all.

By announcing their existence as pro-BDS Jews, these students help unravel the false equivalence of Jewish identity with support for Israel, making it much more difficult for opposition groups to slander divestment activists as "Jew-haters," for pro-Israel students to claim that divestment creates an unsafe climate for Jewish students, and for administrators to apply bureaucratic sanctions against SJP. On more and more campuses, situations are occurring like that described by JVP student Jacob Manheim at the 2013 UCLA divestment hearing—"When a council member said that divestment was an attack on Jewish students . . . another council member specifically pointed to the UCLA JVP chapter as evidence for diverse views within the Jewish community."

By standing beside their Palestinian, Arab, and Muslim friends in SJP, Jewish students can shield their comrades from repression and backlash. For example, in 2013 pro-Israel students at Barnard College, which partners with Columbia University, worked with opposition groups to pressure administration to remove SJP's banner from campus by claiming that the banner, which depicted the undivided contours of historic Palestine, was offensive to Jewish students. "In contrast," explained outraged student and JVP cofounder Eva Kalikoff in a personal interview in 2015,

> this spring's Israeli Apartheid Week forestalled any charges of antisemitism because of the strong and visible presence of JVP. Chris and I wrote an op-ed[13] in the *Columbia Spectator* that firmly separated Zionism and Judaism, effectively taking that argument off the table. I really strongly believe that if JVP had existed the way it does now when the banner went up, there would have been enough of a critical mass to prevent its removal.

When JVP students make their voices heard, the specter of antisemitism is shown to be ephemeral and lacking substance, while the vocal minority of pro-Israel Jewish students who had conjured it into being are shown to be a spectacle, designed to conceal the great diversity of views held by the Jewish community they claimed to represent.

Intersectionality

But when real antisemitism does rear its ugly head on campuses, how can JVP students stake out their own position against the backlash machine? Students at UC Davis faced this question in February 2015, when, after a swastika was scrawled upon a Jewish fraternity, the backlash machine quickly swung into formation. While UC Davis Hillel blamed the swastika on a recently passed divestment resolution, opposition groups quickly whipped up a national media frenzy—during which, bizarrely, comedian Roseanne Barr tweeted, "I hope all the Jews leave UC Davis and then it gets nuked"—insisting that BDS had created an unsafe campus climate for Jewish students.[14]

Writing in their campus paper, Jewish students at UC Davis called on their peers and the public, not to scapegoat Muslims or drop weapons of mass destruction on a public university, but to take a sober and honest look at inequities on campus. After condemning the graffiti in the "harshest terms," they insisted that

> while this individual incident is undeniably chilling, in general the institutional Jewish community enjoys great support and immense privilege—yet as Jews supporting justice in Palestine, that community is often closed to us. . . . Muslim and Arab students, especially those working for Palestinian human rights, have been subjected to censure and discrimination for years at UC Davis . . . [but] the administration has not condemned a single instance of Islamophobic, anti-Palestinian or anti-Arab racism on campus. In contrast to this position, the administration quickly reached out and denounced the vandalism that occurred on January 31. This double standard should not stand.[15]

By quickly blaming the swastika on BDS, the leadership of UC Davis Hillel had turned the campus's sole Jewish space into a mouthpiece of the backlash machine, and had denied support, at a moment of vulnerability, to the many Jewish students scared by the swastika but uncomfortable with bashing BDS. The authors of the op-ed later formed a JVP chapter to create the safe space they greatly needed, and the contrast between the two models of Jewish community became painfully clear. While Hillel sought to isolate Jewish students behind walls of fear, JVP students recognized that this very fearmongering posed, for Jewish students, the graver threat. While Hillel weaponized the anti-Jewish graffiti to launch a further attack on Muslim and Arab students, JVP students insisted that real struggle against antisemitism must remain inseparable from struggles against Islamophobia, anti-Arab racism, and oppression in all its forms.

A few months later, as a wave of protests against anti-Black racism swept campuses across the country, a number of articles appeared in Jewish publications noting that support for BDS had become a mainstay in multi-issue progressive campus coalitions, and worrying that Jewish students were no longer safe or welcome in any of the many movements, from Black Lives Matter to climate justice, that endorsed BDS. In their joint "Statement on Intersectionality," eleven JVP campus chapters across the country set the record straight, mapping a new vision of Jewish identity and struggle against antisemitism:

> As Jewish students who are conscious of Jewish peoples' historical experience of oppression and rightfully proud of our traditions of solidarity and struggle for liberation, we commend all activists, Jewish and non-Jewish, who have

carried on movements for Black lives, Palestinian Liberation, and campuses free from oppression in the face of repression and false accusations of antisemitism. We call on Jewish students across the country to put their hearts into these movements for justice and be unafraid to examine their own societal positions as they trace the intersectional connections between racism in America, Palestine, and around the world.[16]

For JVP students, the only way to bear witness to the historical reality of anti-Jewish persecution is to fight for a campus, and a world, free of oppression and racism in all its forms. This means taking an honest look at the American campus climate, recognizing that, on the whole, Jewish students enjoy high levels of safety, ample access to resources, and freedom from oppression, and demanding that these privileges and freedoms be extended to all, and denied to none.

Conclusion

Today, the campus battle for justice in Palestine sits at the turbulent center of a national firestorm. On and off campuses, while activists are winning the conversation and shaping the worldview of the American public, the backlash machine is forced to rely upon top-down repression, crude bullying, and false antisemitism charges to maintain its slipping grip on the status quo.

In the coming years, new generations of student activists will build on the movement's victories in student government, and will compel their universities to actually divest from occupation profiteers. And as our national consensus moves beyond unconditional support for Israel's occupation and apartheid, history will look kindly upon those Palestinian students who championed the cause of justice for their people; those students of color who connected the dots between the liberation of marginalized communities here and abroad; those allies who practiced joint struggle and demanded freedom for all; and those Jewish students who sought "to transform our own Jewish communities," as students Henry Rosen and Max Fineman wrote in a January 2016 op-ed in *Haaretz*, "to center values of justice and collective liberation rather than exceptionalism and isolation."[17]

I would like to give thanks to Benjamin Balthaser for his help in shaping the ideas that went into this piece, and Adam Horowitz, the JVP 2016 Summer Fellows, and all other editors for their feedback.

Antisemitism on the American College Campus in the Age of Corporate Education, Identity Politics, and Power-Blindness

Orian Zakai

Investigating Israel/Palestine Pedagogy

In the summer of 2015, I underwent a preliminary investigation regarding a possible violation of my school's "anti-discrimination/harassment policy" in connection with a course I taught that included critique of Israel and Zionism.[1] I never learned what specific conduct or behavior I was investigated for except for the fact that some students felt that my course was imbalanced and did not voice enough of "the Israeli side." Eventually, after six long weeks of stress, the procedure found no evidence of misconduct on my part. However, the whole thing startled me deeply, not only because of it threatened my career, but also because it was painful for me to think that my teaching hurt my students. The experience thus generated a long thought process in an attempt to understand why it became almost impossible for me, as an Israeli, to teach conscientiously about Israel/Palestine in the current American college environment.

I should note that the present essay does not deal with the deliberate ways in which allegations of antisemitism are used to persecute Palestinian and pro-Palestine activists. I believe that this crucially important issue will be dealt by others in this volume. From my own relatively privileged and yet precarious position as a contingent faculty teaching Hebrew language and literature, I shall only try to unpack the distress that Jewish students report experiencing in face of scholarly critique of Israel and Zionism, and the way in which this distress interacts with the culture of corporate education and its power-blind version of identity politics.

Also, the following is not meant to be an accusation of or an attack on Jewish and/or Zionist students. I have no doubt in my mind that the students who complained against me are conscientious and socially aware students, and that they experienced real discomfort in my classroom. Moreover, in my experience working with Jewish students, I noticed that investment in Israel is often an outlet for the more socially conscious and caring Jewish youth, the ones who want to belong to something greater than themselves, who care about community and global politics, and who are given the message that support for Israel is a highly regarded way to express their sense of social responsibility. Why wouldn't they feel pain when content learned in the classroom implies that this particular communal investment may mean legitimizing the continued discrimination and human rights violation of others?

A Power-Blind Conversation

It so happened that on the day in which I began writing this essay, I received an email from my school informing me that I am required to take the mandatory online course "Intersections: Preventing Discrimination." The email refers to my school as "the Company" and provides a link to an external site administered by a firm called LawRoom – Inspired Employer Solutions. The course itself contains a series of digital activities designed to educate me about my legal obligations as an employee with regard to discrimination/harassment. It presents ample case studies that demonstrate what discrimination/harassment means in legalistic terms and puts special emphasis on examples of successful and unsuccessful lawsuits. The case studies and testimonies feature mostly white women and men dealing with sexual harassment in the workplace. There are also a couple of stories involving African American women and men and racial discrimination, as well as one gay man speaking of sexual orientation–based micro-aggressions. In the area of religion-based discrimination, we find an example of an unsuccessful lawsuit by an evangelist protesting the non-inclusion of intelligent design in the curriculum. There are also a few cases of people offended by sexual content in the classroom or in art. No ethnicity is discussed, no disability, no LGBTQ folks beyond one white gay man, no intersectionality. The situations are taken mostly from the corporate world or from hard and natural sciences in higher education. The focus of the course is appropriate and inappropriate behavior. There is no mention of concepts such as power, politics, or identity. Indeed, the course seems to lack the basic terminology needed to address the issue at hand. It is so simplistic and schematic, and presents such an alarming analogy between the educational world and the corporate world, that I am surprised to see it used by a higher education institution that employs quite a few scholars who are working and teaching on critical race, ethnicity, sexuality, and gender studies in complex and nuanced ways. The pedagogic value of the course is miniscule, but it does make evident the rift between our scholarly knowledge of issues of difference and marginalization and the procedures that are to govern our behavior in these contexts.

The subjugation of the conversation about "diversity" to corporate culture, and the reification of these conversations into a set of legalistic procedures, designed to protect institutional wealth from possible lawsuits, deserves a much wider discussion than the scope of this essay allows. What needs to be stressed in the present context is that while the allegations of antisemitism directed at critics of Israel are not a new phenomenon, in this day and age they intersect with the rising anxiety among academic administrators about institutions being held accountable for the way social relations of power manifest themselves on campus grounds through acts of aggression and micro-aggression against students of traditionally underrepresented populations.

The recent elaboration of the legalistic discourse regarding discrimination/harassment is related to the 2011 reinterpretation of the federal Title IX regulations, known as the "Dear Colleague Letter."[2] While Title IX originally intended to protect equal opportunities for female student-athletes, the Dear Colleague Letter justly defines sexual violence in terms of discrimination on the basis of sex and gender, insofar as it creates a hostile environment, which limits survivors' access to educational opportunities. Compliance with this new interpretation of Title IX came to require mandatory training of campus communities on issues of sexual and gendered violence and mandatory reporting of any knowledge of possible violation to a centralized authority. In this context, my institution, like many other institutions across the country, revised its own anti-harassment/discrimination policy. The new policy takes on the principle elaborated by the Dear Colleague Letter, namely that an experience of aggression based on one's identity may "interfere with or limit a student's ability to participate in or benefit from the school's program,"[3] and expands it to include discrimination/harassment on the basis of "actual or perceived sex, sexual orientation, gender identity or expression, race, creed, color, place of birth, ancestry, ethnicity, religion, national origin, age, disability, marital status or other *characteristics* as defined and protected by law in the location where a particular program is operating." The expansion itself is undoubtedly justified as gender and sex cannot be regarded as the only realm in which harassment/discrimination occur. However, as someone who has spent much time and energy advocating and educating about issues of sexual violence,[4] my concern is with the shift from thinking of discriminatory aggression in terms of the systems of power it replicates and bolsters to thinking of it in terms of the protection of individual identity "characteristics."

Understanding discrimination in terms of power means understanding that categories such as "race," "gender," "ethnicity," and others are not merely "characteristics" of the individual who needs to be protected from discrimination. Rather, they represent the placement of individuals and communities within sociopolitical hierarchies that are *already* discriminatory insofar as they unequally distribute access to resources (such as education) and institutional support, and unevenly determine the likelihood of a person to be mocked, humiliated, restricted, silenced, excluded, put under surveillance, detained, arrested, violated, injured, or killed.[5]

When the systems of power that shape social relations of power are excluded from or marginalized in diversity and inclusivity discourses, discrimination becomes a matter of hurt emotions and uncomfortable feelings, which may be easily pinned to a "protected characteristic" in order to shut down the teaching of uncomfortable contents. No doubt the emotional composure of college students is often fragile, and I for one believe that a good pedagogue should carefully take this into account in order to maximize students' openness to learning. But this is a different conversation; a pedagogic, rather than a legalistic conversation. In the case of Jewish students and the critique of Israel, when we lose sight of power, we are left with an identity constructed in the realm of nationalist ideology, fixated by pro-Israel Jewish education, and fraught with questions that have no place to be aired, largely because of the boundaries on discourse set by the political agenda of Jewish organizations, boundaries which the instructor is expected to keep intact even if they conflict with their scholarly judgment. When we lose sight of power in this case, it is very easy for the system to coopt diversity discourse to protect these boundaries and the power structures that produce them.

Indeed, in a power-blind system that produces power-blind policies, the social justice context in which activists have fought against discrimination dissipates, and theoretically there is nothing to prevent, for example, a white man from complaining about being discriminated against in a feminist or critical race studies class. In the present context, we may argue that Jewish students complaining that they are being discriminated against or harassed when confronted with critique of Israel may be equated with that hypothetical white man. This analogy is of course limited because there indeed is a legacy of discrimination against Jews in higher education in the United States, albeit its residues are almost negligible now. However, the distress over Israel experienced by Jewish students today cannot be situated solely in relation to the Jewish history of real discrimination in this country. Rather it has to also, and primarily, be read in against the backdrop of the politics of power in Israel/Palestine.

The subjective experience of this distress, however, is located in a space where Israel's power politics remain comfortably ambiguous. This is the place where a false perception of Israel as weak, as being "singled out," unfairly treated, surrounded by enemies, is imbricated with a students' experience of discomfort vis-à-vis the challenges of a critical discussion of Israel/Palestine. Discomfort is here magnified through its reverberations in the national story, as the students experience the feeling of not being able to apply the various *hasbara* "defenses" of Israel in a scholarly context as being "singled out," rendered "defenseless" against the indefensible images of human rights violations, just as Israel itself is "singled out" and "defenseless" in the pro-Zionist imagination. Class discussions then tend to escalate, if allowed, into the apocalyptic realm where the possibilities of a Holocaust happening in America and the destruction of Israel by a coalition of Arab countries are juggled as if they were as real as the occupation itself.

A metonymic relation is therefore established between the student challenged in the classroom and the State of Israel. In literary studies, a metonym is the relation between two things (objects, images, systems, narratives), that come to represent each other either by being posited side by side or in a relation of the part to the whole. Within the framework of nationalism, the relation between the individual life-story and a national grand narrative is constructed as metonymic, and it is often the work of national ideology to produce, elaborate, and nurture this metonymic relation. In this context, we may understand how the real experience of Jewish students in a classroom critical of Israel, or vis-à-vis "Pro-Palestine" campus activism, comes to be metonymic of the ideological construct of "Israel as victim." The vicious cycle in which the personal and the national narratives sustain each other is often complicated and painful to break through.

Politics, Identity, and Hierarchies of Power

One question that I was struggling with in my investigation as a possible violator of my institution's anti-harassment/discrimination policy was in regard to the relations between political opinion and identity. Notably, political opinion is not one of the protected "characteristics" that the policy names. Indeed, in an educational setting political expression should be protected in the name of academic freedom, which was inappropriate as grounds for my investigation, because, of course, a discussion of Israel/Palestine politics in the American campus centered on academic freedom would necessarily highlight the protection that should be awarded to the critics of Zionism. Discrimination, harassment, and antisemitism are therefore much more fruitful discursive environments for those wishing to set boundaries for the conversation.

Here again we may observe the transition of the conversation from politics of power to power-blind identity politics. Students often report to me that they are crystal clear about their political positions regarding Israel/Palestine, despite having little to no knowledge of the politics and history of the conflict. I see this as an outcome of non-academic Jewish education facilitated in settings such as Hebrew schools, Birthright trips, and Hillel, which constructs the identification with Israel as a matter of Jewish identity rather than politics. In this frame of thought, support for Israel neatly derives from one's identity and therefore does not need to, and indeed ought not, be examined and shaped in the realm of real politics.

To be clear, I do not think there is a fixed borderline between identity and politics. Indeed the very premise of identity politics, as I understand it, is that one's political position is bound with one's identity as *shaped by systems of power*. An African American student's antiracist politics would undoubtedly derive from their experience of racism, and they should be protected from racist politics in the classroom. However, a white student whose white supremacist politics derive from their experience of privilege should not be afforded the same protection in my mind. Identity politics loses its ethical gravity in a power-blind system. Looking at Jewish students' identification with Israel through the prism of power, it should be very clear that students side with state power on this matter. And while Israel's security concerns are often cited in attempt to portray Israel as a vulnerable state and justify its use of violent state power, there is no way of denying the gross asymmetry of power between Israel and the Palestinians.

There is, however, another, more complicated, matter that comes up in this context—the relationship between American Jews and power in the United States. To be clear, I do not believe that American Jews enjoy the same privileges as non-Jewish white people. In my school, it is still quite difficult for a student to get a kosher meal, not to mention a Passover kosher meal, or to observe Yom Kippur and still meet their academic commitments. In fact, as someone who is new to the Jewish American campus reality, I was surprised by how little attention is bestowed upon such practical issues that affect Jewish students' well-being on campus (some of my students were literally starving on Passover week) in comparison to the protection of the Jewish

American identification with Israel. However, if we are to compare Jewish power to Palestinian power on my campus, we would observe that Jewish students compose a large percentage of the student body while the percentage of Palestinian students is miniscule; that we have a strong Hillel and an almost non-existent Students for Justice in Palestine; and that in any given semester, there are several courses on Israel but almost never ones devoted to Palestinian history and culture.

If we are to examine the Jewish American identification with Israel against the backdrop of all relevant hierarchies of power, which entail, I would maintain, not only (and not even predominantly) the hierarchy of power between Jews and non-Jews in the United States, but also the hierarchies of power between Jews and Palestinians in Israel and in this country, it should become clear that the equating of the critique of Zionism with antisemitism reflects a misunderstanding of the relations between power and racism, a misunderstanding that is unfortunately prevalent within the framework of power-blind corporate education.

To Cry Fire

Paradoxically, while the challenge to my own academic freedom occurred in the name of Jewish American identification with Israel, I mostly feel foreign, as an Israeli lefty, within the Jewish American discourse of Israel/Palestine. And, moreover, often when my American Jewish students and colleagues speak of their sense of belonging to the Jewish state, I am painfully reminded of my own sense of non-belonging to a society that gradually ostracizes me and my kind.

When I was teaching about Israel/Palestine in 2015, it was in the wake of my visit to Israel in July 2014, during the war on Gaza, when I was roaming the streets of Tel Aviv, gazing at the once-so-familiar and homey sights of people flooding the cafés, the bars, the squares—and they all seemed unreal. In Tel Aviv, across from the IDF headquarters, they have renovated the buildings of the old "German Colony," and have built a new leisure center with restaurants, cafés, galleries, and picnic tables. One of the restaurants came up with the cute idea to sell picnic baskets so you can have yourself a nice family picnic across from the iron gates of the headquarters, from which orders of killing were sent while you were picnicking. In the summer of 2014, anti-war protests were named illegal and protesters were assaulted. That summer, while marching against the war, I saw a woman in a car pressing her entire body outside the passenger window to shout at us. Her voice was extremely loud and it overcame both the noise of the busy street and the anti-war chants. I was asked by my English-speaking partner to translate, and I did. She was shouting in Hebrew, "Kill all the children, kill them all."

So when I was teaching in spring of 2015, I felt like someone who was trying desperately to report a fire. People kept saying that the report was not balanced enough, but how can you report a disaster in a balanced way? Where is the sacred balance to be located in a situation that is so ostensibly unbalanced? How can a "balanced" pedagogy of Israel/Palestine be scholarly or ethically justified when the very core of the subject matter is the unbalanced power of one people over another? In fact, I would argue, a balanced approach to Israel/Palestine is possible only within the US-centric framework that governs Israel/Palestine pedagogy in the United States, where it almost seems as if the main conflict at hand is that between American "pro-Israel" and "pro-Palestinian" students and scholars. Here, despite constant attempts to delegitimize pro-Palestinian activism, and despite the fact that on many campuses like my campus, Palestinian students have much less institutional support, visibility, and opportunity to speak, it is easier to pretend there is balance since all participants more or less equally possess "citizenship" in the educational communities.

In this framework the realities of Israel/Palestine and the realities of the occupation are relegated to the margins. The real face of unbalanced power in Israel/Palestine—movement restrictions, humiliations at checkpoints, land grabs, house demolitions, settlers' abuse of Palestinians, daily arrests of children, violent suppression of protest, torture, administrative detention, the cheapening of Palestinian lives that makes possible mass killings of Palestinian civilians every few years—all of this is relegated to the margins of the debate, while Jewish American crisis of identity is centralized.

I am no stranger to crisis of identity, and nor do I want to minimize its real pangs for young people. To an extent, I think that the class I taught in the spring of 2015 became the site of a clash between my own crisis of identity as an Israeli and that of some of my Jewish students. Indeed as a pedagogue, what I learned from the experience is how my critical perspective of the country of which I am a citizen intervenes in an American conversation whose parameters are at times foreign to me because they have at least as much to do with American campus politics as they do with the realities of Israel/Palestine. Pedagogically speaking, there is no way for me to proceed without taking this into account, and yet, forgoing considerations of power, committing to fake balance, accepting the intellectual deadlock of a symmetrical approach to "the conflict"—these seem to me like easy ways out, catering to American wishful thinking and to the power-blindness of corporate education. My work as a teacher should be harder than that.

Chilling and Censoring of Palestine Advocacy in the United States

Dima Khalidi

David Horowitz, a right-wing ideologue that the Southern Poverty Law Center describes as "a driving force of the anti-Muslim, anti-immigrant and anti-Black movements,"[1] plastered posters all over University of California campuses in the spring of 2016. One poster, with a picture of Angela Davis, read "Communist Anti-Israel BDS Supporter—#StopTheJewHatred." Another poster found on multiple campuses, featuring a picture of what appear to be Hamas fighters, stated "Boycott, Divest, Sanction—a Hamas-inspired genocidal campaign to destroy Israel, the world's only Jewish State." Preceding a list of students and faculty at each campus believed to promote BDS, the poster said, "The following students and faculty ... have allied themselves with Palestinian terrorists to perpetrate BDS and Jew Hatred on this campus."[2] The names of students and faculty were culled from the website Canary Mission, an anonymous cyberbullying endeavor dedicated to profiling advocates for Palestinian rights in an effort to malign them and ruin their reputations and career prospects.

The chilling effect that such blacklists have on students who speak out for Palestinian rights, or who wish to speak out but are too afraid to be similarly defamed, are difficult to measure. Palestine Legal has fielded dozens of calls from students and others who fear how such blacklisting will affect their career prospects. At least two leaders of SJP groups resigned their positions out of such fears. This is precisely the intended effect of these efforts: to intimidate advocates for Palestinian rights into silence and inaction.

David Horowitz and his "Freedom Center" are too much even for more mainstream Israel advocacy organizations to swallow. Some groups, including San Diego State's Hillel chapter and UCLA's J Street U chapter, condemned Horowitz's tactic of naming students.[3] Yet Horowitz represents the extreme end of a spectrum of Israel advocacy groups that have the same intent, even if their tactics vary: to conflate criticism of Israel, including via public advocacy for BDS, with antisemitism and support for terrorism. While not all Israel advocacy groups use Horowitz and Canary Mission–style tactics of public blacklists and intimidation, many engage in inflammatory, false, and hyperbolic rhetoric about those who support Palestinian rights, contributing to the atmosphere of fear, intimidation, and public condemnation that activists face, and sometimes resulting in serious consequences for activists who are exercising their First Amendment rights.

To give one recent example, an ad hoc group of students at CUNY's Brooklyn College recently protested a faculty council meeting by holding a brief "mic check" to raise their concerns about issues such as tuition increases, campus diversity, and surveillance. Although two of the nine students that participated were leaders with the Brooklyn College Students for Justice in Palestine (SJP) chapter, it was an unaffiliated third student whose actions drew controversy when she reportedly yelled "Zionism out of CUNY" during the mic check, and allegedly called the Jewish professor chairing the meeting "Zionist."[4] Almost immediately, the Zionist Organization of America complained to CUNY, enumerating this and other alleged incidents of antisemitism at CUNY, and calling for SJP to be banned from its campuses. The New York State Senate passed a resolution soon thereafter to cut $485 million in funding from CUNY because of the alleged antisemitism, and thirty-five New York legislators wrote to CUNY demanding that it ban SJP from the university system.[5]

Meanwhile, media outlets broadcasted that SJP was responsible for "antisemitic rhetoric," and Brooklyn College president Karen Gould swiftly declared, before any investigation was conducted, that the students had made hateful anti-Jewish remarks. Following an investigation targeting only four of the nine protesters, only the two SJP students were ultimately charged with disciplinary violations, and underwent a lengthy disciplinary process, which eventually vindicated them.[6] This vindication, however, only came after they were smeared in the press and by their university president. After Gould's statement, one of the students was harassed with messages calling her "Muslim trash" and "scum" for her "heinous acts," and found a poster on campus with her picture on it defaced, her eyes blacked out.[7]

As revealed in the excerpt below from *The Palestine Exception to Free Speech*, the 2015 report released by Palestine Legal and the Center for Constitutional Rights, the deployment of false accusations of antisemitism is one of several tactics used to malign, censor, and punish Palestinian rights activists. Yet it is the most prevalent. Of the 171 incidents of suppression that Palestine Legal responded to in the first half of 2016 (a 22 percent increase from the same period in 2015), 51 percent involved false accusations of antisemitism, roughly equivalent to the 59 percent documented in the first half of 2015. Thirty-three percent of these incidents involved false accusations of support for terrorism, up from 29 percent in the first half of 2015.[8] This reflects a continuation of the trends identified in the report analyzing 2014 and 2015 data. The most prevalent tactic to intimidate advocates for Palestinian rights into silence is still to falsely accuse individuals, groups, and the movement for Palestinian rights as a whole of being motivated by antisemitism and support for terrorism.

It's no coincidence that the two tactics often overlap, and go hand in hand. It is, after all, much easier to sow the idea that those who promote Palestinian rights are antisemitic if they are also depicted as pro-terrorist. These kinds of accusations are now at a fever pitch, to the point where lawmakers around the country are introducing and often passing unconstitutional legislation condemning and punishing those who endorse BDS.[9] They justify such legislation by labeling BDS as "antisemitic," as Senator Chuck Schumer recently did while vowing to introduce federal legislation against BDS;[10] and by linking BDS with terrorism, as Governor Andrew Cuomo has done in justifying his executive order, signed in June 2016, requiring New York state to divest from companies and institutions that engage in or promote BDS. Cuomo called BDS "a new brand of warfare," and stated that the "Hamas tunnel" he visited on a propaganda trip to Israel in the midst of Israel's brutal 2014 offensive on Gaza "was not nearly as frightening as continued efforts to boycott, divest from and sanction Israel."[11]

Some university heads are also repeating such insinuations. In an especially egregious response to the David Horowitz posters described above, San Diego State University president Elliot Hirshman not only failed to denounce the defamatory posters; he also exacerbated the effect on the targeted students, making statements implying that they had brought the posters' accusations upon themselves, and stating that BDS supporters share a "common goal" with terrorists.[12]

When government officials—legislators and university heads included—adopt the language and repeat the insinuations of the most extreme Israel advocates, it is a sign that the widespread efforts to conflate criticism of Israel with antisemitism and support for terrorism are succeeding at the highest levels. This is even occurring as such tactics are being rejected and defied at the grassroots level, as evidenced by a continually growing movement for Palestinian rights. Challenging this tactic, exposing the anti-Palestinian and anti-Muslim fervor that fuels it, and advocating on behalf of those who are targeted by it continues to be a priority for Palestine Legal in its mission to protect the right to stand for justice.

—Dima Khalidi, June 2016

The following is excerpted from The Palestine Exception to Free Speech: A Movement under Attack in the US.[13]

In reaction to the growing movement for Palestinian rights, a number of organizations that staunchly support Israeli policy have sought to suppress and silence criticism of Israel through a broad range of tactics. From January 2014 through June 2015, Palestine Legal interviewed hundreds of students, academics, and community activists who reported being censored, punished, subjected to disciplinary proceedings, questioned, threatened, or falsely accused of antisemitism or supporting terrorism for their speech in support of Palestinian rights or criticism of Israeli policies.

In 2014, Palestine Legal responded to 152 incidents of censorship, punishment, or other burdening of advocacy for Palestinian rights and 68 requests for legal assistance in anticipation of such actions. The organization responded to 140 such incidents and 33 such requests for assistance in anticipation of potential suppression in the first six months of 2015, the vast majority (89 percent in 2014, 80 percent in 2015) involving college students, university professors, or academic associations.

Because these incidents often involve recognizable patterns in strategies and tactics, the Report classifies them in the following categories:

1. False and Inflammatory Accusations of Antisemitism and Support for Terrorism
2. Official Denunciations
3. Bureaucratic Barriers
4. Administrative Sanctions
5. Cancellations and Alterations of Academic and Cultural Events
6. Threats to Academic Freedom
7. Lawsuits and Legal Threats
8. Legislation
9. Criminal Investigations and Prosecutions

These strategies of suppression often have their intended effect: intimidating or deterring Palestinian solidarity activists from speaking out. The fear of punishment or career damage discourages many activists from engaging in activities that could be perceived as critical of Israel. For example, several students told Palestine Legal that they feared that false accusations of antisemitism or supporting Hamas (designated as a terrorist organization by the US government) would hinder their ability to find a job or travel.[14] The speech activities of Palestinian-American, Arab-American, and Muslim students routinely subject them to heightened harassment, intimidation, and discriminatory treatment in the midst of a post-9/11 climate in which their communities already face infringements of their civil liberties.[15]

The Report seeks to identify and criticize the ways certain groups staunchly supportive of Israel choose to stigmatize, silence, and suppress constitutionally protected activism that promotes Palestinian human rights or criticizes Israeli policies. The Report does not address advocacy in support of Israeli government practices that does not seek to suppress differing viewpoints. Any conflation of these distinct concepts merely evidences a failure to apprehend the free speech principles this Report sets out to defend.

Actors

Israel Advocacy Organizations

A network of lobbying groups, watchdog groups, public relations entities, and advocacy groups funded by, working in coordination with, and/or staunchly supportive of the policies and practices of the Israeli government primarily drives efforts to silence speech on behalf of Palestinian rights. Organizations dedicated to countering Palestinian rights activism—often in ways that seek to unlawfully suppress protected speech, as detailed in this Report—have proliferated in response to the increasing effectiveness of the movement for Palestinian rights. Prominent groups engaged in suppression include the Louis D. Brandeis Center for Human Rights Under Law (Brandeis Center), the Zionist Organization of America (ZOA), the AMCHA Initiative, Hillel International, Shurat HaDin–Israel Law Center, StandWithUs, the Anti-Defamation League (ADL), the American Israel Public Affairs Committee (AIPAC), the Jewish Federations of North America, the Jewish Council for Public Affairs, Scholars for Peace in the Middle East, the American Jewish Committee, the Committee for Accuracy in Middle East Reporting in America (CAMERA), Divestment Watch, the Israel on Campus Coalition, Campus Watch, the David Project, and the David Horowitz Freedom Center.[16]

These groups are not monolithic and pursue distinct strategies to suppress speech critical of Israel. Hillel International, the largest Jewish campus organization in the world, prohibits campus Hillel affiliates from hosting speakers supportive of BDS.[17] The Brandeis Center, which focuses on confronting the "resurgent problem of antisemitism and anti-Israelism on university campuses,"[18] the AMCHA Initiative, and ZOA have filed complaints alleging violations of Title VI of the Civil Rights Act of 1964, arguing that speech critical of Israel creates a hostile educational environment for Jewish students (see section B, part 7c). AMCHA and the David Project have mounted campaigns to malign individual students and faculty members.[19] StandWithUs, which boasts of a "sizeable team . . . dedicated to supporting students' efforts to promote and defend Israel amid the virulent anti-Israel movement on college campuses,"[20] reportedly works closely with the Israeli government[21] and keeps dossiers on pro-Palestinian speakers.[22] Shurat HaDin, an Israel-based organization that "fight[s] academic and economic boycotts and challeng[es] those who seek to delegitimize the Jewish State,"[23] acknowledges working with Israeli intelligence agencies and law enforcement[24] and has threatened or initiated legal action against several organizations that have contemplated or passed BDS initiatives, including the Presbyterian Church (USA), the ASA, and the Park Slope Food Coop.[25] While more mainstream groups sometimes criticize activities of groups that occupy the far right of the spectrum,[26] their collective efforts to suppress speech produce the same effect: suspicion and heightened scrutiny of individuals critical of Israeli government actions toward Palestinians.

These groups spend considerable time and resources combating what they deem to be efforts to "delegitimize" Israel. The "delegitimization" framing, which the Israeli government and many US officials have adopted,[27] allows Israel advocacy organizations to cast criticism of Israeli state practices as a challenge to the state's "right to exist." The Reut Institute, an Israeli think tank, characterized the BDS movement itself as a "delegitimization challenge" and an "existential threat" in a 2010 paper.[28] The Reut Institute recommended that Israel respond by "sabotag[ing] [delegitimization] network catalysts"[29] and "attack[ing] catalysts"[30]—that is, those who question Israel's policies and practices. Building on the Reut Institute's suggestions, Israel advocacy groups have committed vast resources to responding to "delegitimization challenges."

In October 2010, the Jewish Federations of North America and the Jewish Council for Public Affairs launched the Israel Action Network, a $6 million campaign to counter "delegitimization" activities and monitor groups advocating for Palestinian rights through BDS and other actions.[31] The Jewish Agency for Israel declared in 2013 that it was developing a plan that would eventually commit $300 million to this effort and "would combine donor dollars from the United States with Israeli government funds to create what is likely the most expensive pro-Israel campaign ever."[32] In June 2015, casino mogul Sheldon Adelson and media proprietor Haim Saban convened a summit that reportedly raised "at least $20 million" to combat BDS efforts.[33]

The Israeli government itself identified "delegitimization" as a threat and set aside resources to combat it.[34] Prime Minister Benjamin Netanyahu reportedly convened a meeting of top Israeli ministers in February 2014 to discuss ways to combat the BDS movement. The officials discussed using lawsuits "in European and North American courts against [pro-BDS] organizations," "legal action against financial institutions that boycott settlements ... [and complicit] Israeli companies," and "encouraging anti-boycott legislation in friendly capitals around the world."[35] Officials understood that undertaking such efforts would require "activat[ing] the pro-Israel lobby in the US."[36]

These Israel advocacy organizations, many of which have operated for decades, are increasingly focused on countering the Palestine solidarity movement, BDS, and campus activism in particular.

Universities and Other Institutions

As universities have become ground zero in the clash between advocates for Palestinian human rights and the counter-campaign to silence criticism of Israel, university administrators have emerged as key decision-makers regarding whether to condemn, limit, or sanction Palestine advocacy. Universities, along with other institutions that host or sponsor events related to Palestinian rights, often come under substantial pressure from Israel advocacy organizations able to mobilize donors, community members, and sympathetic media. As detailed throughout the Report, university administrations have canceled programs, sanctioned students, fired professors, and scrutinized departments in response to external pressure. In so doing, universities treat students who speak out on Palestine differently than other students, indicating that the viewpoint of the speech, and not the facially neutral explanations often put forward, drives the censorship. Viewpoint-based restrictions at public institutions, including universities, violate the First Amendment.

Other institutions have similarly acceded to pressure from Israel advocacy organizations by canceling events and otherwise closing off forums for discussion and debate on Palestinian human rights.

Government Officials

US government actors have also contributed to the suppression of advocacy for Palestinian rights. The executive branches of federal and local governments, which include local police, the Department of State, the Department of Education, the Federal Bureau of Investigation (FBI), and the Department of Homeland Security (DHS), as well as other law enforcement agencies and prosecutors' offices, have engaged in targeted surveillance, investigations, raids, and criminal prosecutions on the basis of Palestine advocacy. Lawmakers have proposed and passed legislation that impinges upon free speech and other civil liberties. These activities sometimes take place with significant encouragement and input from Israel advocacy groups and Israeli officials.

Tactics

False and Inflammatory Accusations of Antisemitism and Support for Terrorism

The primary tool in the arsenal of Israel advocacy organizations is public vilification of supporters of Palestinian rights—and their advocacy campaigns—as antisemitic or pro-terrorism. These accusations subject students, scholars, and other advocates to significant personal and professional harm and deter many from publicly criticizing Israel's actions. Character attacks also force students and scholars to spend significant time combating accusations that could ruin their careers. As one student who was falsely accused of associating with terrorists noted, "the underlying message" is "that if you speak out too loudly or work too hard . . . anti-Palestinian activist[s] will smear you just like [they] tried to smear me."[37] Even where the threat does not result in self-censorship, accusations of antisemitism and support for terrorism often persuade campus authorities to restrict or punish protected speech.

Monitoring and Surveillance to Facilitate Accusations

To facilitate false accusations of antisemitism and support for terrorism, Israel advocacy organizations monitor Palestinian rights advocates on social media, scrutinize them in public, and sometimes infiltrate private settings. Through social media monitoring, organizations identify out-of-context quotations, Facebook posts, and other material that can serve as fodder for character attacks. For example, in January 2015, the Reut Institute reportedly held a "hackathon," in which Israeli officials and a number of other Israeli advocacy groups participated, aimed at exploring ways to gather intelligence on and target individuals involved in Palestine solidarity work.[38] In its June 2015 strategy document, the Reut Institute highlighted the need to "out-name-shame the delegitimizers" as a strategy to fight BDS, recommending the use of "all available fire-power—financial, social, legal, etc."[39]

In spring 2015, an anonymously run website, Canary Mission, published names, photos, biographical information, and links to Facebook profiles for dozens of students, professors, and other activists in order "to expose individuals and groups that are anti-Freedom, anti-American and antisemitic" to schools and prospective employers.[40] Canary Mission relies on little or no evidence, using innuendo and guilt by association to accuse dedicated activists and organizations of connections to terrorism. Campus Watch, led by far-right Israel activist David Horowitz, has long engaged in such activities, maintaining and publishing dossiers on students and faculty and urging readers to "alert university stakeholders" to the "problems in Middle East studies."[41] Organizations like StandWithUs also reportedly keep dossiers on activists.[42]

Students and other activists have reported being videotaped and photographed at demonstrations and other events for Palestinian rights. Students at DePaul University, for example, told Palestine Legal that an Israeli consular entourage videotaped and photographed them as they canvassed campus during a divestment referendum campaign. Such surveillance can affect students of Palestinian origin in particular, some of whom have expressed concern that documentation of their Palestine rights advocacy may lead Israel to deny them entry to visit family in Israel and Palestine.[43]

Surveillance also sometimes goes beyond public monitoring and involves in-person infiltration of student groups in private settings. In one instance, leaked documents revealed that a student spying for the AMCHA Initiative at UC Santa Cruz traveled as part of a university-sponsored student delegation to Israel and Palestine. The student wrote a confidential report to AMCHA that included details about other delegation participants, including reflections about the trip posted to a private group on social media.[44] In another instance, someone reporting for David Horowitz's website, Jew Hatred on Campus, attended an SJP meeting at UCLA and published notes, including students' comments about how to respond to posters that branded SJP as an antisemitic, pro-terrorist organization.

Equating Criticism of Israel with Antisemitism

False and inflammatory allegations of antisemitism underlie many attacks on Palestinian rights activists in the United States. Of the 152 incidents Palestine Legal responded to in 2014, 76 (50 percent) involved accusations of antisemitism based solely on speech critical of Israeli policy; in the first six months of 2015, 83 of 140 incidents (59 percent) involved false accusations of antisemitism. Accusations of antisemitism chill discussion and debate on Israel/Palestine.

In two cases during the spring semester of 2015, for example, students were blocked from even discussing boycott and divestment. At the University of Toledo (UT) in Ohio, Israel advocacy groups claimed that a divestment resolution would create an antisemitic environment on campus.[45] In response, the UT student government barred the public's attendance at a divestment hearing, in violation of Ohio's Open Meetings Act; restricted the attendance of SJP members, forcing them to sit in a separate room from Hillel students; and blocked student senators from voting on the resolution. After significant outcry, the student government allowed the resolution to go forward; it passed overwhelmingly. At Northeastern University, the student government blocked the student body from voting on a divestment referendum because students, backed by Israel advocacy groups, argued that discussing divestment would in and of itself create an antisemitic climate.[46]

In some cases, Israel advocacy groups even charge that academic content covering Palestinian history, culture, or social movements is antisemitic. For example, in spring 2015, AMCHA demanded the cancellation of a student-led course at UC Riverside called "Palestinian Voices," which sought to explore "Palestinian voices through contemporary literature and media."[47] The course assigned reading materials that focused on Palestinian historical narratives, literature, and cultural production and included readings by Edward Said and Rashid Khalidi, as well as a spectrum of Israeli Jewish writers, from Benny Morris and Eyal Weizman to David Grossman and Neve Gordon. AMCHA argued that the course's "clear intent [was] to politically indoctrinate students to hate the Jewish state and take action against it."[48] While the university allowed the course to go forward, the student instructor became the target of anti-Muslim hate mail and misogynist cyberbullying as a result of the campaign.[49]

AMCHA similarly objected to Palestine-related course material at UCLA in spring 2012, arguing that the inclusion of BDS-related links on the website of a course taught by Professor David Shorter violated university policy and state and federal law. After receiving several letters from AMCHA that claimed the BDS materials were akin to antisemitism, the chair of UCLA's Academic Senate conducted an investigation without notifying Professor Shorter and shared disputed information about the investigation with the press. The Academic Senate's Academic Freedom Committee ultimately found that posting the links fell within Professor Shorter's right to academic freedom.[50] Nevertheless, Shorter suffered considerable damage as a result: several major publications carried stories about AMCHA's campaign against him,[51] which generated hate mail, death threats, and a reputational smear that resulted in the loss of consulting contracts.[52]

Israel advocacy groups have increasingly promoted the "State Department definition" of antisemitism, which erroneously includes criticism of Israel as a nation-state in the definition.[53] Departing from the conventional understanding of antisemitism as hate and ethno-religious bias against Jewish people, the redefinition defines antisemitism to include "demonizing Israel," "applying a double standard to Israel," and "delegitimizing Israel," also referred to as the "three Ds."[54] This redefinition serves to chill debate and justify legislation and other punitive actions against advocates for Palestinian rights.

For example, AMCHA cited the "State Department definition" to support its claims against the course at UC Riverside.[55] During the spring of 2015, Israel advocacy groups urged the University of California,[56] Stanford,[57] Northwestern,[58] and Northeastern[59] to adopt the redefinition. AMCHA's Tammi Rossman-Benjamin explained that such a move would render BDS and other common forms of campus activism, such as replicas of Israel's wall or talks by former Israeli soldiers about abuses they witnessed, antisemitic by definition.[60] At the time of publication, no university has adopted the redefinition, but student governments at UC Santa Barbara[61] and UCLA have passed resolutions that condemn antisemitism on campus and incorporate the "three Ds."[62]

In 2012, the California legislature passed a resolution officially branding speech supporting Palestinian rights "antisemitic." House Resolution No. 35 calls for the regulation of speech critical of Israel on California college campuses and defines antisemitism even more broadly and vaguely, to include "language or behavior [that] demonizes and delegitimizes Israel" and "student- and faculty-sponsored boycott, divestment, and sanction campaigns against Israel."[63] In contravention of well-established First Amendment principles, the resolution also condemns "speakers, films, and exhibits . . . that falsely describe Israel, Zionists, and Jews" or claim that "Israel is a racist, apartheid, or Nazi state [or] is guilty of heinous crimes against humanity such as ethnic cleansing and genocide."[64] It further calls for "strong leadership from the top . . . [to ensure] that no public resources will be allowed to be used for antisemitic or any intolerant agitation."[65]

Conflating criticism of Israel with antisemitism also fuels the false narrative that genuinely antisemitic incidents like swastika vandalism stem from pro-Palestine activities. For example, in the spring of 2015, Israel advocacy groups quickly attributed swastika graffiti found on the property of a Jewish fraternity at UC Davis to a recent student government vote to divest from companies aiding in Israel's occupation, despite lacking evidence of any such connection. A few months later, at Stanford University, Israel advocacy organizations similarly speculated that swastika graffiti stemmed from a recent BDS campaign, though police later identified a teenage perpetrator with no known connections to the Stanford campus or to the Israel/Palestine issue.

SJPs are not the sole targets of false accusations—groups like Jewish Voice for Peace (JVP), the emerging Open Hillel movement, and even J street, a liberal "pro-Israel" organization, have all faced accusations of contributing to antisemitism.[66] The ADL's annual list of "top ten anti-Israel groups" regularly includes organizations that promote Palestinian rights, like JVP and SJP, on the basis that they "employ rhetoric that is extremely hostile to Israel, Zionists and/or Jews."[67] Such accusations ignore the track record of groups that advocate for Palestinian rights as part of a larger commitment to equality and justice for all people.

Antisemitism accusations carry great potency, particularly given the historical memory of the Holocaust, the long history of bona fide antisemitism in the US, recent instances of swastika graffiti on campuses, and violence against Jews in North America and Europe. Yet, labeling critics of Israel antisemitic chills protected speech, ruins reputations, and intentionally diverts the conversation away from Israel's violations of Palestinian rights and toward the allegedly sinister motivations of individuals. When students wish to raise questions about Israel's human rights record—for example, through a divestment referendum or a student-led course on Palestinian literature—they must redirect their resources away from discussing Israel/Palestine issues in order to defend themselves against false accusations. As the co-president of NYU's SJP explained:

> If you can say that they're a self-hating Jew or they're antisemitic, it draws attention away from the issues we're talking about, so suddenly we're not discussing home demolitions, we're having to defend ourselves and say, no, we don't actually hate Jewish people—we're just trying to draw attention to Palestine.[68]

Conflating criticism of the Israeli government with antisemitism also undermines and distracts from the fight against genuine antisemitism. To address instances of anti-Jewish animus, educators and students alike must be able to identify them, but this becomes impossible when the meaning of the word is diluted. As a Jewish student from Stanford explained, "As Jews, we must be vigilant in fighting antisemitism on campus. We must be equally vigilant in fighting the abuse and misuse of the term."[69]

Conclusion

Let the Semites End the World!
On Decolonial Resistance, Solidarity, and Pluriversal Struggle

Alexander Abbasi

There is a zone of nonbeing, an extraordinarily sterile and arid region, an utterly naked declivity where an authentic upheaval can be born.
—Frantz Fanon, *Black Skin, White Masks*

I am a Semite for two reasons. Firstly, I am what we might call a "biological" Semite—I am an Arab Palestinian, Muslim male who descends from the "races" of the Semitic-speaking peoples among the civilizations of Africa and Asia. Secondly, I am a Semite because I see the world from its underside, from the zone of nonbeing that Fanon mentions above. The figure of the Semite in the Western consciousness is one that has continuously agitated from the outside looking in. It is a figure that has been a victim of Europe—Semites were the original Others outside the borders of Europe's conceptualization of Self, and have had to look in from the periphery at what Europe defines as the center. The rise of Europe over the world for the past five hundred–plus years has allowed Semites—by the very definition of their being-as-Other—to provide a critical view of the world in which we live. Semites, and all those who have become Other-like-Semites, therefore pose a challenge to the world as it is known.

Let us be clear about what this world is though. It is no coincidence that the world is the way it is. The issues and problems of our day do not arise from thin air. They have been created, and persist, because of sources known to be unknown. The issue—as prophets and revolutionaries have eternally taught us—is that we live with a veil covering our eyes. Not only our eyes. This veil wraps itself around the deepest essence of our being, strangling the way we view, sense, touch, and breathe within the world we "know." While different times and places have assigned to this veil different terms that made sense in their contexts, we must make clear the name of the veil of our times. The world itself is our veil.

The veil that blinds us is one of internal and external colonization. It is one in which Eurocentrism is shoved so rapidly and stealthily down our throats that we only think and act through the lens of Western Man. We enter schools from a young age to learn, yet exit to be enslaved to a system of existential alienation, imprisoned in cages mental and physical, and crossed by borders and markets that don't have our permission to do so. For those of us who continue our education, whether through the so-called higher bastions of education or the school of hard knocks, we continue to encounter the same blinding force of being mentally, physically, spiritually and emotionally "Westoxicated"—drunk with the West. So much so, that even when we think we are being critical of Empire, the struggles of the Global North often forget and step on the feet of the humans, ecology, and cosmos of the Global South. And in the South, humans look up to imitate and adore their masters in the North. This is the cycle of "the world" as it is known.

As long as humans remain enchanted by the world, we will continue to vaguely, unconsciously, unknowingly be engulfed by its unjust hierarchies of power. If the world we know is not the world we want to live in, what are the options we have to end it? In this chapter, utilizing the contestation regarding the question of anti-Semitism and the figure of the Semite, I will argue that decolonial resistance, solidarity, and pluriversal struggle are our options for ending the world. The issue of anti-Semitism plays an integral role in understanding how the world has become the way it is, and also how we can choose to say no to that world. The frameworks needed to de-link from the veil of Western Man require an act of disobedience in thought and praxis. To think and act in a way contrary to that veil is to further a movement breathing life into a world of death. From Ferguson to Gaza, Baltimore to Kerala, Cape Town to London—we are in a moment that requires a decolonial turn locally and globally—in arms with comrades who are ready to exit the hell that enrages us to fight. The Semites of the world, both old and new, must unite in this joint struggle to end the world, while providing the reflections needed to birth another anew.

Semites and Anti-Semitisms

How did the world get this way? The figure of the Semite helps us open that door. The word "Semite" was developed at the height of scientific thought during the European colonial Renaissance. In the eighteenth century, French and German orientalist scholarship attempted to organize Arabic, Aramaic, and Hebrew under a single linguistic canon. The category of "Semite" eventually solidified in the work of nineteenth-century French scholar Ernest Renan. It has become common to mainly associate the terms "Semite" and "anti-Semitism" with Jews and historical anti-Jewish practices. Yet, medieval Christendom and Europe for a long time viewed a number of Semitic figures as their subhuman Other—including the Black African, Arab, Muslim, and Jew from the South and the Orient—all of whom share what can be categorized as Semitic language and culture. It therefore would prove useful (and historically accurate) to rather speak of "Semites" and "anti-Semitisms" in the plural.[1]

In the context of Iberian Christendom in the Middle Ages, Muslims and Jews were classified by Iberian Catholic authorities as those who carried *raza*, meaning "defect" in medieval Castilian. Many argue this is where the concept of "race" comes from. In 1492, the Iberian Catholic crown settler-colonized the remaining Islamic sultanate of Al-Andalus in Granada and intensified a process of ethnically cleansing the Muslims and Jews from those lands on the basis of their view that Muslims and Jews did not have *limpieza de sangre*, or "purity of blood." Their blood and being were considered dirty and defective in comparison to their European Christian counterparts. The figure of the Semite, as I have defined it above—combining the characteristics of being non-Christian and non-white—became in the view of the European colonizers the racial prototype for the rest of the world's others.

Shortly after the final conquest of Al-Andalus, the famed European crusader Christopher Columbus was patronized by Spanish Catholic King Ferdinand and Queen Isabella to embark on a mission to find an eastern route to "India" within the same year that Granada fell, on January 2, 1492. When Columbus and his *conquistadores* fell upon the New World on October 12, 1492, and encountered the "Indians" (Aztec, Maya, Inca, etc.)—a diverse people they had never known before—they approached them through their already developed anti-Semitic worldview. This is evidenced in one example by the Europeans calling the Indian sites of worship "mosques" and "synagogues."[2] It is also materially evidenced by European Catholics utilizing on the Indians the same tactics for conversion, torture, and genocide they had used on the Muslims and Jews in the Iberian Peninsula. The colonizers cross-fertilized these tactics back and across the Atlantic and Indian Ocean on their old and newfound subjects.[3] The colonization of the Indians in tandem with the enslavement of Africans in the New World's plantation economy in the sixteenth century laid the material and metaphysical foundations of an emerging modern Western civilization that was to soon envelope the earth.

It is important to note that the "religion"-based *raza* system that produced anti-Semitism in the Iberian Peninsula is different from the later concept of biological race developed during the European Renaissance and Enlightenment periods. Yet, given the long histories of otherization that continue to regurgitate, revamp, and resurface in the world we now live in, knowing the historical development of both is necessary to understand the complex, interconnected nature of these persisting race and ethnic hierarchies. Whereas religion had in a sense been racialized in the Andalusian world, race becomes worshipped in the post-Andalusian world—the White Man becomes God—and the false idols of Western Man enchant those of us still blinded by the veil that He hath laid over our eyes. Anti-Semitism allowed for the figures of the Moor, Indigenous, Black, and many others across Europe's world-encompassing colonial landscape to share a sameness in their Otherness as old and new Semites.

Beginning the chapter with an analysis of how anti-Semitism is intertangled with the foundations of modern racism and imperial power allows for an entry into the discussion of how deep our current systems of oppression really are. Again, if we are to end the world as it is, we must first critically understand it from an anti-normative perspective—meaning, from the viewpoint of those on the margins and periphery, from the experience of those beings and things that are not considered "normal." The moment of 1492 marks the beginning of "modernity," which is the "space and time" norm we now forcibly live under. Thus, to be "modern" means to be normal, to be white, to be Westernized, to be male, to be capitalist, to be a heterosexual, to be intoxicated by the glamour of European imperial expansion and its multiple hierarchies of oppression.

The Coloniality of Power

Black feminist Kimberlé Crenshaw coined the term "intersectionality" (1989) as a tool to understand the various ways in which systems of oppression (as well as systems of resistance) are thoroughly interconnected and codependent upon one another.[4] As Black feminist revolutionary Audre Lorde famously stated, "There is no thing as a single-issue struggle because we do not live single-issue lives."[5] Contrary to Western supremacist rationale, humans are not one-dimensional and linear beings. Humans are a relation—a walking, breathing multitude of relations between Self and Other. Like the world, humans are a microcosm of overlapping geographies, rationalities, diasporas, and seasonal comings and goings between borders of space and time, land and life forms. We are self/social conduits who bring meaning to each other through the exchange of a multiplicity of issues and experiences, systemic relations of power and powerlessness included. Therefore, it is useful to understand the modern world—including its human relations—as one that contains not just one hierarchy of power separated from another, but rather "heterarchies" of power, or multiple hierarchies of power that are intersectional.

In following this line, Latin American decolonial thinker Ramón Grosfoguel describes the heterarchy of the world as "European/capitalist/military/Christian/secular/patriarchal/white/heterosexual/male."[6] If you were a renegade Moor in Granada, Black African slave in the US South, invisibilized Indigenous of the Americas, or casted-out Dalit in India in the last five hundred years, this heterarchy would describe the hegemonic world emerging over you, in one way or another. Grosfoguel names this heterarchy of power relations the "coloniality of power." The coloniality of power penetrates our paradigms of living so that the residues as well as still-alive systems of slavery, colonialism, and domination are inhaled with each breath we take, knowingly or not. From global socioeconomic class hierarchies; to hierarchies of language, knowledge, spirituality, sexuality, gender, race/ethnicity, aesthetics, pedagogy, and media/technology production; to theories and practices of human aging, nature/ecology, and space/time itself, the veil of these Eurocentric heterarchies within the coloniality of power is vast and immanent. To put it simply, the world is colonized nearly to its core.[7]

While I cannot fully unravel many examples of these hierarchies in the scope of this essay, I do think that when putting forward frameworks for joint struggle we must at the bare minimum stay conscious of how these Eurocentric hierarchies play out systemically and interpersonally. We must remember that the coloniality of power is a highly sophisticated system of oppression that has been mastering itself for over five hundred years. To identify and name it as the major veil that blinds us is not to negate other hierarchies or systems of oppression that have previously or simultaneously existed; for example, the Brahminist caste system in South Asia, forms of anti-Blackness in the Middle East, or the history of premodern forms of colonialism in Native American and Black African communities. These are important and necessary to include in our analyses as well, but they are not the *main* system we are dealing with now.[8] A certain shift took place over the past five hundred years that subsumed all these previous hierarchies and systems to fit within—or under—the coloniality of power. To identify the coloniality of power is to speak of the material persistence of a well-developed force that is the most dominant today in oppressing us all; including those with privilege (white, male, heterosexual, etc.), who do damage to themselves by not recognizing and seeking to subvert their privilege. What is needed to make possible the existence of alternative forms of living and being in the world is a move toward strengthening decolonial resistance, solidarity, and pluriversal struggle.

Decolonial Resistance

The epigraph that opens this chapter by Frantz Fanon speaks of a place. An "extraordinarily sterile and arid region" outside of the normal, outside of the world as it appears. It is the zone of nonbeing. A zone where supposed humans don't have the opportunity to descend into hell because—as Afro-Jewish philosopher Lewis Gordon says—they are already living it.[9] It is the zone of the enslaved, encaged, and enraged who have been given a cosmic "no" in response to their attempts at self-determination and communal autonomy. The world itself is the *zone of being*, a place where those with privilege assume human reciprocity and dignity in their trials and tribulations. A place where privilege and power is not questioned; it is Reality. The zone of nonbeing, on the other hand, is the underworld, the Unreal, and the enflamed. It is the zone of Semites and all Others encaged by the coloniality of power. We go to the zone of nonbeing in understanding the world from its underside, naked and unveiled. And we must continuously dwell in that place to be able to succeed in our upheaval against the world. To go beyond the normal world (the zone of being)—by not merely reforming or fine-tuning, but instead dismembering and burning to ashes its most venomous tentacles—is to recapture our being-in-the-world on dignified and just terms. The zone of nonbeing is the point of departure; it is where we begin the process of decolonial resistance, solidarity, and pluriversal struggle. One of the first steps of decolonial resistance is to re-understand oneself and community, as the saying goes: "No knowledge, no self. Know knowledge, know self." Decolonizing the self is necessary so that we de-link from the Imperial Ego and universal Story of the West that we've been brainwashed with, and re-link with a multitude of histories of resistance that inspire us to turn the world anew. Remembering our various human ancestors and movements is very helpful for this process of resistive renewal. From prophets Moses to Mohammad (peace be upon them), Malcolm X to Mao Zedong, Angela Davis to Frida Kahlo, Celia Sanchez to Houria Bouteldja, there are a plethora of old and new figures of liberation—from a variety of locations, times, and perspectives—who are models for engaging resistance against oppression. In terms of movements, in 1498 (just six years after the fall of Granada) in the South Asian city of Kerala, the Malabar Muslims declared *jihad*, or struggle, against Portuguese colonizers, successfully fighting off European invasion for centuries thereafter. The Haitian revolution (1792–1804) saw a Maroon army of self-liberated African slaves throw off the clutches of the French and gain independence while abolishing slavery, sending shockwaves of resistance across the world. The Bandung Conference was held in 1955 by twenty-nine newly independent African and Asian countries to strengthen their commitment to fighting colonialism and neo-colonialism. I mention these figures and movements to remind us that we are not necessarily doing anything particularly new in our turn toward decolonization. There have always been currents of those fighting for the end of the world and an upheaval from the zone of nonbeing. It is important to re-learn and re-connect to those (our) histories of resistance, so as to decolonize the Self and have a counter-historical, liberating understanding of ourselves in relation to the oppressive "history" the world teaches us.

International and Transnational Solidarity

On another level, furthering decolonial resistance means thinking internationally and operating transnationally, in solidarity with forces local and global. To exit the borders within which the master has placed us, the wise words of Martin Luther King Jr. ring true: "An injustice anywhere is a threat to justice everywhere." Or as the South African protest chant goes, "An injury to one is an injury to all!" Internationalism asks us to remain in a state of in-betweenness. Of having, for example, one foot in the struggles for justice in the Global North, in addition to consciousness of, and possibly even the other foot in, the struggle for justice in the Global South (and even to realize there is a South in the North and a North in the South!). It means to embody a type of "border thinking," as Chicana feminist Gloria Anzaldúa coined it.[10] To know and act from the peripheries—those borders lining the zones of being and nonbeing—creates an ethical commitment to always center the narratives of the marginalized and oppressed. It is to see the militarized US-Mexico death border, to see the apartheid wall in occupied Palestine, to see checkpoints and police in Jerusalem and Ferguson as locations where land and life meet through the intensity of Euro-American colonial forces sharing resources and tactics to christen their New Semites.

The Latin root of "trans" means "across, beyond, or to go beyond." Transnational solidarity means to speak across or beyond the borders of nation-states and exclusionary nationalisms, and to stand firmly in the earth that binds the co-resistance work that is done across boundaries. It means to reach not only in between, but to go over and around the limits of colonial nation-states. From the anti-Semitic Warsaw ghettos under Nazism to the anti-Semitic ghettos of Gaza under Zionism, it means getting our hands dirty by digging tunnels underneath and blasting holes through the walls that marshal us into zones of being/nonbeing. Palestine solidarity work is a prime example of transnational solidarity. In learning from the transnational solidarity struggle to overcome juridical-political South African apartheid, Palestinians civil society has called on global citizens and societies to engage in Boycott, Divestment and Sanctions (BDS movement) against apartheid Israel. What is unique about Palestine solidarity work is that it fits the needs and desires of any locale, and adapts well to forming intersectional alliances in all places of the world. Whether one is a Marxist, an Islamist, or even a "good-hearted liberal," Palestine solidarity is ideologically adaptable to both single and multi-coalitional frameworks that choose local targets to boycott (companies, products, etc.), divest from (pension funds, university investments, etc.) or sanction (Israeli ambassadors, trade relations with Israel, etc.)—it clears the space needed for seeing the interrelated nature of such systems as the prison- and military-industrial complexes across the world. Practicing transnational solidarity produces critical frameworks to end the occupation of indigenous land from Turtle Island/Abya Yala to Palestine/Bilad al-Sham, and to smash materially linked networks of colonial occupation and racist apartheid on a local and global scale.

Challenging Epistemic Racism

One of the most important keys of decolonial resistance is challenging and going beyond epistemic racism. What does this mean? It means we need to be able to think and act in a way that goes beyond Eurocentrism in our approach to the ideologies and knowledges we employ in our struggles for justice. One way epistemic racism often shows up in social justice movements is in relation to the Westernized Left. That is, Leftists who attempt to put forward an anti-normative position, but in reality, end up providing what we might call "a Eurocentric critique of Eurocentrism." When I say "Westernized" I also refer to people of color who are Westoxicated, meaning they have internalized the Eurocentric hierarchies of the coloniality of power, especially in regard to knowledge systems. How do the problematics of the Westernized Left play out in our movements? Let's take the issue of political theory as a case study. For example, secular or atheist Communists often assume that the religious vs. secular binary (i.e., that secular = political and public, religion = apolitical and private) is a universal story for the world, when in fact, that framework cannot be applied so easily to non-European contexts. Latin American Catholic liberation movements, Islamists in Africa and Asia, Black liberation theologies in North America, and indigenous

Aymara activists in Latin America are examples of both Abrahamic and non-Abrahamic faith traditions that publicly put forward politics and systems of governance based on a non-Eurocentric knowledge tradition. They challenge the Eurocentricity of the Westernized Left, and show that there are a variety of ways to engage social justice struggle beyond the confines of Marxist fundamentalism. Of course, this doesn't mean that Socialists and Marxists do not deserve space or are "gentiles" that should be excommunicated. On the contrary, Marx himself was a Semite (his contemporaries called him a "Moor"!) who gave us a powerful tool to critique the coloniality of power and to include in a much larger tool box of liberation. Combatting epistemic racism (and sexism), for example, would ask us not only to interpret the politics and ethics of struggles through the lens of Michel Foucault, Karl Marx, and Jacques Derrida but also through that of Enrique Dussel, Ali Shariati, and Audre Lorde. Another mistake that the Westernized Left often makes is to think that the main problem we are dealing with is a clash of socioeconomic *classes*. This classical economic reductionism is problematic. What they fail to see is that we are not only dealing with a clashing of classes, but a much larger clash of *civilizations*, within which classes are included—economic, racial, gendered, and so forth. I would like to provocatively argue that Samuel Huntington's now infamous thesis was right—he was just on the wrong side! We *are* confronted with a continued civilizational war of the West over "the Rest" as demonstrated by the coloniality of power (and yes, the Rest can become Westernized too). In terms of how we may reconcile the problematics of Westernized Leftists, we must challenge the Westernized Left to allow space for dialogue among multiple critical approaches to struggle. Possible examples could include how the Islamic concepts of *jihad* or *tawhid*, the Jewish concept of *tikkun olam*, the Pan-African Bantu concept of *ubuntu*, or the Aymara concept of *pachamama* may also be interlocated within our tool boxes for building social justice movements. One success of the contemporary Black Lives Matter (BLM) movement is that it has combatted epistemic racism, sexism, and homo/transphobia from the very level of its leadership. BLM was founded and is led by three queer Black women, which comes as an intersectional critique of the "old boys' club" of Afro-American liberation movements in the past who did not take as seriously the voices of women, LGBTQI, or gender nonconforming folks. BLM includes these diverse voices and approaches to its framework, in addition to maintaining an internationalist and global vision of solidarity with movements in Palestine, Mexico, and indigenous communities elsewhere. Contemporary student movements in South Africa (known by the hashtags

#FeesMustFall and #RhodesMustFall) are another great example of decolonial resistance and intersectional struggle. These movements are seeking free education at the higher education level, the decolonization of knowledge and power in universities (in curriculum and in the removal of colonial symbols of power such as the Cecil Rhodes statue), undoing patriarchy and sexism, and maintaining solidarity with laborers within the university fighting for a more dignified wage. The South African student movements' nuanced and multi-faceted framework for approaching struggle sheds light on the urgent need for pluriversal approaches to struggle.

Pluriversal Struggle

The advantage of decolonial resistance is that it combats epistemic racism by taking non-Western theories and knowledges of liberation, economics, and development seriously. In doing so, the framework of pluriversality is born. A pluriversal framework urges us to move from "universal" notions of Justice, Democracy, and Human Rights to "pluriversal" notions of these concepts so as to fully integrate a multiplicity of non-Eurocentric standards for establishing sustainable human and ecological dignity. "Pluriversal" means that we allow a multitude to inform the way we relate to each other. We allow for a pluralistic expression of political ideology and social organizing approaches while still being committed to points of unity. A pluriversal approach means that Muslims can fight for a decolonial caliphate while indigenous Bolivian activists fight for a decolonial democracy. A pluriversal approach means that Islamic feminism, Black womanism, and *mujerista* approaches to gender justice be considered legitimate in their own right, and can be in critical dialogue with white feminism. A pluriversal approach means being able to hold a critical dialogue between the UN Universal Declaration of Human Rights and the conceptions of human rights and dignity that challenge that charter, such as those from an Islamic liberation theology perspective or Pan-Africanist conceptualization. Pluriversality allows, as the Zapatista slogan goes, that we fight "for a world with space for many worlds." Thus, the binary of the zone of being/nonbeing is shattered, and we are able to build a new humanity and ecology between North and South, East and West, First and Third Worlds on more dignified and liberating terms.

Conclusion: Let the Semites End the World!

Lastly, and again, the world must end. Not because we adore violence or seek to make universal the truth of the wretched of the earth. The world must end because there are no other options at this point. The Semites of the world are sick and tired of hell. The veil has made us blind toward nonbeing, choked into not breathing and confused as to whom it is that snuck on the white masks in the first place. The civilizational war we face by the West-over-the-Rest complex has sowed the seeds of extremism among our Semitic kin, and they—that is the fundamentalists of all stripes from our ranks who are problematic but not *the* problem—are in need of alternative guidance. The cycle of the world will continue to spit us out raw if we simply copy what the master has taught his slaves—we must not seek to do to the world what the world has done to us. Our ancestors—who refused to die in hell twice and fought for us to breathe another generation—have left us with the tools for intersectional strategizing and pluriversal horizons. To become disenchanted with the world, to de-link from the coloniality of power, and to embody the frameworks of decolonial resistance are tools that allow for thinking and doing otherwise. We have the right to unveil by any means necessary, but only so that we do not re-create the zone of nonbeing. Destroying the world is an act of restorative justice. And rebuilding another is ultimately a process of revolutionary love—how else must the previously silenced teach our children that time reveals shadows, and shadows are never silent in times of war? Let the Semites unite, and let us fight to end the world!

Building toward the Next World

Rabbi Alissa Wise

Redemption is the quintessential Jewish project. Secular Jews may find it in socialism, Orthodox Jews have it in the concept of the *moshiach* (messiah), liberal Jews speak of *tikkun olam*—healing the world. Still others might find it in moments of connection and courage. The Jewish concept of *olam ha'bah* (literally, "the world to come") is often understood as the next world, a messianic future at the end of days, a world of possibility and of justice. *Olam ha'zeh* (literally, "this world") where we reside, has been left unfinished and imperfect, and is a place of need, fear, shame, distraction, and defeat. Our work while we are alive and able is to build bridges from *olam ha'zeh* to *olam ha'bah*. This book is a bridge-building project.

Talking about antisemitism isn't easy. We at JVP dragged our feet on taking up this project in large part because it felt too fraught and frustrating. Fraught because defining antisemitism elicits strong feelings and multiple analyses that felt daunting to reconcile with one another. Frustrating because while we always address the isolated incidents of real antisemitism when they do arise in our movement, we need to focus on strategies for ending the occupation that more urgently need our attention. We put it off for too long. The antisemitism of the white supremacist far right has become closer to power through the Trump campaign/administration, defended by some Jewish pro-Israel advocates because of their Zionist stances. In the meantime, as so many of the contributors describe in detail, pro-Israel advocates have redoubled their efforts to deflect responsibility to ensure Palestinians have basic rights by lobbing accusations of antisemitism and even attempting to push legislation that would define critique of Israel to be antisemitic. Ultimately, we realized that we were leaving our movement partners in the lurch through our reluctance to tackle this question. And being part of a movement means doing what is needed by the collective, not just what is comfortable for us. This is part of building those bridges to *olam ha'bah*.

The truth is that everyone who organizes for justice in Palestine must wrestle with antisemitism, either because a false accusation is being lobbed at them, or because of a need to be vigilant to ensure that critique of the Jewish state doesn't become blanket criticism of Jewish people. It is the deliberate strategy of pro-Israel advocates to blur the lines between justified critique of Israel's oppressive policies and hatred of Jews. This intentional blurring leaves us all confused—and vulnerable.

For over a decade JVP has been partnering with churches as they seek to align their values (*olam ha'bah*) with their investments (*olam ha'zeh*) by divesting from companies profiting from the Israeli occupation. As I've built relationships with these interfaith partners, I have been asked countless times: "How do I deflect accusations that I am antisemitic?" I always respond: "Well, are you?" While there is nothing inherently antisemitic in critiquing Israel, that does not mean one isn't also harboring antisemitic sentiments toward Jews or isn't behaving in antisemitic ways.

Just as I challenge Christian and other partners to interrogate the antisemitism they may harbor, white Jewish Americans must ask ourselves how we benefit from and act in ways that support white supremacy. Similarly, all Jews must look at how support for Israel, defended by fear of antisemitism, legitimates dispossession of Palestinians. Unfortunately, such thoughtful self-reflection (an *olam ha'bah* activity) rarely gets our attention as we are busy addressing antisemitism as a red herring.

Taken together, these essays reflect widespread pain and frustration about accusations of antisemitism. In the essays by the Jewish contributors, I can hear the sadness wrought by the blacklisting, slander, and ridicule they have been subject to by the mainstream Jewish world. From writers outside the Jewish community, I hear a longing to be able just to speak their minds and hearts and be heard. All too often the real issues of life, death, suffering, human rights, and democracy never even get debated. Shaul Magid argues in his piece that the accusation of antisemitism is "often a tool of control that emerges when one form of Jewish identity become hegemonic and thus deems all others a threat to the Jews." It is downright traumatic for many Jews when they are evicted by their fellow Jews from synagogues, Hillels, and other Jewish community spaces. Those who believe the project of Israel requires the continued subjugation and suffering of Palestinians want to deem the outcry by the subjugated and their supporters the offense. By crying foul and linking critique of the state to hate speech, they all too often succeed in deflecting from their actual complicity in and commission of a decade of massive, national-level crimes.

The essays collected here reflect well the multiplicity of perspectives and experiences in our movement. This movement is rooted in a shared commitment to justice for all people, which includes fighting antisemitism alongside all systems of oppression. This book is the first meditation on antisemitism to include the voices of Muslim and Christian Palestinians as well as Jewish and Christian African Americans, all of which bring critical perspectives on power, supremacy, and tribalism. The contributors articulate unapologetically the often invisible ways the pro-occupation right wields accusations of antisemitism. While it makes sense for us as Jewish Voice for Peace to initiate this exploration of antisemitism, our study would be incomplete without the voices outside of the Jewish community so often silenced. My own understanding of antisemitism has deepened through seeing how my partners and colleagues have been hurt by antisemitism. Their struggles for recognition and liberation are stymied by the relentless privileging of antisemitism in debates about Israel/Palestine over and above racism and Islamophobia.

So many of the writers contribute to demystifying the strategies used by those who wish to silence dissent and critique of Israel, particularly on college campuses. JVP's campus coordinator, Ben Lorber, sums up the problem well in his piece: "The cruel and tragic irony of the situation is clear—in conjuring the specter of antisemitism, opposition groups weaponize the real and painful legacy of anti-Jewish persecution, and use it to bludgeon into submission the struggles of marginalized communities in our own time." Similarly, Orian Zakai, a member of JVP's Academic Advisory Council, writes about how challenging it is for her as a Jewish Israeli to critique Israel in large part because the landmines on American campuses are so illogical, having more to do with campus politics than with the realities of Israel/Palestine. With exasperation she describes the intellectual and ethical sacrifices she is being asked to make, ones that JVP is all too familiar with: refusing to acknowledge the power differentials at play and insisting there are two symmetrical sides. Her conclusion packs a wallop: "My work as a teacher should be harder than that." So it should.

These political maneuvers of course extend beyond the campus environment. In church settings a similar type of manipulation is used, aided by many liberal Christians' guilt for the church's complicity in fomenting anti-Jewish hatred for centuries. In the lead up to three successive Presbyterian General Assemblies where the issue of divestment from the Israeli occupation was being debated, Jewish pro-Israel advocates have threatened to cut ties with their Presbyterian colleagues if they voted in favor of divestment, claiming a vote for divestment was an antisemitic act. In 2014 the Reform movement's leader, Rabbi Rick Jacobs, went as far as to offer the leaders of the Presbyterian church a meeting with Benjamin Netanyahu if they voted down divestment, a move that was met with anger and resentment by Presbyterians who understood this as an attempt to silence them. Similarly, in the halls of Congress and state legislatures we see a serious dumbing down of the debate to the point where a call for "balance" becomes indifference to Palestinian suffering. Throughout the 2015–16 legislative season, over a dozen bills moved through state legislatures that prohibit state contractors to boycott companies profiting from Israeli occupation, likening those boycotts to "antisemitic ideology." These efforts are meant to intimidate those who advocate for BDS as a nonviolent way to pressure Israel to change, the result being an endorsement of a nearly fifty-year brutal occupation with no end in sight. Thanks to the great work these essays have done exposing the mechanisms of how pro-occupation advocates wield antisemitism to quash activism for justice, we are better able to interrupt them. In fact, we have an obligation to do so because we understand better how the false accusations work, and what actual anti-Jewish sentiment and behavior look like. With this new understanding we can develop smart, effective strategies to address true antisemitism and sort through the propaganda, making space for creative solutions, building bridges from *olam ha'zeh* to *olam ha'bah*.

Of course none of this work is possible without understanding that our vision for liberation has to be intersectional and collaborative. All of our contributors approach their exploration of antisemitism with an understanding that it does not operate in a vacuum. This reminds us that our strategies for liberation must likewise be multiracial, collaborative, mutually dependent. Failure to do so leads to devastating consequences for Palestinians and other people of color, including Jews of color, living under Israeli rule. When all the Jewish community sees is antisemitism, racist and supremacist attitudes are given free range and urgent civil rights struggles—such as the Movement for Black Lives are sidelined or even undermined. We are also challenged by Chanda Prescod-Weinstein's reminder that to support Israel's existence in its current form is to hold that supremacy, religious or racial, is sometimes acceptable, leaving us susceptible to supporting and maintaining white supremacy in this country.

While the contributors have various perspectives on how antisemitism functions, they all share a commitment to combatting antisemitism as part of our work to challenge all forms of oppression. Our hope is that this book will serve to transform the conversation about antisemitism and the struggle for a just peace in Israel/Palestine. I hope you will be emboldened by the perspectives of not just Jews, but Christians, Muslims, Palestinians, and other people of color weighing in on a topic that many in the Jewish world wish to remain verboten to non-Jews. We hope that this type of exploration, employing a holistic assessment from all those affected by a particular oppression—not just those targeted by that oppression—can be a useful model for cultivating solidarity for all struggles. This approach reveals how we are all impacted by oppression, and the depth of understanding we can glean allows us to make smarter choices for our organizing.

This book is a snapshot of a moment in time. For those of us who feel berated by false accusation of antisemitism and are confused on how to fight actual antisemitism, the struggle can feel eternal, but it is not. Jewish history—indeed, all histories—are dynamic. My understanding of the ebbs and flows of openness and insularity in Jewish history leaves me confident that the American Jewish community will become more receptive to the idea that justice means all of us. We can see evidence of that shift even as I write, as the generational divide on this issue in the American Jewish community grows wider by the second. While we may choose to harken back to some other time in Jewish history to figure out what to do today, we don't have to, as meaningful and grounding as that practice may be. We can look to Torah, Talmud, the Bund, or Matzpen for guidance, but these essays remind us we must also look outside the Jewish community.[1] Understanding antisemitism in the United States today is simply incomplete without the reflections from our Christian, Muslim, and other partners. Likewise, we must dig deeper within, challenging ourselves to interrogate how we have blind spots in our analyses and understandings. Of course we must also vision forward toward *olam ha'bah*. Let the testimonies and teachings of this book remind us we are a part of history—it is not happening to us. We can reach *olam ha'bah* even as we sit in *olam ha'zeh*.

This book holds up a mirror to the American debate on Israel/Palestine, and the challenge to us now is not to look away. How do we reveal that fighting antisemitism is not a replacement for working to end the subjugation of millions of Palestinians? How do we engage with the real history of antisemitism and work to end its current manifestations without falsely privileging it? How do we realize *olam ha'bah*?

Ranking oppressions in a way that obscures their relationships and urgency is the stuff of *olam ha'zeh*. Likewise, McCarthyite policies that divide communities, like those of Hillels on campuses, are short-sighted and ill-conceived strategies of those stuck in *olam ha'zeh*. False accusations of anti-semitism that distract from real manifestations of anti-Jewish persecution are classic *olam ha'zeh* strategies. But, refusing what's easy and pushing past our comfort zones is the work toward *olam ha'bah*. Forming diverse coalitions to struggle against all forms of oppression, including antisemitism, is *olam ha'bah*. The decades-long organizing to end the Israeli occupation, ensure equal rights for all citizens of Israel, and realize the right of return for Palestinian refugees—that is *olam ha'bah* in *olam ha'zeh*.

I believe *olam ha'bah* is possible in *olam ha'zeh*—what divides them is an ethical border, not a temporal one. One moment on top of the other, that is how we will reach *olam ha'bah*. Each moment we choose Other over self is a moment when we cross the ethical border between the two worlds. When we are in *olam ha'bah*, it is only and always together. Let's go.

Appendix I:
JVP Statements on Antisemitism

#1: JVP's Understanding of Antisemitism in the United States

Jewish Voice for Peace is dedicated to working toward justice, dignity, and equality for all people, and to actively opposing all forms of oppression. Fighting antisemitism is an important part of our work for a more just world.

As a community rooted in Jewish traditions, we understand antisemitism as discrimination against, violence towards, or stereotypes of Jews for being Jewish. Antisemitism has manifested itself in structural inequality, dispossession, expulsion, and genocide, with the most well-known examples being in Europe with the Spanish Inquisition, the expulsion of Jews from Spain in 1492, and the Nazi Holocaust in the 1940s. Antisemitism does not impact all of us who identify as Jewish in the same way. The experiences and histories of Jews of color and/or Sephardi/Mizrahi Jews are distinct from those of white, Ashkenazi Jews.[1] Jewish communities around the world have had different experiences with discrimination, bigotry, and violence. In this statement, we will be focusing on two forms of antisemitism that resonate in the United States today: Christian antisemitism and racial antisemitism.

Christian hegemony—the fact that Christian values and beliefs dominate US culture in everyday and pervasive ways—impacts all religious minorities in the United States.[2] Despite the many liberation theologies that can and do inspire Christian communities to work towards justice for all people, there are some denominations of Christianity in the United States that use antisemitic religious interpretations of Christian scripture. These interpretations treat Judaism as inferior to Christianity, or cast blame on "the Jews" for the death of Jesus.[3] Additionally, we see the theology of Christian Zionism, which encourages Jewish return to Israel as a means to achieve Christian redemption, as similarly founded on antisemitic interpretations of scripture.

Racial antisemitism, and the term "antisemitism" itself, developed alongside pseudo-scientific theories of race in nineteenth-century Europe. These theories identified and classified different categories of people, then placed them in a racial hierarchy. This racist logic still echoes in US white supremacist, "alt-right," and neo-Nazi circles, which have moved from the fringes to the mainstream since the election of Donald Trump. At various points in history, this form of antisemitism has had secular institutional and governmental support, reaching its apex in the mass violence against Jews and other groups during the Nazi Holocaust. In the United States today, even as the Trump administration emboldens and empowers antisemitism in the form of incidents of bigotry, violence, or speech, it is not currently reinforced by state institutions in the same ways that racism, anti-immigrant prejudice, and anti-Muslim bigotry are through state violence, mass incarceration, and surveillance. We commit to fighting racism, Islamophobia, and antisemitism—we all need to be vigilant as we expect these forms of bigotry and oppression to gain greater intensity in the coming years.

Historically, European Jewish immigrants to the United States were marginalized along with many other immigrant groups, but have largely been racialized as white over time.[4] In the United States, many Jewish institutions focus on white Ashkenazi history when discussing antisemitism, ignoring the histories of Mizrahi/Sephardi Jews and the existence of Ashkenazi Jews of color. Those of us who are white Ashkenazi Jews have a responsibility as white people who benefit from white privilege to challenge and disrupt white supremacy and systematic racism, notwithstanding our histories and experiences with antisemitism.

Contemporary expressions of antisemitism include treating Jewish people as a monolithic group, stereotyping Jewish people as rich or greedy, and demonizing Jews as all-powerful or as secretly in control of political events.[5] These tropes are evident when the United States is exempted from responsibility for its unconditional support of Israeli apartheid, and instead the US-Israel relationship is blamed solely on Jewish power. The white nationalists known as the "alt-right," for example, staunchly support Israel even as they disseminate and perpetuate antisemitic myths of Jewish control and power.[6]

Antisemitism does not operate in a vacuum; we must fight it along with Islamophobia, sexism, classism, and homophobia, as well as anti-Arab, anti-Black, and other forms of racism, as part of the work of dismantling all systems of oppression. JVP is committed to challenging Ashkenazi dominance and racism as we oppose antisemitism and Islamophobia. The just world we seek depends on it.

#2: Inaccurate and Misleading Definitions of Antisemitism

As we fight antisemitism, we must also examine how inaccurate, misleading, or problematic definitions of antisemitism have a harmful impact on movements for justice. We see these harmful definitions most often in attempts to defend Israeli policies, in anti-Muslim rhetoric and policies, and sometimes even in progressive movements.

Definitions of antisemitism that treat criticism of Israel or of Zionism as inherently antisemitic are inaccurate and harmful. The majority of Jews are not Israeli, and not all citizens of Israel are Jewish. Israel is a state; Zionism is a political ideology; Judaism and Jewish identity encompass a diversity of religious and secular expressions and a robust, varied set of traditions, cultures, and lived experiences. The misplaced focus of those who demonize Palestinian rights advocacy while ignoring or defending the antisemitism of white supremacists dilutes the understanding of antisemitism and makes it ever more difficult to fight.

JVP's criticism of Israeli policies comes from a desire to see justice realized for all peoples in the region. For many of us, such criticism is rooted in our Jewish values and traditions. While it is antisemitic to criticize the State of Israel solely on the basis of the Jewish identity of most Israeli citizens or leaders, criticism of the Israeli state that is based on its past and present actions is not antisemitic. Likewise, advocating for justice for Palestinians, including recognizing their right of return, is not antisemitic. Israel should be held accountable for its discriminatory policies, which systematically deny Palestinians, and to varying degrees Mizrahi, Sephardi, and Ethiopian Jews, access to equal treatment and human rights.

We are also concerned by definitions of antisemitism that posit that Jewish people are perpetually victims, or that antisemitism is a cyclical or permanently recurring feature of human society. These definitions of antisemitism often function to divert attention from the power and privilege that some Jews exercise, either as beneficiaries of white privilege or as Jewish citizens of Israel, where Jewish people are privileged at the expense of non-Jews. These definitions of antisemitism have three kinds of effects that harm movements for justice: they single out antisemitism as an exceptional form of bigotry; they reinforce a narrative of perpetual victimhood; and they equate antisemitic microaggressions with structural inequality.[7] It is essential for progressive movements to include analysis about Israel as we fight antisemitism. The campaign and election of Donald Trump have clarified the ways one can be a committed Zionist and a staunch antisemite. We are alarmed by the growing power of antisemitic, racist white nationalists. Nevertheless, we recognize that the policies of the Trump administration will most likely impact Muslim Americans and people of color the hardest.

Those seeking to maintain the status quo in Israel/Palestine routinely use false charges of antisemitism, and harmful and inaccurate definitions of antisemitism, in an attempt to silence voices critical of Israeli policies towards Palestinians.[8] No one should underestimate the power of an accusation of antisemitism, and when false charges of antisemitism are used to deflect Israel's responsibility for the dispossession of Palestinians, they should be recognized as censorship. At the same time, supporters of Palestinian rights are not immune from racist, sexist, and/or antisemitic behavior, and this behavior must be addressed when it occurs. Likewise, one can be antisemitic or condone antisemitism and emphatically support the far-right government of Israel.

There is a disturbing trend of incidents of antisemitism being blamed on Muslims and/or Arabs, despite a lack of evidence to support those accusations. This gives antisemites, most often white supremacists, a free pass to vent their bigotry and racism while harming people who are particularly vulnerable to discrimination in our society. The "alt-right" feeds off this dynamic, which is a major failure of the institutional Jewish community. We've also seen examples where anti-Muslim stereotypes about Muslim antisemitism manifest in cases of entrapment by law enforcement and promote a harmful false narrative of a clash between Jews and Muslims. These false charges do a disservice to the fight against antisemitism, have extremely harmful effects on Muslim and/or Arab communities, and serve as a way to suppress the struggle for equality and freedom for all people.

At JVP, we have seen how false accusations of antisemitism have muddied the understanding of antisemitism in all areas of our work. We hope these statements will strengthen the movement for justice in Palestine in the United States by clarifying the difference between expressions of antisemitism and support for Palestinian human rights. Given that the current political moment is rapidly shifting, we will continue to be vigilant to understand and name antisemitism in relation to all forms of oppression. Our own commitment to fighting all forms of oppression grounds our organizing for justice for all people.

Addendum: The original version of this statement was written in the first half of 2016. In November 2016, in the wake of Donald Trump's election and appointment of staff and advisors with deep roots in white nationalist and antisemitic movements, we have revised this statement to reflect how white nationalism in the United States has now been galvanized by its proximity to power and is an indicator of institutional support for antisemitism, along with Islamophobia, misogyny, homophobia, and racism. You can find the most updated version at jvp.org/antisemitism.

Appendix II:
Discussion Guide
and Additional Readings

Questions for Discussion

1. Where do the various working definitions of antisemitism used by authors in this volume agree and disagree? What are the political implications of those agreements, disagreements, or contradictions? Do you agree with some authors more than others? Why?

2. How can the analyses provided by authors in this book help us build a stronger movement for justice?

3. What tools do these readings provide to identify and challenge antisemitism when it occurs? What tools do they provide to identify and challenge false charges of antisemitism?

4. What are some assumptions about antisemitism that you had prior to reading this book? Which of those were challenged, if any?

5. Does antisemitism show up in your own life and political work? How and where?

6. Do false charges of antisemitism show up in your life and political work? How and where?

7. How do false charges of antisemitism negatively affect progressive activism? How can we push back against those false charges?

8. How did this book complement or challenge your understanding of Israel/Palestine? What was new for you and what do you still have questions about?

9. What analyses or perspectives were missing from this book? What do you wish had been included?

10. Many pieces in the book take on antisemitism in conjunction with racism and Islamophobia. How does antisemitism relate to and intersect with other forms of bigotry and discrimination?

11. Many argue that Zionism arose as a response to European anti-semitism. What role does Zionism play in different pieces in the book?

12. How do these authors distinguish between antisemitism and anti-Zionism? What questions do you have about the differences?

13. As many authors in this volume point out, antisemitism is often misused. Have you seen examples of antisemitism invoked to further an Islamophobic message or policy? To defer responsibility for benefiting from white privilege? To censor criticism of Israel?

Additional Readings

This is not intended as a complete list. We do not necessarily agree with or endorse all readings listed here, but we do see them as important to discussions of antisemitism.

On the Definition of Antisemitism

Beller, Steven. *Antisemitism: A Very Short Introduction*. New York: Oxford University Press, 2007.

Berger, David. "Antisemitism: An Overview." In *History and Hate: The Dimensions of Antisemitism*, edited by David Berger, 3–14. Philadelphia: Jewish Publication Society, 1986.

Engel, David. "Away from a Definition of Antisemitism: An Essay in the Semantics of Historical Description." In *Rethinking European Jewish History*, edited by Jeremy Cohen and Moshe Rosman, 30–53. Oxford: Littman Library of Jewish Civilization, 2009.

Halperin, Ben. "What Is Antisemitism?" *Modern Judaism* 1 (1981): 251–62.

Langmuir, Gavin. *History, Religion, and Antisemitism*. Berkeley: University of California Press, 1990.

———. *Toward a Definition of Antisemitism*. Los Angeles and Berkeley: University of California Press, 1996

Zimmerman, Moshe. *Wilhelm Marr: The Patriarch of Anti-Semitism*. New York: Oxford University Press, 1986.

On Histories of and Experiences with Antisemitism

Biale, David. *Power and Powerlessness in Jewish History*. New York: Schocken Books, 1986.

Kivel, Paul. *Living in the Shadow of the Cross: Understanding and Resisting the Power and Privilege of Christian Hegemony*. Vancouver: New Society Publishers, 2013.

Lerner, Michael. *The Socialism of Fools: Anti-Semitism on the Left*. Oakland: Tikkun Books, 1992.

Lester, Julius. "A Report on Black Anti-Semitism." *Jewish Currents* (1992).

Levins Morales, Aurora. "Latin@s, Israel and Palestine: Understanding Anti-Semitism." March 15, 2012, www.auroralevinsmorales.com/blog/latins-israel-and-palestine-understanding-anti-semitism.

Nelson, Jack. *Terror in the Night: The Klan's Campaign against the Jews*. New York: Simon & Schuster, 1993.

Oppenheimer, Yochai. "The Holocaust: A Mizrahi Perspective." *Hebrew Studies* 51 (2010): 303–28.

Pulzer, Peter G. J. *The Rise of Political Anti-Semitism in Germany and Austria*. Cambridge: Harvard University Press, 1964.

Rosenwasser, Penny. *Hope into Practice: Jewish Women Choosing Justice Despite Our Fears*. San Bernardino, CA: Penny Rosenwasser, 2013.

On Race, Racism, and Judaism

Adams, Maurianne, and John H. Bracey. *Strangers & Neighbors: Relations between Blacks & Jews in the United States*. Amherst: University of Massachusetts Press, 1999.

Alexander, Michelle. *The New Jim Crow*. New York: The New Press, 2010.

Arsenault, Raymond. *Freedom Riders: 1961 and the Struggle for Racial Justice*. Oxford: Oxford University Press, 2006.

Baldwin, James, and Nat Hentoff. *Black Anti-Semitism and Jewish Racism*. New York: R.W. Baron, 1969.

Ball, Howard. *Murder in Mississippi: United States v. Price and the Struggle for Civil Rights*. Lawrence: University of Kansas Press, 2004.

Bashkin, Orit. *The New Babylonians: A History of Jews in Modern Iraq*. Palo Alto: Stanford University Press, 2012.

Bauman, Mark K., and Berkley Kalin. *The Quiet Voices: Southern Rabbis and Black Civil Rights, 1880s to 1990s*. Tuscaloosa: University of Alabama, 1997.

Brodkin, Karen. *How Jews Became White Folks and What That Says about Race in America*. New Brunswick, NJ: Rutgers University Press, 1998.

Chetrit, Sami. "Mizrahi Politics in Israel: Between Integration and Alternative." *Journal of Palestine Studies* 29, no. 4 (2000): 51–65.

Davis, Kristian Bailey. "Black-Palestinian Solidarity in the Ferguson-Gaza Era." *American Quarterly* 67, no. 4 (2015): 1017–26.

Diner, Hasia R. *In the Almost Promised Land: American Jews and Blacks, 1915–1935*. Westport: Greenwood Press, 1977.

Forman, Seth. *Blacks in the Jewish Mind: A Crisis of Liberalism*. New York: New York University Press, 1998.

Goldstein, Eric. *The Price of Whiteness: Jews, Race, and American Identity*. Princeton: Princeton University Press, 2008.

Greenberg, Cheryl Lynn. *Troubling the Waters: Black-Jewish Relations in the American Century*. Princeton: Princeton University Press, 2006.

Kaye-Kantrowitz, Melanie. *The Colors of Jews: Racial Politics and Radical Diasporism*. Bloomington: Indiana University Press, 2007.

Khazzoom, Loolwa, ed. *The Flying Camel: Essays on Identity by Women of North African and Middle Eastern Jewish Heritage*. New York: Seal Press, 2003.

Lavie, Smadar. "Blow-ups in the Borderzones: Third World Israeli Authors' Gropings for Home." *New Formations* 18 (1992): 84–106.

———. *Wrapped in the Flag of Israel: Mizrahi Single Mothers and Bureaucratic Torture*. New York: Berghahn Books, 2014.

Shohat, Ella. "Sephardim in Israel: Zionism from the Standpoint of Its Jewish Victims." *Social Text* 19/20 (1988): 1–35.

———. "The Invention of the Mizrahim." *Journal of Palestine Studies* 29, no. 1 (Autumn 1999): 5–20.

Sundquist, Eric J. *Strangers in the Land: Blacks, Jews, Post-Holocaust America*. Cambridge, MA: Belknap of Harvard University Press, 2005.

Tobin, Diane, Gary A. Tobin, and Scott Rubin. *In Every Tongue: The Racial & Ethnic Diversity of the Jewish People.* San Francisco, CA: Institute for Jewish & Community Research, 2005.

Tsoffar, Ruth. "'A Land that Devours Its People': Mizrahi Writing from the Gut." *Body and Society* 12 (2006): 25–55.

On Israel/Palestine

Abunimah, Ali. *The Battle for Justice in Palestine.* Chicago: Haymarket Books, 2014.

Barghouti, Omar. *Boycott, Divestment, Sanctions: The Global Struggle for Palestinian Rights.* Chicago: Haymarket Books, 2011.

Bennis, Phyllis. *Understanding the Palestinian-Israeli Conflict: A Primer.* New York: Olive Branch Press, 2015.

Gorenberg, Gershom. *The Accidental Empire: Israel and the Birth of the Settlements, 1967–1977.* New York: Owl Books, 2007.

Hochberg, Gil. *In Spite of Partition: Jews, Arabs and the Limits of Separatist Imagination.* Princeton: Princeton University Press, 2007.

Khalidi, Rashid. *Palestinian Identity: The Construction of Modern National Consciousness.* New York: Columbia University Press, 2009.

Lynd, Staughton, Alice Lynd, and Sam Bahour. *Homeland: Oral Histories of Palestine and Palestinians.* Northampton, MA: Interlink Publishing Group, 1994.

Pappé, Ilan. *The Ethnic Cleansing of Palestine.* New York: OneWorld Publications, 2007.

Sacco, Joe. *Palestine.* New York: Fantagraphics Books, 2001.

Said, Edward. *The Question of Palestine.* New York: Vintage, 1992.

On Islamophobia and Orientalism

Bulkin, Elly, and Donna Nevel. *Islamophobia and Israel.* New York: Route Books, 2014.

Bunzl, Matti. *Anti-Semitism and Islamophobia: Hatreds Old and New in Europe.* Boston: Prickly Paradigm Press, 2007.

Ghosh, Amitav. *In an Antique Land.* New York: Knopf, 1992.

Kalmar, Ivan Davidson, and Derek J. Penslar, eds. *Orientalism and the Jews.* Waltham, MA: Brandeis University Press, 2005.

Kumar, Deepa. *Islamophobia and the Politics of Empire.* Chicago: Haymarket Books, 2012.

Magid, Shaul. "Islamaphobia, Antisemitism, the Holocaust, and a 'New' Jewish Culture." *Zeek*, August 20, 2010.

Said, Edward. *Orientalism.* New York: Pantheon Books, 1978.

On Zionism

Boyarin, Daniel. *Unheroic Conduct: The Rise of Heterosexuality and the Invention of the Jewish Man.* Berkeley: University of California Press, 1997.

Butler, Judith. *Parting Ways: Jewishness and the Critique of Zionism.* New York: Columbia University Press, 2012.

Rosen, Brant. *Wrestling in the Daylight: A Rabbi's Path of Palestinian Solidarity.* New York: Just World Books, 2012.

Said, Edward. "Zionism from the Standpoint of Its Victims." *Social Text* 1 (1979): 7–58.

Contributors

Alexander Abbasi is a Calistinian (Palestinian + Californian) born and raised in Los Angeles, Khaliphaztlán. He is currently a PhD candidate in religion studies at the University of Johannesburg, South Africa, where he focuses on Islamic liberation theology and decolonial theory, and is somewhere between an academic in activist clothing and an activist in academic clothing.

Omar Barghouti is a Palestinian human rights defender and co-founder of the Palestinian-led BDS movement. He holds bachelor's and master's degrees in electrical engineering from Columbia University in New York City, and a master's in philosophy (ethics) from Tel Aviv University. He is the author of *BDS: The Global Struggle for Palestinian Rights* (Haymarket Books, 2011).

Tallie Ben Daniel is the Academic Advisory Council coordinator for Jewish Voice for Peace. She completed her PhD in cultural studies from the University of California, Davis, in 2014. She is currently working on a book titled *Gay Capital: San Francisco, Tel Aviv and the Politics of Settler Colonialism.*

Rachel Ida Buff is co-coordinator and a founding member of Milwaukee Jewish Voice for Peace. She teaches history and comparative ethnic studies at the University of Wisconsin–Milwaukee. Her book, *Against the Deportation Terror*, will appear in 2017; she is also completing a novel. She blogs on politics and other stuff at atlasofadifficult.wordpress.com.

Judith Butler is Maxine Elliot Professor in the Department of Comparative Literature and the Program of Critical Theory at the University of California, Berkeley. She is also active in gender and sexual politics and human rights, antiwar politics, and serves on the Advisory Board of Jewish Voice for Peace.

Ilise Benshushan Cohen is a Sephardic-Mizrahi Jewish scholar, teacher, activist, and mom. An Atlanta native, she leads JVP-Atlanta and is a member of the Jews of Color/Mizrahi and Sephardi Caucus. She is an IFPB (Interfaith Peace-Builders) delegation leader, board member, and former chair. She is committed to justice for Palestinians, decolonization, and building authentic community.

Walt Davis is a Presbyterian minister and professor emeritus of the Sociology of Religion at San Francisco Theological Seminary. He holds an MDiv degree in theology from Union Theological Seminary and a PhD in social ethics from Boston University. From 2008 to 2014 he was chair of the education committee of the Israel-Palestine Mission Network of the Presbyterian Church (USA).

Arthur Goldwag is the author of *The Beliefnet Guide to Kabbalah, Isms & Ologies, Cults, Conspiracies, and Secret Societies*, and, most recently, *The New Hate: A History of Fear and Loathing on the Populist Right*. His political commentary has appeared in *Salon*, the *Atlantic, Boing Boing*, the *Chicago Tribune*, the *Washington Spectator*, the SPLC's *Hatewatch* blog and *Intelligence Report*, and the *New York Times*.

Rev. Graylan Hagler has served as the senior minister of Plymouth Congregational United Church of Christ, Washington, DC, since 1992. He is also the executive director of Faith Strategies, an organizing body and think tank of clergy in operation since 2012 that advises labor, social, and political campaigns on ways to embrace and engage faith communities in movements and campaigns. Under his leadership, Plymouth Congregational United Church of Christ has become the focal point of organizing and a solidarity center with progressive causes in the Washington, DC, community and around the world. He traveled with a delegation of Black cultural artists and activists to the West Bank in 2014. The last time he was in Israel/Palestine was 1974; a forty-year gap between experiences.

Dima Khalidi is the founder and director of Palestine Legal and cooperating counsel with the Center for Constitutional Rights. Founded in 2012, Palestine Legal is the only legal organization in the United States exclusively dedicated to supporting the movement for Palestinian rights.

Antony Lerman is Senior Fellow at the Bruno Kreisky Forum for International Dialogue, Vienna, and Honorary Fellow at the Parkes Institute for the Study of Jewish/Non-Jewish Relations, Southampton University. He was founding editor of *Antisemitism World Report* from 1992 to 1998 and is associate editor of the international academic journal *Patterns of Prejudice.*

 Aurora Levins Morales is a Puerto Rican Ashkenazi Jewish feminist writer and is a sixth-generation radical. She has been part of many social justice movements, including the women's movement of the 1960s–70s, the Puerto Rican independence movement, and movements for Latin America solidarity, environmental justice, disability justice, and Middle East peace and justice. She was a member of New Jewish Agenda, and has been a member of Jewish Voice for Peace since soon after it was founded. She is active in the JVP Artists Council and Jews of Color in Solidarity with Palestine, which works in close collaboration with JVP. She worked as an elder and poet in residence with Jews for Racial and Economic Justice in New York City in 2015–16. She can be reached at www.auroralevinsmorales.com.

 Ben Lorber works as campus coordinator with Jewish Voice for Peace, supporting student activists across the country in their movement for justice in Israel/Palestine. He has written for a variety of online and print publications, and has also organized in the labor and migrant justice movements. He lives in Chicago, Illinois.

 Shaul Magid is the Jay and Jeanie Schottenstein Professor of Jewish Studies, Kogod Senior Research Fellow at the Shalom Hartman Institute of North America, and rabbi of the Fire Island Synagogue in Seaview, New York. He is not a member of JVP and does not support BDS.

 Donna Nevel is a community psychologist and educator as well as a coordinator of PARCEO, a participatory action research center. She has been an organizer for justice in Palestine, against Islamophobia and anti-Arab racism, and for justice in public education.

 Dr. Chanda Prescod-Weinstein is a researcher in theoretical physics. Of Afro-Caribbean and Ashkenazi Jewish heritage, Dr. Prescod-Weinstein is the child and grandchild of Palestine solidarity activists. She first began to confront the problem of Israel and the exclusion of Black Jews in conversations about Zionism and American Judaism when, early in her time at university, the Second Intifada began. Dr. Prescod-Weinstein is a proud member of the Jewish Voice for Peace Academic Advisory Council.

Rabbi Brant Rosen is the Midwestern Regional Director of the American Friends Service Committee and the rabbi of the congregation Tzedek Chicago. He is the cofounder of the Jewish Voice for Peace Rabbinical Council and the author of the book *Wrestling in the Daylight: A Rabbi's Path to Palestinian Solidarity*, published in 2012 by Just World Books.

Linda Sarsour is the executive director of the Arab American Association of New York and cofounder of the first Muslim online organizing platform, MPOWER Change. A Palestinian Muslim American woman, racial justice and civil rights activist, and mother of three, she has been at the forefront of major civil rights campaigns including calling for an end to unwarranted surveillance of New York's Muslim communities and ending police policies like stop and frisk.

Rebecca Vilkomerson is the executive director of Jewish Voice for Peace. She has been a member of JVP since 2001. In 2010 she was named one of the "Forward 50," a list of the most influential Jewish American leaders released by *The Forward*, which also named her one of "14 Women to Watch" in 2014. She lived with her family in Israel from 2006 to 2009.

Kelsey Waxman graduated from the University of California, Berkeley, in 2016 with a BA in history and Arabic language and literature, where she cofounded the Jewish Voice for Peace campus chapter. Originally from Chicago, Illinois, she now works for a human rights law practice in San Francisco, California.

Rabbi Alissa Wise is the deputy director at Jewish Voice for Peace. Alissa was the founding cochair of the JVP Rabbinical Council and the cofounder of Facing the Nakba, which offers educational resources to an American audience about the history of the Nakba and its implications in Israel/Palestine today.

Orian Zakai is a visiting assistant professor of modern Hebrew at Middlebury College. She completed her PhD at the Department of Comparative Literature at the University of Michigan in August 2012. Her research and teaching interests include women and gender in modern Hebrew literature, the interrelations between Hebrew literature and nationalism, intersections of gender, nationality and ethnicity in contemporary Israeli culture, and postcolonial and feminist theories. Orian has published articles on gender and nationalism in *Nashim* and *Prooftexts*. Her collection of short fiction *Hashlem et he-haser* (Fill in the blanks) was published in Hebrew in 2010 by Keter Books. She is a member of Jewish Voice for Peace Academic Advisory Council.

Notes

A Note about the Spelling of "Antisemitism"

1. Wilhelm Marr, *The Way to Victory of Germanism over Judaism* (n.p., 1879).
2. Yehuda Bauer, "In Search of a Definition of Antisemitism," in *Approaches to Antisemitism: Context and Curriculum*, Michael Brown, ed. (New York: American Jewish Committee, 1994), 22–24.

Antisemitism Redefined

1. Irwin Cotler, "Defining the New Anti-Semitism," *National Post*, November 9, 2010, news .nationalpost.com/full-comment/irwin-cotler-defining-the-new-anti-semitism.
2. Brian Klug, "Interrogating 'New Anti-Semitism,'" *Ethnic and Racial Studies* (2012): 8.
3. Ibid, 13.
4. Antony Lerman, *The Making and Unmaking of a Zionist* (London: Pluto Press, 2012), 99.
5. Slavoj Žižek, "A Vile Logic to Anders Breivik's Choice of Target," *Guardian*, August 8, 2011.
6. Jonathan Boyd and Daniel Staetsky, "Could It Happen Here? What Existing Data Tell Us about Contemporary Antisemitism in the UK," *JPR Policy Debate*, May 2015.

Palestinian Activism and Christian Antisemitism in the Church

1. Othering is "the process of perceiving or portraying someone [or some group] as fundamentally different or alien." [Brackets added.] *Your Dictionary*, www.yourdictionary.com /othering. We generally have little knowledge of or empathy with aliens. The more we dehumanize others, the less guilty we feel about mistreating them. In the end, we deceive ourselves and blame them for the harm we do to them in the name of our own security and self-preservation.
2. See Jewish Voice for Peace, *Stifling Dissent: How Israel's Defenders Use False Charges of Antisemitism to Limit the Debate over Israel on Campus*, Fall 2015, jewishvoiceforpeace .org/stifling-dissent.
3. Martha Nussbaum, "Narrative Emotions: Beckett's Genealogy of Love," in *Why Narrative? Readings in Narrative Theology*, Stanley Hauerwas and L. Gregory Jones, eds. (Grand Rapids: Eerdmans, 1989), 217–18.
4. All dates are CE.
5. James Carroll, *Constantine's Sword* (Boston: Houghton Mifflin, 2001), 215–18.
6. Ibid.
7. *La Civiltà Cattolica*, May 1, 1897, cited in Sergio I. Minerbi, *The Vatican and Zionism* (Oxford: Oxford University Press, 1990), 96.

8. In this essay we will not deal with the numerous hate groups in the United States that the Southern Poverty Law Center continues to combat by shedding light on their vitriolic words and heinous acts. Nor will we deal with the pro-Israel groups that label any criticism of Israel antisemitic.

9. The National Council of Churches and numerous mainline Protestant churches have issued study statements in recent years delineating the adverse effects of this form of Christian Zionism.

10. See Don Wagner, "The Mainline Protestant Churches and the Holy Land," in *Zionism and the Quest for Justice in the Holy Land,* Donald E. Wagner and Walter T. Davis, eds. (Cambridge, England: Wipf & Stock, 2014), 139–74.

11. "What is Exceptionalism? All three Abrahamic religions claim to be exceptional in some ways. Exceptionalism is the belief that 'my people' are unusual, unique, or special. On the positive side, all three Abrahamic religions have a special calling to be a blessing for all the nations. Rabbinic Judaism coined the term *tikkun olam* (repairing or healing the world) to express this call. On the negative side, exceptionalism exempts the chosen from the need to conform to normal rules, laws, or general principles that we use to hold other peoples accountable. Exceptionalist beliefs have a sacred quality and lead to exceptionalist attitudes and actions involving double standards in behavior and often in law. When holding political power, each Abrahamic faith has been susceptible to the merger of theological and ethical exceptionalism that puts believer-insiders above the law they expect nonbeliever-outsiders to obey. Christian exceptionalism has often taken the form of antisemitism, the theological support of slavery followed by Jim Crow segregation, as well as ethnic cleansing and genocide against Native American Indians. The dark side of Zionist exceptionalism today is the ethnic cleansing and land confiscation of Palestinians, justified by an appeal to God's will derived from biblical texts." Israel/Palestine Mission Network of the Presbyterian Church (U.S.A.) (IPMN), *Zionism Unsettled: A Congressional Study Guide,* 2014, 7.

12. Jewish Voice for Peace, executive summary of *Stifling Dissent.*

13. Nussbaum, "Narrative Emotions," 224.

14. IPMN, *Zionism Unsettled,* 17.

15. Brant Rosen, *Wrestling in the Daylight: A Rabbi's Path to Palestinian Solidarity* (Charlottesville, VA: Just World Books, 2012), 16.

16. Carroll, *Constantine's Sword,* 271.

17. Ibid., 273.

18. Rosemary Ruether, *Faith and Fratricide: The Theological Roots of Anti-Semitism* (Eugene, OR: Wipf & Stock, 1996): 206, quoted in Carroll, *Constantine's Sword,* 340.

19. Carroll, *Constantine's Sword,* 361.

20. Robert Michael, "Luther, Luther Scholars, and the Jews," *Encounter* 46, no. 4 (Autumn 1985): 342.

21. The omission in *Nostra aetate* of any mention of the contribution of Christian antisemitism to the Holocaust remains a profound disappointment to many. See David Glick, "Reflections on the Holocaust," *Pastoral Psychology* 44, no. 1 (1995): 26.

22. "Hosanna Preaching Seminars," Israel/Palestine Mission Network of the Presbyterian Church (U.S.A.), www.israelpalestinemissionnetwork.org/main/study-resources/hosanna-seminar.

Black and Palestinian Lives Matter

1. Diane Tobin, Gary A. Tobin, and Scott Rubin, *In Every Tongue: The Racial & Ethnic Diversity of the Jewish People* (San Francisco: Institute for Jewish & Community Research, 2005).

2. I use the term "anti-Jewish prejudice" out of recognition that the term "anti-Semitism," although introduced to describe a distaste for Jews, belies the fact that Palestinians are Semites as well.

3. Here I must distinguish between Judaism and Zionism. Israel proclaims itself to be a Jewish state, but it in fact operates as a Jewish supremacist apartheid state. In my view, Jewish supremacy, which has one manifestation in Zionism, is antithetical to any form of Judaism that I would like to claim presently or in future.

4. Jack Nelson, *Terror in the Night: The Klan's Campaign against the Jews* (New York: Simon & Schuster, 1993); Kiese Laymon, *Long Division: A Novel* (Chicago: Bolden, 2013).

5. Julius Lester, "A Report on Black Anti-Semitism," *Jewish Currents* (1992): 5–9.

6. Howard Ball, *Murder in Mississippi:* United States v. Price *and the Struggle for Civil Rights* (Lawrence: University of Kansas Press, 2004); Raymond Arsenault, *Freedom Riders: 1961 and the Struggle for Racial Justice* (Oxford: Oxford University Press, 2006).

7. Kristian Davis Bailey, "Black–Palestinian Solidarity in the Ferguson–Gaza Era," *American Quarterly* 67, no. 4 (2015): 1017–26.

8. "Israel Palestine Conflict 101," Jewish Voice for Peace, jewishvoiceforpeace.org/israeli-palestinian-conflict-101; Noura Erakat, "The Nakba and Anti-Blackness," *The Nakba Files*, May 18, 2016, nakbafiles.org/2016/05/18/the-nakba-and-anti-blackness.

9. Michelle Alexander, *The New Jim Crow* (New York: The New Press, 2010).

10. Gideon Levy and Alex Levac, "What It's Like to Be a 12-year-old Palestinian Girl in Israeli Jail," *Ha'aretz*, April 29, 2016, www.haaretz.com/opinion/.premium-1.716838.

11. Bailey, "Black–Palestinian Solidarity."

12. Maurianne Adams and John H. Bracey, *Strangers & Neighbors: Relations between Blacks & Jews in the United States* (Amherst: University of Massachusetts Press, 1999).

13. Eliza Gray, "Thetans and Bowties," *New Republic*, October 5, 2012, newrepublic.com/article/108205/scientology-joins-forces-with-nation-of-islam.

14. Hasia R. Diner, *In the Almost Promised Land: American Jews and Blacks, 1915–1935* (Westport, CT: Greenwood, 1977); Mark K. Bauman and Berkley Kalin, *The Quiet Voices: Southern Rabbis and Black Civil Rights, 1880s to 1990s* (Tuscaloosa: University of Alabama Press, 1997); Adams and Bracey, Strangers & Neighbors; Eric J. Sundquist, *Strangers in the Land: Blacks, Jews, Post-Holocaust America* (Cambridge, MA: Harvard University Press, 2005); Cheryl Lynn Greenberg, *Troubling the Waters: Black-Jewish Relations in the American Century* (Princeton, NJ: Princeton University Press, 2006).

Intersections of Antisemitism, Racism, and Nationalism

1. I use "Sephardi" (the Hebrew word for "a Jew of Spanish origin," also known as "Sephardic") to mirror "Mizrahi" (the Hebrew word that means "Eastern Jew" or, in its more historical and derogatory use, "Oriental Jew"). I use these together because my ancestors were expelled from Christian Spain but had been part of an Islamic world for centuries before it became Catholic. After expulsion, they journeyed through the Ottoman Middle East, eventually settling in what is modern-day Turkey. For this reason, I use both Sephardi/Mizrahi identity markers, acknowledging both the expulsion from Spain and the rootedness in the Middle East. In my experience growing up in the United States, "Mizrahi" was not a term used to describe Jews who had Sephardic linguistic heritage and roots. However, politically I align with a critical movement of Mizrahi scholars and activists who reclaim their full identities, ancestries, histories and values.

2. See Penny Rosenwasser, *Hope into Practice: Choosing Justice Despite Our Fears* (Penny Ros-

enwasser, 2013) on internalized antisemitism, and Cherie Brown, "Beyond Internalized Antisemitism: Healing the Collective Scars of the Past," *Tikkun*, March–April 1995, ncbi.org/wp-content/uploads/2013/07/beyond-internalized-antisemitism_-healing -the-collective-scars-of-the-past.pdf, which discusses fear and trauma.

3. Jewish Council for Public Affairs, "A 'Purple State Strategy' for Jewish Community Relations," blog post, January 12, 2016, jewishpublicaffairs.org/2016/01/12/a-purple -state-strategy-for-jewish-community-relations. In the post, David Bernstein discusses the split in community relations in the mainstream Jewish community after the 1990s, when "American Jews felt safer than ever before." Gary Phillip Zola and Marc Dollinger, eds., *American Jewish History: A Primary Source Reader* (Boston: Brandeis University Press, 2014), 325.

4. For an example of a "middle agent" description, see April Rosenblum, "The Past Didn't Go Anywhere: Making Resistance to Antisemitism a Part of All Our Movements," April 2007, www.buildingequality.us/prejudice/antisemitism/rosenblum/the-past.pdf.

5. For a more in-depth history on Christian hegemony see Paul Kivel, *Living in the Shadow of the Cross: Understanding and Resisting the Power and Privilege of Christian Hegemony* (Vancouver: New Society Publishers, 2013).

6. See Edward Said, *Orientalism* (New York: Pantheon Books, 1978) for a prolific discussion of Orientalism and its foundations and discursive practices.

7. These evils are all present in our communities, especially with the growing number of both Jews of color and Jews benefiting from the privileges that come from white Jewish identity.

8. Also see Michael Lerner, *The Socialism of Fools: Anti-Semitism on the Left* (Oakland: Institute for Labor and Mental Health, Tikkun Books, 1992).

9. Cherie Brown might suggest this is because of the remnants of the terror connected to a traumatic history of antisemitism. See Cherie Brown, "Unhealed Terror," *Tikkun* (Winter 2011), www.tikkun.org/nextgen/unhealed-terror.

10. Karen Brodkin, *How Jews Became White Folks and What that Says About Race in America* (New Brunswick, NJ: Rutgers University Press, 1998), 25–52.

11. Not to mention the disregard or erasure of indigenous peoples or American Indians.

12. Even today, antisemitism in the Middle East is seen through the lens of European antisemitism and Orientalism.

13. This is the case for Rosenblum's and Brown's contributions about antisemitism and Jewish terror and trauma.

14. This was different for my mother and her generation, where the experience of racism by the dominant Ashkenazi Jewish community was painful and more overt. My grandfather, who was a Sephardic rabbi, did as much as he could to try to unify the community so that it would be insignificant whether one was Sephardic or Ashkenazi; however, this required a certain element of assimilation and erasure.

15. My reflections on Orientalism and the experience of Sephardi/Mizrahi Jews have been influenced and inspired by Ella Shohat. See Ella Shohat, "Sephardim in Israel: Zionism from the Standpoint of Its Jewish Victims," *Social Text* 19/20 (1988): 1–35.

16. See Smadar Lavie, *Wrapped in the Flag of Israel: Mizrahi Single Mothers and Bureaucratic Torture* (New York: Berghahn Books, 2014).

17. See Ella Shohat, "The Invention of the Mizrahim," *Journal of Palestine Studies* 29, no. 1 (Autumn 1999): 5–20.

18. There are other ways to describe antisemitism. I have chosen this popular definition in order to grapple with and interrogate the contradictions of being a victim and an oppressor at the same time, not just outside of one's community but also internally. I hope this analy-

sis is relevant in a way that suggests that every community must work to address injustices and freedom in a meaningful way.

19. By "white Christians," I am referring to those raised Christian or benefiting from secular Christian culture and Christian privilege.

20. Arab and Middle Eastern bodies include and are not limited to Arab-Jews, Arab-Muslims, Arab-Christians, Arab-Druze, Turkish-Muslims, Turkish-Jews, Kurds (Iraqi and Turkish), Iranian-Muslims, Iranian-Zoroastrians, Iranian-Bahai, and Iranian-Jews.

21. This is not to say this is a religious conflict but to address its cultural and ideological contexts.

22. This also likely assumes that most Jews are European and belong to the same racial group as white Christians. For these purposes, they can be forgiven for their failure to accept Jesus because they can pass as white.

23. Sometimes they make excuses such as, "Oh, that one [Christian] person is known to be unreasonable," after having claimed that the Jewish people run the banks, but don't feel a need or responsibility to confront this kind of antisemitism.

24. This is not to demean the significance and meaning Jesus has to Christians but to highlight that Jewish discussions about Jesus take place usually because we are forced to talk about Jesus, even though he is not someone that is in our texts or history. As a Jewish person, I want to respect the importance of Jesus and G-d to Christians and the Christian community.

25. Though Christianity was imposed on Black people and later became a form of resistance during slavery and the horrors of racism, this doesn't take away how Christianity remains hegemonic.

26. Non-European Jews include Mizrahi/Sephardi/Ethiopian Jews.

27. They don't have to be a real obstacle, but the effort by the Israeli state to be identified as Western and European has been the case since before independence and certainly with the arrival of hundreds of thousands of Jews from the Arab and Muslim world.

28. Rita Giacaman, director of the Bir Zeit University Public Health program, conversation with author. I remember a presentation to the Interfaith Peace-Builders delegation that I brought to Israel/Palestine and this conversation over a decade ago in which she described the Israeli military occupation and its effects on the Palestinian people as a public health crisis. Solvable mental, physical safety, and health issues could be addressed but were under assault throughout the occupation. This made it less possible for the Palestinian people to address the public health needs of their communities.

29. This effectively denies the right of Palestinian people to exist with any meaningful aspirations, while also conveniently assuming they must be controlled, or even worse, labeled as terrorists.

30. The Atlanta Jewish Federation is connected to a larger umbrella organization, Jewish Federations of North America. The Jewish Federations do philanthropic work on behalf of the Jewish communities in their respective cities, in Israel, and around the world. The Atlanta Federation's mission is for "caring for those in need, deepening engagement in Jewish life and strengthening Jewish identity, and creating connections among Jews locally and around the world." Jewish Federations of North America, "Federation Impact," jewishfederations.org/federation-impact-stories.

31. I could have asked this of Sephardi and Mizrahi lives in relation to Ashkenazi lives as well.

32. See Institute for Middle East Understanding (IMEU), "50 Days of Death and Destruction: Israel's 'Operation Protective Edge,'" September 10, 2014, imeu.org/article/50 -days-of-death-destruction-israels-operation-protective-edge.

33. IMEU, "Putting Palestinians 'On a Diet': Israel's Siege & Blockade of Gaza," August 14, 2014, imeu.org/article/putting-palestinians-on-a-diet-israels-siege-blockade-of-gaza;

UN Office of the Coordination of Humanitarian Affairs, *The Gaza Strip: Humanitarian Impact of the Blockade,* July 2015, www.ochaopt.org/documents/ocha_opt_gaza_blockade _factsheet_july_2015_english.pdf.

34. Adam Horowitz, "Read the Genocidal Sermon a Notable Atlanta Rabbi Gave This Rosh Hashanah," *Mondoweiss,* October 3, 2014, mondoweiss.net/2014/10/genocidal-atlanta -hashanah.

35. JVP-Atlanta, "Following Shocking Sermon, Atlanta JVP Calls on Area Rabbis to Challenge Racism in the Jewish Community," *Mondoweiss,* October 9, 2014, mondoweiss .net/2014/10/following-challenge-community.

36. AJC's work in supporting anti-BDS legislation affects First Amendment rights in various states in the United States—including the right to free speech. Palestine Legal, the Center for Constitutional Rights, and Jewish Voice for Peace have been working to combat these bills suppressing free speech. Jewish Voice for Peace's *Stifling Dissent* and Palestine Legal's *The Palestine Exception to Free Speech: A Movement under Attack in the US* discuss suppression of Palestinian advocacy, critique of Israel, and claims of antisemitism.

37. There is a difference between gatekeeping and racist disciplining. Institutional Jewish communities, expecting to form an alliance on the basis of Judeo-Christian "values," will shame or guilt white and often Christian communities who they know favor a more human rights–based approach to Israel/Palestine. This gatekeeping draws attention away from claims of injustice, therefore the legitimate critique of Israel gets diverted into a discussion on antisemitism. Whereas when communities of color speak out for justice, especially in Israel/Palestine, and it prompts the censure of the institutional Jewish community, racist disciplining is used as a threat or punishment. The institutional Jewish community withdraws resources, distances itself, and resorts to posturing to influence communities of color to retract their position on human rights, specifically on Palestinian rights. We can see this today in the responses of the more prominent actors in the institutional Jewish community to the Black Lives Matter platform. In the past, racist disciplining has worked and taken a toll, but today many communities of color understand this dynamic and do not buckle under the pressure.

38. I also conducted formal interviews with communities of color in Atlanta and San Francisco in 2003–4 about this phenomenon and its impact on silencing communities in order to keep other social justice work continuing.

39. Discrimination toward minoritized Jews in Israel, including Sephardi/Mizrahi and Ethiopian Jews, has occurred in multiple forms. Upon immigration to Israel, different Mizrahi communities experienced a variety of harsh (mis)treatment. Ringworm radiation of North African Jewish children and the kidnapping of Yemeni babies are two examples. See the documentary *The Ringworm Children,* directed by David Belhassen and Asher Hemias (2004; Israel: Casque D'or Films), and Shoshana Madmon-Gerber, *Israeli Media and the Framing of Internal Conflict: The Yemenite Babies Affair* (New York: Palgrave Macmillan, 2009). Furthermore, discrimination against African asylum seekers in Israel has been documented toward foreign workers in Israel as well. See Bureau of Democracy, Human Rights, and Labor, *2010 Human Rights Report: Israel and the Occupied Territories* (Washington, DC: US Department of State, 2011), www.state.gov/j/drl/rls/hrrpt/2010/nea/154463. htm; Committee on the Elimination of Racial Discrimination, UN Human Rights Office of the High Commissioner, "Consideration of Reports Submitted by States Parties under Article 9 of the Convention," March 9, 2012, www2.ohchr.org/english/bodies/cerd /docs/CERD.C.ISR.CO.14-16.pdf; and David Sheen, "Ethiopian-Israelis Protest Police Brutality, but Do Black Lives Matter in Israel if They're Not Jews?," *Alternet,* May 4,

2015, www.alternet.org/world/ethiopian-israelis-protest-police-brutality-do-black-lives-matter-israel-if-theyre-not-jews.

40. Iris Marion Young names these faces of oppression explicitly in her essay "Five Faces of Oppression," in *Diversity, Social Justice, and Inclusive Excellence: Transdisciplinary and Global Perspectives*, Seth N. Asumah and Mechthild Nagel, eds. (Albany: State University of NY Press, 2014), 3–32.

41. This kind of thinking has been used by Israeli leadership, government officials in the United States and Canada, and organizations such as JJAC (Justice for Jews in Arab Countries) and JIMENA (Jews Indigenous to the Middle East and North Africa). See Yehouda Shenhav, "Arab-Jews, Population Exchange, and the Palestinian Right of Return," in *Exile and Return: Predicaments of Palestinians and Jews*, Ann M. Lesch and Ian S. Lustick, eds. (Philadelphia: University of Pennsylvania Press, 2005).

42. This was the case for decades with the Israeli identity cards that were issued to all citizens, Jerusalem residents, and those in the occupied territories. For Jews, the Israeli identity card named their nationality as Jewish rather than Israeli. Palestinians had an Arab nationality rather than an Israeli one. Now there are other strategies to identify who is a Jewish Israeli and who is not. Ofra Yeshua-Lyth, "Discrimination Is Legal, There Are No Israelis: Reading the Supreme Court's Decisions on Israeli Nationality," *Mondoweiss*, June 3, 2014, mondoweiss.net/2014/06/discrimination-decisions-nationality.

43. It is also important to talk about the Palestinian diaspora as a whole.

44. In Israel and in the occupied territories.

45. Sephardi/Mizrahi Jews, Ethiopian Jews, etc.

46. Foreign workers in Israel from Nigeria, Thailand, the Philippines, etc., as well as African asylum seekers.

47. Arabs practice many different religions including Muslim, Christian, and Druze.

48. This is a particular eschatology that is central to some evangelical Christians and Christian Zionists (presentation by Jennifer Roberts, Agnes Scott College, 2016). Besides this, there are other problematic aspects to the relationships over the last two decades between the Israeli government and Christian Zionists.

49. See Ilise Benshushan Cohen, *Israeli State Violence/Mizrahi Resilience: An Ethnography of Mizrahi Experiences of War and Eviction and Their Intersection with Palestinian Experiences* (PhD dissertation, California Institute of Integral Studies, 2013).

50. Even though many southern Jews survived by assimilating as much as possible with the white and Christian population to avoid being targeted, as Black people were during Jim Crow.

51. See Daniel Boyarin, "Masada or Yavneh? Gender and the Arts of Jewish Resistance," in *Jews and Other Differences: The New Jewish Cultural Studies,* Jonathan and Daniel Boyarin, eds. (Minneapolis: University of Minnesota Press, 1997), 306–29.

52. Israel exports its militarization without regard to where the arms will be used and the impact on those who will be victims of this militarization. See Jeff Halper, *War against the People* (London: Pluto Press, 2014).

53. Israel for years has been receiving at least $3 billion of US military aid a year, a substantial portion of which must be spent on US arms. This military funding and the weapons that come with it aids Israel in sustaining the occupation. The US Campaign to End the Israeli Occupation works on this issue and is one of many groups that calls for the end of US military aid to Israel until the occupation ends (see US Campaign to End the Israeli Occupation, "Military Aid to Israel," www.endtheoccupation.org/section.php?id=208). Proposals to increase this military aid annually to at least $4 billion are being considered. This aid also supports the arms industry of Israel.

54. Rashid Khalidi, *Brokers of Deceit: How the US Has Undermined Peace in the Middle East* (Boston: Beacon Press, 2013).

55. Other phrases are Ashkenazi "centrism," "hegemony," and "supremacy."

56. See Sami Shalom Chetrit, *Intra-Jewish Conflict in Israel: White Jews, Black Jews* (London: Routledge, 2009); Eran Kaplan, *Beyond Post-Zionism* (New York: State University of NY Press, 2015), 107; Yfaat Weiss, *A Confiscated Memory: Wadi Salib and Haifa's Lost Heritage* (New York: Columbia University Press, 2011); Arnon Golan, "The Spatial Outcome of the 1948 War and Prospects for Return," in *Israel and the Palestinian Refugees*, Eyal Benvenisti, Chaim Gans, and Sari Hanafi, eds. (Berlin: Springer, 2007).

57. This is similarly true in the United States but has been changing since the recent emergence of the Black Lives Matter movement and as intersectionality continues to gain momentum.

58. He believes Mizrahi Jews are responsible for most of the racism toward Palestinians while he is righteous in working for Palestinian rights. However, there are plenty of Ashkenazi Jews that are also responsible for maintaining the occupation and racism in Israel.

59. This is manifested as Christian hegemony, white supremacy, and male dominance.

60. The email reads that Zionists "are directly involved in . . . creating and funding of ISIS (Daesh); creation of Boko Haram in Africa and their inhumane treatment of Africans; genocide being committed by Saudi Arabia against people of Yemen under supervision of Zionists; daily car-bombs all over the Middle Eastern countries planted by CIA (Blackwater agents)/Mossad, masqueraded as Shiit/Suni [*sic*] ethnic conflict." Email message to author, May 18, 2016.

61. Grant Foster, "'Holy Spirit' Almost Serves Up Holy Dinner at Kruger," *SA Promo Magazine*, March 9, 2016, www.sapromo.com/holy-spirit-almost-serves-up-holy-dinner-at -kruger/10395.

62. This quote comes directly from the Facebook post (March 10, 2015) along with a photo of a person being attacked by two lions.

63. See Hennie Pretorius and Lizo Jafta, "'A Branch Springs Out': African Initiated Churches," in *Christianity in South Africa: A Political, Social, and Cultural History*, Richard Elphick and Rodney Davenport, eds. (Berkeley: University of California Press, 1997), 217–18.

On Antisemitism and Its Uses

1. Jews, especially in Germany, played a role in the development of race science. See John Efron, *Defenders of the Race: Jewish Doctors and Race Science in Fin de-Siècle Europe* (New Haven: Yale University Press, 1994). David Engel notes that "there is no compelling evidence that at the time of its introduction the stem 'antisemit-' was generally understood as implying an attitude toward Jews rooted in race. Actually, there is evidence to the contrary." See David Engel, "Away from a Definition of Antisemitism: An Essay in the Semantics of Historical Description," in *Rethinking European Jewish History*, Jeremy Cohen and Moshe Rosman, eds. (Oxford: Littman Library of Jewish Civilization, 2014), 36, note 4.

2. This issue has been written about at least since the early 1980s. See, for example, Robert Alter, "Deformations of the Holocaust," *Commentary Magazine* 71, no. 2 (1981); Ismar Schorsch, "The Holocaust and Jewish Survival," *Midstream* 21, no. 1 (1981): 38–42; Jacob Neusner, *The Jewish War against the Jews: Reflections of Golah, Shoah, and Torah* (New York: Ktav, 1984); Shaul Magid, "Islamaphobia, Antisemitism, the Holocaust, and a 'New' Jewish Culture," *Zeek*, August 20, 2010; "The Holocaust and Jewish Identity in America: Memory, the Unique, and the Universal," *Jewish Social Studies* 18, no. 2 (2013): 100–35; "The American Jewish Holocaust 'Myth' and 'Negative Judaism': Jacob Neusner's Contribution

to American Judaism," in *A Legacy of Learning: Essays in Honor of Jacob Neusner*, Alan J. Avery-Peck et al., eds. (Leiden: Brill, 2014), 321–40. Most recently, see Gershon Goremberg, "Tragedy Shouldn't Be the Defining Feature of Modern Judaism," *Moment Magazine*, January–February 2016, www.momentmag.com/opinion-the-victimhood-olympics.

3. See Jonathan Woocher, *Sacred Survival: The Civil Religion of American Jews* (Bloomington, IN: Indiana University Press, 1986).

4. On an appraisal similar to Herzl, see Lucian Wolf, "Antisemitism," in *Encyclopedia Britannica*, 11th ed. (New York: Encyclopedia Britannica, 1910), ii, 134–46. On a long mediation on the "Jacob hates Esau" motif, see R. Naftali Berliner of Volozhin, Naftali Zvi Berlin (Neziv), *"Se'ar Yisrael,"* first published in his *Rinat Yisrael* and then again as an appendix to Neziv's commentary to Song of Songs. On the Neziv, see Gil Perl, *The Pillar of Volozhin: Rabbi Naftali Zvi Yehuda Berlin and the World of Nineteenth-Century Lithuanian Torah Scholarship* (Boston: Academic Studies Press, 2013). Neziv's small tract on antisemitism was published in English as Howard Joseph, *Why Antisemitism? A Translation of "The Remnant of Israel"* (New Jersey: Jason Aronson, 1996). On Herzl's theories of antisemitism's economic roots, see Theodore Herzl, "A Solution to the Jewish Question," in *Israel in the Middle East: Documents and Readings on Society, Politics, and Foreign Relations, Pre-1948 to the Present*, 2nd ed., Jehuda Reinharz and Itamar Rabinovich, eds. (Waltham, MA: Brandeis University Press, 2007), 16–20. Cf. Herzl, *The Complete Diaries of Theodor Herzl* (New York: Herzl Press, 1960), 9–10.

5. I want to thank my colleague and friend John Efron for bringing this Pinsker reference this to my attention.

6. See Ruth Wisse, *Jews and Power* (New York: Schocken, 2007), and Meir Kahane, *Never Again! A Program for Survival* (Los Angeles: Nash, 1971). In *Never Again!* Kahane takes this to its logical conclusion to suggest that the Nazis in one sense were not to blame for the Holocaust since they were simply acting according to their nature. The blame should go to those (in America and beyond) who did not stop them from acting in such a manner.

7. David Engel, "Away from a Definition of Antisemitism," 35.

8. The classic study of definitions is Gavin Langmuir's *Toward a Definition of Antisemitism* (Los Angeles and Berkeley: University of California Press, 1996). Cf. Ben Halperin, "What is Antisemitism?," *Modern Judaism* 1, no. 3 (1981): 251–262; David Berger, "Antisemitism: An Overview," in *History and Hate: The Dimensions of Antisemitism*, D. Berger, ed. (Philadelphia: JPS, 1986), 3–14; and most prominently in my view, Engel, "Away from a Definition of Antisemitism," 30–53.

9. Another more recent focus is the antisemitism that is playing itself out on some American college campuses. Although this too is an important topic, it is more complicated because the separation between anti-Israelism or anti-Zionism and antisemitism is a complicated story.

10. There were notable examples during the Almohad period in Spain and medieval Yemen. There is a large body of literature on this question as it relates to the way many German Enlightenment thinkers created the "Golden Age of Spain," arguing that Islam was a much more tolerant civilization than Christendom for the Jews. For a succinct analysis of these trends see Mark Cohen, *Under Cross and Crescent: The Jews in the Middle Ages* (Princeton: Princeton University Press, 1995), 4–14.

11. On this see Yosef Hayyim Yerushalmi, *Zakhor* (Seattle: University of Washington Press, 1996).

12. See Alan Dershowitz, *The Case For Israel* (New York: John Wiley and Sons, 2004), 13–21, and Edward Said, *The Question of Palestine* (New York: Vintage Books, 1992), 56–82.

13. See Magid, "Butler Trouble: Zionism, Excommunication and the Reception of Judith Butler's Work on Israel/Palestine," *Studies in American Jewish Literature* 33, no. 2 (2014): 237–59. There is a growing body of literature that, while gesturing to the potential legitimacy of non- or even anti-Zionism as being distinct from antisemitism, in most cases, that gesture soon disappears as anti-Zionism, either in the form of Jewish groups such as Jewish Voice for Peace or non-Jewish ones such as Students for Justice in Palestine, becomes cast as an expression of antisemitism. For a recent example of this see Leil Lebovitz, "Anti-Zionism Is Antisemitism: Get Over It," *Tablet Magazine*, April 13, 2006, www.tabletmag.com /jewish-life-and-religion/199847/anti-zionism-is-antisemitism. By citing numerous examples of anti-Zionist rhetoric that, I agree, borders on antisemitism in student newspapers at Stanford and Oberlin, Lebovitz illustrates what is to my mind a sophomoric analysis that asserts liberal Jewish engagement with anti-Israelism (that is, a deep critique of its policies) or anti-Zionism is being naïve if it thinks it exists outside the antisemitic orbit. He concludes with the dripping sarcasm that is to my mind a substitute for thinking throughout the essay: "And those Jews who believe that their liberal sophistication will somehow save them from the wrath of bigotry should strongly reconsider: Never send to know for whom the anti-Semites troll; they troll for thee." One must support Israel, this suggests, because if one does not, one is giving strength to antisemitism, intentionally or not. One could only hope a more crisp argument could be made to give his view the intellectual heft it sorely needs. I agree with Lebovitz that the Oberlin and Stanford examples are troubling and that the term "antisemitic" may indeed apply in those cases. But to universalize those examples without any real argument is not the responsible way to treat this important issue. It illustrates to me the flippant way many in the Jewish media use the term "antisemitism" for self-serving ends.

14. I say "openly" because polls show that the predominant instances of hate crimes in America are still against Jews. The FBI's Uniform Hate Crime Statistics in 2014 show that 57 percent of reported hate crimes in the United States were against Jews while 16 percent were against Muslims. Yet the public perception seems to suggest the opposite. See the 2014 Hate Crimes Statistics at www.fbi.gov/about-us/cjis/ucr/hate-crime/2014/topic -pages/victims_final.

15. Butler, *Precarious Life: The Powers of Mourning and Violence* (London: Verso, 2006), 111. Noam Pianko makes a similar argument in his *Jewish Peoplehood: An American Innovation* (New Jersey: Rutgers University Press, 2016), 70. "Still deeply influenced by the nationalist paradigm, peoplehood advocated doubling down on the function of peoplehood as a code word for modified Zionist claims about the meaning of Jewish collectivity. The rhetoric of peoplehood serves as a ballast against post-Zionism and the perception of a distancing between American Jews and Israel." Cf. 27, 56, 67. Cf. Alexandre Adler, *Le Sionisme et le monde contemporain*, 240–241, cited in Ivan Segré, "The 'Communitarian' Ideology," in *Reflections on Antisemitism*, Alain Badiou, Eric Hazan, and Ivan Segré, eds. (London and New York: Verso, 2013), 67.

16. See Charles Liebman, *Pressure without Sanctions* (Cranbury, NJ: Associated University Presses, 1977), 199–200. Cf. Dov Waxman, *Trouble with the Tribe: The American Jewish Conflict over Israel* (Princeton: Princeton University Press, 2016), 18–54.

17. Cited in Michael Staub, *Torn at the Roots: The Crisis of Jewish Liberalism in Postwar America* (New York: Columbia University Press, 2004), 203.

18. "Israeli Ambassador in U.S. Sends Out Holiday Gift Packages with Settlement Products," *Haaretz*, December 23, 2015.

19. This is arguably the foundation of Hannah Arendt's critique of David Ben-Gurion's statist Zionism in her essay "To Save the Jewish Homeland," in *Hannah Arendt: The Jewish*

Writings (New York: Schocken Books, 2007), 388–401.

20. This point is developed in perhaps a more nuanced way by Judith Butler in her reading of Lawrence Summers in her *Precarious Life*.

21. On "negation of the Diaspora" and its contemporary relevance, see Eliezer Schweid, "The Rejection of the Diaspora in Zionist Thought: Two Approaches," in *Essential Papers on Zionism*, Jehuda Reinharz and Anita Shapira, eds. (New York and London: NYU Press, 1996), 133–60. More recently, see Arnold Eisen, "Zionism, American Jewry, and the 'Negation of the Diaspora,'" in Michael A. Meyer and David N. Myers, eds. *Between Jewish Tradition and Modernity: Rethinking an Old Opposition* (Detroit, MI: Wayne State University Press, 2014), 175–91.

22. See Butler, *Precarious Life*, citing and examining Lawrence Summers' comment, 100–127. Writing about Jean-Claude Milner, a former French Parliamentarian, Alain Badiou notes, "For Milner being antisemitic does not necessarily involve intention. It is not an explicit ideology. It is not a matter of consciousness, a project, or decision. Certain choices that appear to be far removed from it—in which 'Jew' does not appear—are none the less antisemitic. . . . The great victory of Milner and his whole current has been to create 'objective' antisemitism, leading to an interesting possibility declaring almost anything, or anyone, antisemitic." Badiou, "What Interests, What Aims?," in *Reflections on Antisemitism*, 28.

23. The emergence of Jewish survivalism as a kind of civil religion of many contemporary Jews attests to the extent to which the worldview of Meir Kahane (albeit not necessarily his tactics) has been absorbed by a large swath of Jews in the early twenty-first century, in Israel and in the Diaspora. See my article, "Antisemitism as Colonialism: Meir Kahane's 'Ethics of Violence,'" *Journal of Jewish Ethics* 1, no. 2 (Summer 2015): 231–61.

24. For an examination of this, see Badiou and Hazan, "The Role of Israel," in *Reflections on Antisemitism*, 29–32. I would add here that one could ask how many pro-Zionist communities such as evangelical Christians are really using Zionism as a vehicle for antisemitism. See, for example, Rony Brauman's interview in *Mouvements*, cited in "Appendix: Mass Culture and 'the Jews,'" in *Reflections*, 231.

25. It is not only the Orthodox who make this claim. For example, in the film *Gentleman's Agreement* (1947), the character Professor Lieberman, a world-renowned physicist (played by Sam Jaffe), challenges the idea that being a Jew is a matter of racial descent. "I have no religion, so I am not Jewish by religion. Further, I am a scientist, so I must rely on science, which tells me I am not Jewish by race, since there's no such thing as a distinct Jewish race." See Susan A. Glenn, "In the Blood? Consent, Descent, and the Ironies of Jewish Identity," *Jewish Social Studies* 8, no. 23 (Winter–Spring 2002): 146.

26. See Jeremy Stolow, "Nation of Torah: Proselytism and the Politics of Historiography in a Religious Social Movement," (PhD dissertation, York University, 2000). On a new investigation of Jewish peoplehood that views it largely as an American invention, see Noam Pianko, *Jewish Peoplehood*.

27. For another rendering of the symmetry between Zionism and antisemitism, see Daniel Boyarin, "The Colonial Drag: Zionism, Gender, and Mimicry," in *Unheroic Conduct* (Berkeley and Los Angeles, 1997), 271–312.

28. See Emanuel Feldman, "The 'Jude' on the Yellow Star," *Cross-Currents*, August 24, 2005, www.cross-currents.com/archives/2005/08/24/the-judeon-the-yellow-star. Cf. Yael Feldman, "On Trauma and Selective Memory: Could the Shoah Resistance Call 'Not as Sheep to Slaughter!' Have a Medieval Pedigree?" (unpublished essay, 13). Feldman's paper was presented at a seminar of the Katz Center for Advanced Judaic Studies in January 2016.

29. In terms of aiding and abetting real antisemitism, this is a legitimate concern and those

non-antisemitic supporters of these alternatives must grapple with it seriously and police its borders carefully. But we also have to recognize that aiding and abetting antisemitism also exists with certain forms of militaristic Zionism as that kind of Zionism simply gives fodder to antisemitism the way Donald Trump's anti-Muslim campaign as part of his the 2016 US presidential bid gives fodder to ISIS.

30. Jennifer Thompson, *Jewish on Their Own Terms: How Intermarried Couples Are Changing American Judaism* (New Jersey: Rutgers University Press, 2014).

31. Thompson, *Jewish on Their Own Terms*, 29.

32. See Arthur Hertzberg, ed., *The Zionist Idea* (Philadelphia, PA: Jewish Publication Society, 199), 625.

33. See J. J. Goldberg, "First Step to Reflecting Jewish Values: Focus Less on Israel," *The Forward*, January 22, 2016, forward.com/opinion/331169/want-to-rebuild-the-jewish-public-agenda-start-by-listening-to-actual-real/?attribution=home-conversation-headline-3.

34. For an early analysis of this problem and possible solutions see Jacob Neusner, *The Jewish War against the Jews*; my *American Post-Judaism* (Bloomington: Indiana University Press, 2013), 186–232; and "The Holocaust and Jewish Identity in America: Memory, the Unique, and the Universal," *Jewish Social Studies* 18, no. 2 (2012): 100–135.

Antisemitism, Palestine, and the Mizrahi Question

1. Of course, this erasure is not isolated to the United States. The term "Mizrahi," which means "Eastern" in Hebrew, is an imperfect umbrella term that refers to the Jewish communities descended from the Middle East and North Africa, including but not exclusively Iraq, Syria, Bahrain, Kuwait, Iran, Lebanon, Kurdistan, Yemen, Turkey, Uzbekistan, Libya, Tunisia, Algeria, Morocco, Afghanistan, and Pakistan.

2. Michael Dumper, ed., *Palestinian Refugee Repatriation: Global Perspectives* (New York: Taylor & Francis, 2006) 6. Until 2011, Palestinians constituted the largest refugee population in the world. From 2011 to the present, the Syrian refugee population has been the largest.

3. For more on this, see Rhoda Kanaaneh's *Birthing the Nation: Strategies of Palestinian Women in Israel* (Berkeley: University of California Press, 2002).

4. Please see Eric Davis, *Memories of State: Politics, History and Collective Identity in Modern Iraq* (Berkeley: University of California Press, 2005), and Derek Gregory, *The Colonial Present* (Malden: Blackwell Publishing, 2004).

5. Orit Bashkin, *The New Babylonians: A History of Jews in Modern Iraq* (Stanford: Stanford University Press, 2012), 110.

6. Although I am focusing for the moment on the Jews of Iraq, many non-European Jewish communities underwent similarly exploitative treatment in Israel, and often worse. See Rachel Shabi, *We Look Like the Enemy: The Hidden History of Israel*, and Shohat, "Sephardim in Israel," 1–35.

7. Shabi, *We Look Like the Enemy*, 23; Smadar Lavie, "Mizrahi Feminism and the Question of Palestine," *Journal of Middle East Women's Studies* 7, no. 2 (2011): 56–88. There is an argument to be made that the banning of Yiddish in Israel is connected to a kind of European assimilation as well. See Dovid Katz, *Words on Fire: The Unfinished Story of Yiddish* (New York: Basic Books, 2007).

8. Lavie, "Mizrahi Feminism," 57.

9. Shohat, "Sephardim in Israel," 15.

10. See Edward Said, *Orientalism* (New York: Pantheon Books, 1978).

11. See Kimberlé Crenshaw's seminal work, "Mapping the Margins: Intersectionality, Identi-

ty Politics, and Violence against Women of Color," *Stanford Law Review* 43, no. 6 (1991): 1231–99.

12. Brodkin, *How Jews Became White Folks.*

13. Keith Feldman, *A Shadow over Palestine: The Imperial Life of Race in America* (Minneapolis: University of Minnesota Press, 2015).

14. Feldman, *Shadow over Palestine,* 10.

15. From my research, it seems Rosenblum's zine borrows heavily from the thinking of Cherie Brown. I have come across versions of this theory in multiple progressive Jewish spaces. My hope is that my writing here is taken as my own honest attempt to work through what I find problematic about this analysis, not an indictment of those who may find it useful.

16. Rosenblum, "The Past Didn't Go Anywhere," 2–3.

17. Ibid., 8.

18. See Edward Said, *The Question of Palestine* (New York: Vintage, 1992); Ran Greenstein, *Zionism and Its Discontents: A Century of Radical Dissent in Israel/Palestine* (New York: Pluto Press, 2014); and Ilan Pappé, *The Ethnic Cleansing of Palestine* (New York: One World Publications, 2007).

19. Rosenblum, "The Past Didn't Go Anywhere," 8.

20. In 1938, Jews were banned from owning or possessing firearms in Nazi Germany, one of many anti-Jewish laws throughout the decade before the Holocaust, and there have been other points in history—under Catholic rule in the Middle Ages, for example—where similar laws were enacted. However, it is factually inaccurate to say that Jews "were legally banned from being allowed to carry weapons for substantial periods under Christian and Muslim rule." For more, see David Biale, *Power and Powerlessness in Jewish History* (New York: Schocken Books, 1986).

21. See Daniel Boyarin, *Unheroic Conduct: The Rise of Heterosexuality and the Invention of the Jewish Man* (Berkeley: University of California Press, 1997).

22. See Tallie Ben Daniel, "Zionism's Frontier Legacies: Colonial Masculinity and the American Council for Judaism in San Francisco," *American Studies* 54, no. 4 (2016): 49–72.

23. Rosenblum, "The Past Didn't Go Anywhere," 8.

24. Sigal Samuel, "I'm a Mizrahi Jew. Do I Count as a Person of Color?," *The Forward*, August 10, 2015, forward.com/opinion/318667/im-a-mizrahi-jew-do-i-count-as-a-person-of-color.

25. Loretta Loss, "The Origin of 'Women of Color,'" *Racialicious*, March 3, 2011.

26. Janani, "What's Wrong with the Term 'Person of Color,'" *Black Girl Dangerous*, March 20, 2013, www.blackgirldangerous.org/2013/03/2013321whats-wrong-with-the-term-person -of-color.

27. Keren Soffar Sharon, "Mizrahi Jews, Jews of Color, and Racial Justice," *Jewschool: Progressive Jews and Views*, April 28, 2016, jewschool.com/2016/04/76596/mizrahi-jews -jews-color-racial-justice/.

28. Richard Silverstein, "San Francisco JCRC steals 'Nakba,'" *Tikun Olam*, May 17, 2016, www.richardsilverstein.com/2016/05/17/san-francisco-jcrc-steals-nakba/.

29. JIMENA, "JIMENA Response to BDS & Campus Anti-Semitism," June 4, 2015, www. jimena.org/bds-anti-semtism-on-campus.

30. Jewish Voice for Peace, *Stifling Dissent.*

31. "JIMENA Response to BDS & Campus Anti-Semitism."

32. I write this conclusion a week after Britain voted to leave the European Union, which many are analyzing as a result of a nationalist, isolationist, and racist campaign.

33. David Biale, *Power and Powerlessness,* 8.

34. David Finkel and Dianne Feeley, "An Interview with Rabab Abdulhadi," *Against Apart-*

heid: The Case for Boycotting Israeli Universities, Ashley Dawson and Bill Mullen, eds. (Chicago: Haymarket Books, 2015), 123–35.

Trump, the Alt-right, Antisemitism, and Zionism

1. Abby Ohlheiser and Caitlin Dewey, "Hillary Clinton's Alt-right Speech, Annotated," *The Fix* (blog), *Washington Post*, August 25, 2016, www.washingtonpost.com/news/the-fix /wp/2016/08/25/hillary-clintons-alt-right-speech-annotated/.
2. Angie Drobnic Holan, "In Context: Hillary Clinton and the 'Basket of Deplorables,'" *Politifact*, September 11, 2016, www.politifact.com/truth-o-meter/article/2016/sep/11 /context-hillary-clinton-basket-deplorables/.
3. "Blow-Out: Breitbart News Sets Traffic Records in July—192 Million Pageviews, 31 Million Uniques, 89 Million Visits," Breitbart News, August 7, 2016, www.breitbart .com/big-journalism/2016/08/07/blow-breitbart-news-sets-traffic-records-july-192 -million-pageviews-31-million-uniques-89-million-visits/.
4. Richard Spencer, "The Conservative Write," *Taki's Magazine*, August 6, 2008, takimag .com/article/the_conservative_write#axzz4JRcIyz7D.
5. Southern Poverty Law Center, "Richard Bertrand Spencer," *Extremist Files*, www.splcenter .org/fighting-hate/extremist-files/individual/richard-bertrand-spencer-0.
6. Richard B. Spencer, "Anti-Zionism for Dummies," *Radix Journal*, AltRight Archive, August 4, 2010, www.radixjournal.com/altright-archive/altright-archive/main/blogs/exit -strategies/anti-zionism-for-dummies.
7. Richard B. Spencer, "Jews, Europeans, and 'Whiteness,'" *Radix Journal*, December 8, 2014, www.radixjournal.com/blog/2014/12/8/jews-europeans-and-whiteness.
8. Hila Hershkoviz, "Ashkenazi Jews Are Not White—Response to *Haaretz* Article," *The Blogs, Times of Israel*, December 5, 2014, blogs.timesofisrael.com/ashkenazi-jews-are -not-white-response-to-haaretz-article/.
9. Southern Poverty Law Center, "Jared Taylor," *Extremist Files*, www.splcenter.org/fighting -hate/extremist-files/individual/jared-taylor.
10. Jared Taylor, "Israel's Operation Wetback," *American Renaissance*, June 22, 2012, www .amren.com/features/2012/06/israels-opereation-wetback/.
11. Heidi Beirich and Mark Potok, "Schism over Anti-Semitism Divides Key White Na- tionalist Group, American Renaissance," *SPLC Intelligence Report*, August 11, 2006, www .splcenter.org/fighting-hate/intelligence-report/2006/schism-over-anti-semitism -divides-key-white-nationalist-group-american-renaissance.
12. "American Renaissance's Jared Taylor Goes Full Anti-Semite," *Anti-Fascist News*, August 26, 2016, antifascistnews.net/2016/08/26/american-renaissances-jared-taylor-goes-full-anti- semite/.
13. Kevin MacDonald, "The Alt Right & the Jews," *Counter-Currents*, September 13, 2016, www.counter-currents.com/2016/09/the-alt-right-and-the-jews/.
14. Greg Johnson, "Reframing the Jewish Question," *Counter-Currents*, October 27, 2015, www.counter-currents.com/2015/10/reframing-the-jewish-question/.
15. Eliza Collins, "David Duke: Voting Against Trump Is 'Treason to Your Heritage,'" *Polit- ico*, February 25, 2016, www.politico.com/story/2016/02/david-duke-trump-219777.
16. Louis Nelson, "Clinton Ad Ties Trump to KKK, White Supremacists," *Politico*, August 25, 2016, www.politico.com/story/2016/08/clinton-ad-kkk-trump-227404.
17. Ari Feldman, "Donald Trump Jr. Retweets the 'Neo-Nazi Movement's Favorite Academ- ic,'" *Forward*, September 1, 2016, forward.com/news/national/348960/donald-trump-jr

-retweets-the-neo-nazi-movements-favorite-academic/.

18. Anthony Smith, "Donald Trump's Star of David Hillary Clinton Meme Was Created by White Supremacists," Mic, July 3, 2016, mic.com/articles/147711/donald-trump-s-star -of-david-hillary-clinton-meme-was-created-by-white-supremacists#.JLmQkpfgS.

19. Andrew Anglin, "Happening: Trump Retweets Two More White Genocide Accounts Back-to-Back," Daily Stormer, January 25, 2016, www.dailystormer.com/happening -trump-retweets-two-more-white-genocide-accounts-back-to-back/.

20. Jared Taylor, "What Is the Alt Right?," *American Renaissance*, October 11, 2016, www .amren.com/news/2016/10/what-is-the-alt-right-jared-taylor/.

21. Alan Rappeport and Noah Weiland, "White Nationalists Celebrate 'an Awakening' After Donald Trump's Victory," *New York Times*, November 19, 2016, www.nytimes.com /2016/11/20/us/politics/white-nationalists-celebrate-an-awakening-after-donald-trumps -victory.html?hp&action=click&pgtype=Homepage&clickSource=story-heading&module =a-lede-package-region&region=top-news&WT.nav=top-news&_r=1.

22. Joseph Goldstein, "Alt-Right Gathering Exults in Trump Election With Nazi-Era Salute," *New York Times*, November 20, 2016, www.nytimes.com/2016/11/21/us/alt-right -salutes-donald-trump.html?_r=0

23. Allum Bokhari and Milo Yiannopoulos, "An Establishment Conservative's Guide to the Alt-Right," Breitbart News, March 29, 2016, www.breitbart.com/tech/2016/03/29/an -establishment-conservatives-guide-to-the-alt-right/.

24. Quoted in Ben Shapiro, "Responding to the Alt Right: Are They Bigots, or Just Stupid Children?," *Daily Wire*, March 24, 2016, www.dailywire.com/news/4396/responding-alt -right-are-they-bigots-or-just-ben-shapiro.

25. Lauren Gambino, "Journalist Who Profiled Melania Trump Hit with Barrage of Antisemitic Abuse," *Guardian*, April 28, 2016, www.theguardian.com/us-news/2016/apr /28/julia-ioffe-journalist-melania-trump-antisemitic-abuse.

26. Dana Schwartz, "An Open Letter to Jared Kushner, from One of Your Jewish Employees," *Observer*, July 5, 2016, observer.com/2016/07/an-open-letter-to-jared-kushner-from-one -of-your-jewish-employees/.

27. Arthur Goldwag, "Putting Donald Trump on the Couch," *New York Times*, September 1, 2015, www.nytimes.com/2015/09/01/opinion/putting-donald-trump-on-the-couch.html?_r=0.

28. Tweet by @RosieGray, October 13, 2016: "I'm told Trump's speech today was a joint Stephen Miller/Steve Bannon production," twitter.com/RosieGray/status/786659018425012224.

29. Cleve R. Wootson Jr., "Sen. Al Franken Claims That Donald Trump's New Ad on the Economy Is Anti-Semitic," *The Fix* (blog), *Washington Post*, November 6, 2016, www .washingtonpost.com/news/the-fix/wp/2016/11/06/sen-al-franken-claims-that-donald -trumps-new-ad-on-the-economy-is-anti-semitic/.

30. Jesse Singal, "Yes, Steve Bannon Asked Why a School Had So Many Hanukkah Books," *Daily Intelligencer* (blog), *New York* magazine, November 15, 2016, nymag.com/daily /intelligencer/2016/11/yes-steve-bannon-asked-why-a-school-had-many-hanukkah -books.html.

31. Kimberley A. Strassel, "Steve Bannon on Politics as War," *Wall Street Journal*, November 18, 2016, www.wsj.com/articles/steve-bannon-on-politics-as-war-1479513161.

32. Alan M. Dershowitz, "Assessing the Bannon Appointment," *Jewish Press*, November 20, 2016, www.jewishpress.com/indepth/opinions/alan-dershowitz-assessing-the-bannon -appointment/2016/11/20/.

33. Joel B. Pollak, "The Psychosis of Palestinian Nationalism," Breitbart News, November 19, 2014, www.breitbart.com/national-security/2014/11/19/the-psychosis-of-palestinian

-nationalism/.

34. Michael Wolff, "Ringside with Steve Bannon at Trump Tower as the President-Elect's Strategist Plots 'an Entirely New Political Movement,'" *Hollywood Reporter,* November 18, 2016, www.hollywoodreporter.com/news/steve-bannon-trump-tower-interview-trumps -strategist-plots-new-political-movement-948747.

35. Larry Solov, "Breitbart News Network: Born in the USA, Conceived in Israel," Breitbart News, November 17, 2015, www.breitbart.com/big-journalism/2015/11/17/breitbart -news-network-born-in-the-usa-conceived-in-israel/.

Centering Our Work on Challenging Islamophobia

1. "Stories & Strategies: An Interview with Bina Ahmad," *Network against Islamophobia* newsletter, no. 2, jewishvoiceforpeace.org/wp-content/uploads/2015/07/Network-Against -Islamophobia-Newsletter.pdf.

2. Alex Kane, "Author Deepa Kumar on the Imperial Roots of Anti-Muslim Sentiment," *Mondoweiss,* July 2, 2012.

Who Am I to Speak?

1. This is a line from my poem "Wings," published in Tony Kushner and Alisa Solomon, eds., *Wrestling with Zion: Progressive Jewish-American Responses to the Israeli-Palestinian Conflict* (New York: Grove, 2003).

"We're Here Because You Were There"

1. UNHCR, "Convention and Protocol Relating to the Status of Refugees," www.unhcr .org/3b66c2aa10.html; Riccardo Bocco, "UNRWA and the Palestinian Refugees: A History within History," *Refugee Survey Quarterly* 28, nos. 2 & 3 (2009): 229–252.

2. Moustafa Bayoumi, "Racing Religion," *CR: The New Centennial Review* 6, no. 2 (Fall 2006): 267–293.

3. George J. Sanchez, "'What's Good for Boyle Heights Is Good for the Jews': Creating Multiculturalism on the Eastside during the 1950s," *American Quarterly* 56, no. 3 (September 2004): 633–661.

4. "The United States v. Rose Kuznitz," in Rose Chernin Case file, Box 27, American Committee for the Protection of the Foreign Born Papers, Labadie Special Collections, University of Michigan.

5. Carol Anderson, *Eyes off the Prize: The United Nations and the African American Struggle for Human Rights, 1944–1955* (New York: Cambridge University Press, 2003); Melani McAlister, *Epic Encounters: Culture, Media and U.S. Interests in the Middle East since 1945* (Berkeley: University of California Press, 2005).

6. John Higham, *Strangers in the Land: Patterns of American Nativism, 1860–1925* (New Brunswick, NJ: Rutgers University Press, 2002).

7. David Cohen, spoken comments recorded in unpublished manuscript in author's possession. See also Bruce Vielmetti, "Immigrant Rights Group, Sheriff David Clark Spar over Records Request," *Milwaukee Journal Sentinel,* May 6, 2015, www.jsonline.com/news/milwaukee /immigrant-rights-group-sheriff-david-clarke-spar-over-records-request-b99495448z1 -302843061.html.

8. Mark Karlin, "Truthout Interviews Max Blumenthal about the 51-Day Israeli Assault on Gaza," *Truthout,* July 19, 2015, www.truth-out.org/progressivepicks/item/31937-truthout -interviews-max-blumenthal-about-the-51-day-israeli-assault-on-gaza.

European Antisemitism

1. Jon Henley, "Antisemitism on Rise across Europe 'in Worst Times since the Nazis,'" *Guardian*, August 7, 2014, www.theguardian.com/society/2014/aug/07/antisemitism-rise -europe-worst-since-nazis.
2. Ibid.
3. Jim Yardley, "Europe's Anti-Semitism Comes Out of the Shadows," *New York Times*, September 23, 2014, www.nytimes.com/2014/09/24/world/europe/europes-anti-semitism -comes-out-of-shadows.html?_r2.
4. Griff Witte, "In a Kosher Grocery Store in Paris, Terror Takes a Deadly Toll," *Washington Post*, January 9, 2015, www.washingtonpost.com/world/europe/paris-kosher -market-seized-in-second-hostage-drama-in-nervous-france/2015/01/09/f171b97e -97ff-11e4-8005-1924ede3e54a_story.html.
5. "Copenhagen Shootings: Police Kill 'Gunman' after Two Attacks," BBC News, February 15, 2015, www.bbc.com/news/world-europe-31475803.
6. Adam Lebor, "Exodus: Why Europe's Jews Are Fleeing Once Again," *Newsweek*, July 29, 2014, www.newsweek.com/2014/08/08/exodus-why-europes-jews-are-fleeing-once -again-261854.html.
7. Jeffrey Goldberg, "Is It Time for the Jews to Leave Europe?," *Atlantic*, April 2015, www .theatlantic.com/magazine/archive/2015/04/is-it-time-for-the-jews-to-leave-europe /386279/.
8. Henley, "Antisemitism on Rise."
9. "Netanyahu to French Jews after Attacks: 'Israel Is Your Home,'" *Yahoo News*, January 10, 2015, www.yahoo.com/news/netanyahu-french-jews-attacks-israel-home-181235447.html ?ref=gs.
10. Barak Ravid, "Danish Chief Rabbi Responds to Netanyahu: Terror Is Not a Reason to Move to Israel," *Haaretz*, February 15, 2015, www.haaretz.com/israel-news/1.642552.
11. Mairav Zonszein, "Jewish Migration to Israel Up 40% This Year So Far," *Guardian*, May 3, 2015, www.theguardian.com/world/2015/may/03/jewish-immigration-israel-jumps-this -year-ukrainians-russians-europe-paris-attacks.
12. Judy Maltz, "Record Number of French Jews Immigrated to Israel in 2015," *Haaretz*, December 16, 2015, www.haaretz.com/jewish/news/.premium-1.692152.
13. Zonszein, "Jewish Migration."
14. "Netanyahu Visits Paris Synagogue, Crowd Breaks into National Anthem," *New York Times*, January 11, 2015, www.nytimes.com/video/multimedia/100000003443029/netanyahu -visits-paris-synagogue-crowd-breaks-into-national-anth.html.
15. "European Jewish Group Slams Netanyahu's Call for French Jews to Immigrate to Israel," *Haaretz*, January 11, 2015, www.haaretz.com/jewish/news/1.636453.
16. Ravid, "Danish Chief Rabbi Responds to Netanyahu."
17. Alissa Rubin and Aurelien Breeden, "Jewish Graves Vandalized in France," *New York Times*, February 16, 2015, www.nytimes.com/2015/02/17/world/europe/french-jews-cemetery -vandalism-latest-sign-of-anti-semitism.html?_r=0.
18. Maud Swinnen, "Danish PM Thorning-Schmidt: 'We Wouldn't Be the Same without the Jewish Community in Denmark,'" *European Jewish Press*, February 17, 2015, ejpress .org/index.php?option=com_content&view=article&id=51586&catid=0.
19. "Radical Islamist Movements: Jidhadi Networks and Hizb ut-Tahrir," Pew Research Center, September 15, 2010, www.pewforum.org/2010/09/15/muslim-networks-and-movements -in-western-europe-radical-islamist-movements-jihadi-networks-and-hizb-ut-tahrir/.
20. Daniel Byman and Jennifer Williams, "Al-Qaeda vs. ISIS: The Battle for the Soul of Jihad,"

Newsweek, March 27, 2015, www.newsweek.com/al-qaeda-vs-isis-battle-soul-jihad-317414.

21. Emmanuel Karagiannis, "Paris Attacks: ISIS Is Not an Existential Threat," *Newsweek*, November 15, 2015, europe.newsweek.com/paris-attacks-isis-threat-336586?rx=us.

22. David Greenberg, "The Roots of Arab Anti-Semitism," *Slate*, October 31, 2001, www.slate .com/articles/news_and_politics/history_lesson/2001/10/the_roots_of_arab_antisemitism .html.

23. Ibid.

24. Jeffrey Goldberg, "Is it Time for the Jews to Leave Europe?," *Atlantic*, April 2015, www .theatlantic.com/magazine/archive/2015/04/is-it-time-for-the-jews-to-leave-europe /386279/.

25. Leonid Bershidsky, "Europe's Haters Aren't So Focused on the Jews Anymore," *Bloomberg*, May 4, 2016, www.bloomberg.com/view/articles/2016-05-04/europe-s-haters-aren-t -so-focused-on-the-jews-anymore.

26. Paul Hockenos, "In Europe, Anti-Semitism and Islamophobia Go Hand in Hand," Al Jazeera America, March 9, 2015.

27. Emran Feroz, "Europe's First Report on Islamophobia Shows the Dangerous Climate Muslims Live In," *AlterNet*, May 4, 2016, www.alternet.org/grayzone-project/europes-first -report-islamophobia-shows-dangerous-climate-muslims-live.

28. Francois Murphy, "Top Rabbi Warns of Far-right Parties Winning Over Some of Europe's Jewish Voters," *Haaretz*, June 1, 2016, www.haaretz.com/jewish/news/1.722560.

29. Peter Foster, "Who Is Norbert Hofer and Should Europe Be Worried about Him Becoming President of Austria?," *Telegraph*, May 23, 2016, www.telegraph.co.uk/news/2016 /05/22/who-is-norbert-hofer-and-should-europe-be-worried-about-him-beco/.

30. Agence France-Presse, "Norway's Muslims and Jews Link Up to Denounce Extremist Violence," *Guardian*, February 21, 2015, www.theguardian.com/world/2015 /feb/21/norways-muslims-and-jews-link-up-to-denounce-extremist-violence.

31. Rifkele, "Please Come to Malmö in the Springtime," *Jewschool: Progressive Jews & Views*, October 12, 2012, jewschool.com/2012/10/29505/please-come-to-malmo-in-the -springtime/.

32. Private email communication.

33. Glenn Greenwald, "Brexit Is Only the Latest Proof of the Insularity and Failure of Western Establishment Institutions," *The Intercept*, June 25, 2016, theintercept.com/2016/06/25 /brexit-is-only-the-latest-proof-of-the-insularity-and-failure-of-western-establishment -institutions/.

34. Paul Krugman, "Israel's Gilded Age," *New York Times*, March 16, 2015, www.nytimes.com /2015/03/16/opinion/paul-krugman-israels-gilded-age.html?_r=0.

35. William Robinson, "The Political Economy of Israeli Apartheid and the Specter of Genocide," *Truthout*, September 19, 2014, www.truth-out.org/news/item/26254-the-political -economy-of-israeli-apartheid-and-the-specter-of-genocide.

36. Aluf Benn, "The Jewish Majority in Israel Still See the Country as a 'Villa in the Jungle,'" *Guardian*, www.theguardian.com/commentisfree/2013/aug/20/jewish-majority-israel-villa -in-the-jungle.

37. Rami Younis, "Israel's Most Racist Soccer Club Isn't Shouting 'Death to Arabs,'" *+972*, April 27, 2016, 972mag.com/israels-most-racist-soccer-club-isnt-shouting-death-to -arabs/118893/.

38. Ofer Aderet, "Right-wing Demonstrators in Tel Aviv Wore Neo-Nazi Shirts," *Haaretz*, July 15, 2014, www.haaretz.com/israel-news/.premium-1.605234.

39. Ali Abunimah, "Israeli Lawmaker's Call for Genocide of Palestinians Gets Thousands

of Facebook Likes," *Electronic Intifada*, May 8, 2015, electronicintifada.net/blogs/ali
-abunimah/israeli-lawmakers-call-genocide-palestinians-gets-thousands-facebook-likes.

40. Sue Surkes, "Far-Right Austrian Party Chief Visits Israel, Tours Yad Vashem," *The Times of Israel*, April 12, 2016, www.timesofisrael.com/far-right-austrian-freedom-party-chief -visits-israel/.

Two Degrees of Separation

1. Theodore Roosevelt, *The Winning of the West* (New York: G. P. Putnam's Sons, 1889).
2. Avi Shlaim, "It Can Be Done," *London Review of Books*, June 9, 1994.
3. Omar Barghouti, "Relative Humanity: Identity, Rights and Ethics—Israel as a Case Study," *PMLA* 121, no. 5 (2006): 1536–43.
4. Birzeit University Institute of Law, *Guidelines: Advocating for Palestinian Rights in Conformity with International Law* (Jerusalem: Civic Coalition for Palestinian Rights in Jerusalem, 2013).
5. Desmond Tutu, "Apartheid in the Holy Land," *Guardian*, April 28, 2002, www.theguardian .com/world/2002/apr/29/comment.
6. Elise Labott, "Arab Citizens of Israel Face Defining Moment in Election," CNN, March 16, 2015, edition.cnn.com/2015/03/16/middleeast/israeli-election-arabs/.
7. BDS Movement, "BDS Movement: Freedom, Justice, Equality," www.bdsmovement.net.
8. Globescan, *Negative Views of Russia on the Rise: Global Survey on Country Influence*, June 3, 2014, www.globescan.com/news-and-analysis/press-releases/press-releases-2014/315 -negative-views-of-russia-on-the-rise-global-survey.html.
9. Itamar Eichner, "Comptroller's Report Highlights Israeli Failure to Fight BDS," *Ynet*, May 24, 2016, www.ynetnews.com/articles/0,7340,L-4807490,00.html; Nathaniel Popper, "Israel Aims to Improve its Public Image," *The Forward*, October 14, 2005, forward .com/news/2070/israel-aims-to-improve-its-public-image.
10. "Israel Has Been Infected by Seeds of Fascism, Says Ex-Prime Minister Ehud Barak," *Haaretz*, May 20, 2016, www.haaretz.com/israel-news/1.720715; Barak Ravid and Gili Cohen, "IDF Deputy Chief Likens 'Revolting Trends' in Israeli Society to Pre-Holocaust Germany," *Haaretz*, May 4, 2016, www.haaretz.com/israel-news/1.717948.
11. Thomas L. Friedman, "Newt, Matt, Bibi and Vladimir," *New York Times*, December 13, 2011, www.nytimes.com/2011/12/14/opinion/friedman-newt-mitt-bibi-and-vladimir.html?_r=0.
12. Ruth Eglash, "Israeli Minister: Criticizing Israel Is the New Anti-Semitism," *Washington Post*, May 4, 2016, www.washingtonpost.com/news/worldviews/wp/2016/05/04 /israeli-minister-criticizing-israel-is-the-new-anti-semitism.
13. BDS Movement, "Palestinian Civil Society Call for BDS," July 9, 2005, www.bdsmovement .net/call.
14. Eli Aminov, "The Mutual Dependency of Zionism and Antisemitism," *AlterNet*, May 28, 2016, www.alternet.org/grayzone-project/mutual-dependency-zionism-and-antisemitism.
15. Adar Primor, "The Unholy Alliance between Israel's Right and Europe's Antisemites," *Haaretz*, December 12, 2010, www.haaretz.com/the-unholy-alliance-between-israel-s-right-and -europe-s-anti-semites-1.330132; Ofer Aderet, "On Holocaust Remembrance Day, Rivlin Slams Likud for Forging Ties With European Extremists," *Haaretz*, May 6, 2016, www.haaretz.com/israel-news/.premium-1.718209.
16. Adalah: The Legal Center for Arab Minority Rights in Israel, "Discriminatory Laws Database," adalah.org/eng/Israeli-Discriminatory-Law-Database.
17. Boycott!, "Supporting the Palestinian BDS Call from Within," www.boycottisrael.info.
18. David Horovitz, "Israel Losing Democrats, 'Can't Claim Bipartisan US Support,' Top

Pollster Warns," *The Times of Israel*, July 5, 2015, www.timesofisrael.com/israel-losing
-democrats-cant-claim-bipartisan-us-support-top-pollster-warns/.

19. "Israeli Army Criticized for Writing I.D. Numbers on Detainees," *Beliefnet*, March 12, 2002,
www.beliefnet.com/faiths/judaism/2002/03/israeli-army-criticized-for-writing-i-d-numbers
-on-detainees.aspx.

20. Jewish Telegraphic Agency, "Israel's Sephardic Chief Rabbi: Gentiles Here to Serve the
Jews," *The Forward*, March 28, 2016, forward.com/news/breaking-news/337161/israels
-sephardic-chief-rabbi-gentiles-here-to-serve-the-jews/.

21. Sharon Pulwer, "Jewish Extremists' Leader: Christians Are 'Blood Sucking Vampires'
Who Should Be Expelled from Israel," *Haaretz*, December 22, 2015, www.haaretz.com/
israel-news/.premium-1.693132.

22. Baz Ratner, "Arson Attack Guts Part of Israel's Church of Loaves and Fishes," Reuters, June
18, 2015, www.reuters.com/article/us-israel-church-fire-idUSKBN0OY0FW20150618.

23. Yossi Gurvitz, "A Court of Non-convictions When the Victim Is Palestinian," *+972*, June 13,
2015, 972mag.com/a-court-of-non-convictions-when-the-victim-is-palestinian/107700/.

24. Patrick Strickland, "Israeli Wedding Party Celebrates Dawabsheh Killings," Al Jazeera,
December 24, 2015, www.aljazeera.com/news/2015/12/israeli-wedding-party-celebrates
-dawabsheh-killings-151224051318762.html; Shahd Abusalama, "The Burning of a Palestinian Child: Not an Exception, but a Result of Zionism," *Mondoweiss*, August 1, 2015,
mondoweiss.net/2015/08/palestinian-exception-zionism/.

25. Chris Hedges, "A Gaza Diary," *Harper's Magazine*, October 2001; Amnesty International,
*Troubled Waters: Palestinians Denied Fair Access to Water—Israel-Occupied Palestinian Territo-
ries*, 2009, www.amnestyusa.org/pdf/mde150272009en.pdf.

26. Giulio Meotti, "The Vatican on Gaza: Israel Is a 'Baby-Killer,'" *Arutz Sheva*, November 11,
2012, www.israelnationalnews.com/News/News.aspx/162368.

27. Joseph Levine, "On Questioning the Jewish State," *New York Times*, March 9, 2013,
opinionator.blogs.nytimes.com/2013/03/09/on-questioning-the-jewish-state/?_r=1.

28. Ibid.

29. Associated Press, "Abbas: 'No Way' to Recognition of Israel as Jewish State," *Haaretz*,
March 9, 2014, www.haaretz.com/israel-news/1.578653; Lisa Goldman, "'I Have a
Dream': Ayman Odeh's Maiden Knesset Speech," *+972*, May 8, 2015, 972mag.com/vid
-i-have-a-dream-ayman-odehs-maiden-knesset-speech/106491/.

30. Levine, "On Questioning."

31. PACBI, "Debating BDS: On Normalization and Partial Boycotts," April 1, 2012, www.
pacbi.org/etemplate.php?id=1850.

32. Omar Barghouti, "Boycotting Israeli Settlement Products: Tactic vs. Strategy," *Electronic
Intifada*, November 11, 2008, electronicintifada.net/content/boycotting-israeli-settlement
-products-tactic-vs-strategy/7801.

33. Omar Barghouti, "Why Israel Fears the Boycott," *New York Times*, January 31, 2014,
www.nytimes.com/2014/02/01/opinion/sunday/why-the-boycott-movement-scares
-israel.html.

34. Human Rights Watch, "Israel, Palestinian Leaders Should Guarantee Right of Return as Part of Comprehensive Refugee Solution," December 21, 2000, www.hrw.org
/news/2000/12/21/israel-palestinian-leaders-should-guarantee-right-return-part
-comprehensive-refugee.

35. Barak Ravid, "Netanyahu: I Don't Want a Binational State, but We Need to Control
All of the Territories for the Foreseeable Future," *Haaretz*, October 26, 2015, www
.haaretz.com/israel-news/.premium-1.682374.

36. US Department of State, Bureau of Democracy, Human Rights, and Labor, *2010 Human Rights Report: Israel and the Occupied Territories* (Washington, DC: US State Department, 2011), www.state.gov/j/drl/rls/hrrpt/2010/nea/154463.htm.
37. United Nations, UN Doc. A/CONF.183/9, "Rome Statute of the International Criminal Court," December 19, 2002, legal.un.org/icc/statute/romefra.htm.
38. Tia Goldenberg, "Israeli Court Rejects Israeli Nationality Status," Associated Press, October 4, 2013, bigstory.ap.org/article/israeli-court-rejects-israeli-nationality-status.
39. Oren Yiftachel, *Ethnocracy: Land and Identity Politics in Israel/Palestine* (Philadelphia: University of Pennsylvania Press, 2006).

The Campus Will Divest!

1. Anna Balzer, "BDS@10: List of 100+ US Victories!" US Campaign to End the Israeli Occupation, June 15, 2016, www.endtheoccupation.org/article.php?id=4503.
2. Jewish Voice for Peace, *Stifling Dissent*.
3. Yardain Amron, "Why Did UCLA Hillel Funnel Cash from Pro-Israel Donor to Student Candidate?," *The Forward*, July 23, 2014, forward.com/news/israel/202616/why-did-ucla-hillel-funnel-cash-from-pro-israel-do/.
4. Alex Kane, "NYC Council Bill to Track Campus Anti-Semitism Is Attack on Palestine Activism, Advocates Say," *Mondoweiss*, March 13, 2015, mondoweiss.net/2016/03/advocates-say-nyc-council-bill-on-anti-semitism-is-attack-on-palestine-activism/.
5. Palestine Legal, "Statement: New NY Bill Unconstitutional," June 13, 2016. palestinelegal.org/news/2016/6/13/dv9bl6v9xt027qbdf2uqzl734siw0i.
6. Center for Constitutional Rights and Palestine Legal, *The Palestine Exception to Free Speech: A Movement under Attack in the US* (New York: Center for Constitutional Rights, 2015), palestinelegal.org/the-palestine-exception/.
7. In 2012–13, the University of California conducted a system-wide "Campus Climate" survey, asking thousands of students from different faith backgrounds about their experience of campus climate. In 2014, a report publishing the survey's results showed that Jewish students reported similar levels of comfort compared to other religious/spiritual groups, with over 90 percent of Jewish students reporting a "very comfortable," "comfortable," or "neutral" campus climate. Regarding both the overall campus climate and the classroom climate in particular, a slightly higher percentage of Jewish students reported feeling "very comfortable" compared to students of other religious groups. The report can be found at campusclimate.ucop.edu/_common/files/pdf-climate/ucsystem-full-report.pdf.
8. Jewish Voice for Peace, "UC Regents Statement on Intolerance Misses the Mark," March 15, 2016, jewishvoiceforpeace.org/uc-regents-statement-intolerance-misses-mark/.
9. Teresa Watanabe, "UC Regents Say Antisemitism Has 'No Place' on Campus but Reject Blanket Censure of Anti-Zionism," *Los Angeles Times*, March 23, 2016, www.latimes.com/local/lanow/la-me-ln-uc-regents-intolerance-20160322-story.html.
10. University of California Students for Justice in Palestine, "University of California Student Petition against HR-35 Surpasses 1,000 Signatures," *Jadaliyya*, January 13, 2013, reviews.jadaliyya.com/pages/index/9528/university-of-california-student-petition-against.
11. Maha Kamel, "'Muslim Students Feel Intimidated' according to UC Climate Survey," The Islamic Center of Southern California, blog.icsonline.org/2012/07/muslim-students-feel-intimidated-according-to-uc-climate-survey.
12. "'Irvine 11': 10 Students Sentenced to Probation, No Jail Time," *Los Angeles Times*, September 23, 2011, latimesblogs.latimes.com/lanow/2011/09/irvine-11-sentenced

-probation-no-jail-time.html.

13. Christopher Godshall and Eva Kalikoff, "We Are Not Waiting," *Columbia Spectator*, March 26, 2015, columbiaspectator.com/opinion/2015/03/26/we-are-not-waiting.

14. Richard Chang and Darrell Smith, "Comic Roseanne Barr Jumps into UC Davis Fray, Says She Hopes Campus 'Gets Nuked,'" *The Sacramento Bee*, February 11, 2015, www.sacbee.com/news/local/education/article9771911.html.

15. "Jews for Divestment," *The Aggie*, February 3, 2015, theaggie.org/2015/02/03/jews-for-divestment/. Since its publication, the article has been removed from *The Aggie* website and replaced with a note that states: "The Guest Opinion includes factual statements regarding StandWithUs. Representatives of that organization have challenged the truthfulness of these statements, and consequently the article has been removed."

16. Jewish Voice for Peace, "JVP Student Network Statement on Intersectionality," January 4, 2016, jewishvoiceforpeace.org/jvp-student-network-statement-on-intersectionality/.

17. Henry Rosen and Max Fineman, "We Anti-Occupation Activists Aren't a 'Danger' to the American Jewish Community," *Haaretz*, January 7, 2016, www.haaretz.com/opinion/.premium-1.695734.

Antisemitism on the American College Campus

1. In the interest of protecting student privacy, I am providing only minimal information about the course. Generally, the issue at hand seemed to be not what the course contained but what the course did not contain.

2. Department of Education, Office for Civil Rights, "Dear Colleague Letter," April 4, 2011, www2.ed.gov/about/offices/list/ocr/letters/colleague-201104.html.

3. Ibid., 3.

4. As a student in Israel, I worked and volunteered for the educational department of the Tel Aviv Rape Crisis Center and for Tel Aviv University's Campus Hotline for Victims of Sexual Harassment.

5. Notably, not all the "characteristics" listed in the cited policy operate in the same way and to the same extent in the way that they unequally distribute power.

Chilling and Censoring of Palestine Advocacy

1. Southern Poverty Law Center, "David Horowitz," www.splcenter.org/fighting-hate/extremist-files/individual/david-horowitz.

2. Stop the Jew Hatred on Campus, "Horowitz Freedom Center Targets BDS Supporters with Campus Poster Campaign," www.stopthejewhatredoncampus.org/horowitz-freedom-center-targets-bds-supporters-campus-poster-campaign.

3. See Jared Sichel, "UCLA Jewish Groups Condemn David Horowitz for Creating #Jew-Haters Posters," *Jewish Journal*, February 26, 2015; Natalie Jacobs, "SDSU Protest Brings Light to Controversial Anti-BDS Activism on College Campuses," *San Diego Jewish Journal*, April 28, 2016.

4. Palestine Legal, "Civil Rights Attorneys Call on Brooklyn College to Drop Politically Motivated Charges against Two Students," press release, May 6, 2016, palestinelegal.org/news/2016/5/6/press-release-civil-rights-attorneys-call-on-brooklyn-college-to-drop-politica?rq=brooklyn%20college.

5. "NY State Senate Says It Will Cut CUNY Funding over Inaction on Anti-Semitism Charges," Jewish Telegraphic Agency, March 21, 2016, www.jta.org/2016/03/21/news-opinion/united-states/ny-state-senate-says-it-will-cut-cuny-funding-over-inaction

-on-anti-semitism-charges.

6. Palestine Legal, "Brooklyn College Students Cleared at Controversial Disciplinary Hearing," press release, May 31, 2016, palestinelegal.org/news/2016/5/31/brooklyn-college -students-cleared-at-controversial-disciplinary-hearing. The independent taskforce commissioned to investigate the Zionist Organization of America's claims about alleged antisemitism on CUNY campuses concluded in September 2016 that the alleged antisemitic incidents could not be attributed to SJP, and that SJP's speech activities were constitutionally protected, noting that the "tendency to blame SJP for any act of anti-Semitism on any CUNY campus" is a "mistake." Palestine Legal, "Independent Investigation Clears CUNY Students for Justice in Palestine," press release, September 9, 2016, palestinelegal.org/news/2016/9/12/press-release-independent-investigation-clears -cuny-students-for-justice-in-palestine.

7. Palestine Legal, "Civil Rights Attorneys Call on Brooklyn College."

8. Palestine Legal, "2016 Mid-Year Report," palestinelegal.org/news/2016/7/25/2016-mid -year-report.

9. Dima Khalidi, "Andrew Cuomo's BDS Blacklist Is a Clear Violation of the First Amendment," *The Nation*, June 23, 2016, www.thenation.com/article/andrew-cuomos-bds-blacklist -is-a-clear-violation-of-the-first-amendment/.

10. Philip Weiss and Adam Horowitz, "Flanked by AIPAC and Israeli Consul, Cuomo Signs Anti-BDS Order," *Mondoweiss*, June 6, 2015, mondoweiss.net/2016/06/flanked -israeli-consul/.

11. Andrew Cuomo, "If You Boycott Israel, New York State Will Boycott You," *Washington Post*, June 10, 2016, www.washingtonpost.com/opinions/gov-andrew-cuomo-if-you-boycott-israel -new-york-state-will-boycott-you/2016/06/10/1d6d3acc-2e62-11e6-9b37-42985f6a265c _story.html?tid=a_inl.

12. Palestine Legal, "San Diego State University Must Defend Students against Harassment," press release, May 12, 2016, palestinelegal.org/news/2016/5/12/san-diego-state -university-must-defend-students-against-harassment?rq=sdsu%20horowitz.

13. The full report can be found at palestinelegal.org/the-palestine-exception. Many thanks to Palestine Legal for allowing us to republish part of their report here.

14. Palestine Legal interview with student (name withheld), May 12, 2015 (concern about family members' travel as a result of false accusations against student); Palestine Legal email interview with student (name withheld), May 27, 2015 (concern about travel as a result of false accusations); Palestine Legal interview with student (name withheld), May 28, 2015 (concern about job prospects upon graduation and her family having difficulty traveling as a result of false accusations); Palestine Legal interview with student (name withheld), June 9, 2015 (concern about job prospects as a result of false accusations); Palestine Legal interview with student (name withheld), August 12, 2015 (concern about job prospects and travel as a result of false accusations).

15. US Commission on Civil Rights, "Federal Civil Rights Engagement with Arab and Muslim American Communities Post-9/11," September 2014, www.usccr.gov/pubs/ARAB _MUSLIM_9-30-14.pdf; Donna Lieberman, "Infringement on Civil Liberties After 9/11," *New York Law School Law Review*, 56 (2011–12), www.nylslawreview.com/ wp-content/uploads/sites/16/2012/02/Lieberman-article.pdf; CCR, case page for *Hassan v. City of New York*, updated January 16, 2015, ccrjustice.org/home/what-we-do/our -cases/hassan-v-city-new-york.

16. For additional information about some of these organizations, their work to silence Palestine human rights advocacy, and their funding sources, see International Jewish Anti-

Zionist Network, "The Business of Backlash," March 2015, www.ijan.org/wp-content /uploads/2015/04/IJAN-Business-of-Backlash-full-report-web.pdf.

17. Hillel, "Hillel Israel Guidelines: Hillel Guidelines for Campus Israel Activities," n.d., www.hillel.org/jewish/hillel-israel/hillel-israel-guidelines.

18. Brandeis Center, "Mission and Values," March 18, 2015, brandeiscenter.com/about/mission.

19. For a summary of AMCHA's tactics and their effects, see Palestine Legal, "Rights Groups Write to UC & CSU Trustees about AMCHA Tactics to Silence Speech on Palestinian Rights," February 21, 2014, palestinelegalsupport.org/2014/02/21/rights-groups-write-to -uc-csu-trustees-about-amcha-tactics-to-silence-speech-on-palestinian-rights/; Kenneth Monteiro, "Commentary on Free Speech and AMCHA Initiative's Attacks on Students and Faculty Across California Campuses," San Francisco State University, 2014, ethnicstudies .sfsu.edu/ethnicst/content/application-statement-current-or-going-circumstances; Ali Abunimah, *The Battle for Justice in Palestine* (Chicago: Haymarket Books, 2014), 169.

20. Stand With Us, "College," www.standwithus.com/campus/college/.

21. Nathan Guttman, "StandWithUs Draws Line on Israel," *The Forward*, November 27, 2011, forward.com/news/146821/standwithus-draws-line-on-israel/.

22. Alex Kane, "Israel Lobby Group Compiles Secret Dossiers on Pro-Palestine Speakers," *Mondoweiss*, February 25, 2014, mondoweiss.net/2014/02/compiles-palestinian-speakers.

23. Shurat HaDin–Israel Law Center, "Overview," n.d., israellawcenter.org/avout/overview/. Shurat HaDin has extensive relationships with the Israeli government and security establishment and has reportedly taken direction from the Israeli government as to which cases to file, according to documents revealed by WikiLeaks. Shurat HaDin has also targeted BDS efforts in other countries (Tom Griffin and David Miller, "BDS Campaigner Targeted by Law Firm with Links to Israeli Intelligence," *SpinWatch*, October 5, 2013, www.spinwatch.org/index.php/blog/item/5550-bds-campaigner-targeted-by-law-firm -with-links-to-israeli-intelligence).

24. Ibid.

25. In June 2015, Shurat HaDin threatened to sue Coca-Cola if the beverage maker did not break its contract with a Palestinian franchise owner who expressed support for BDS in two op-eds (Marissa Newman, "Israeli Group Threatens to Sue Coca-Cola over Palestinian Partner," *The Times of Israel*, June 15, 2015, www.timesofisrael.com/israeli-ngo -threatens-to-sue-coca-cola-over-palestinian-partners-bds-support/).

26. The ADL, for example, criticized the David Horowitz Freedom Center's placement of San Diego State University on a list of top-ten campuses with the worst antisemitic activity (Gary Warth, "Report about Antisemitic Activities at SDSU Disputed," *San Diego Union-Tribune*, February 24, 2015, www.sandiegouniontribune.com/news/2015 /feb/24/sdsu-antisemitism-david-horowitz/).

27. For example, when Secretary of State John Kerry said that Israel "risked becoming an apartheid state," former Illinois representative Bob Dold responded, "We work so hard to combat international attempts to delegitimize the State of Israel, so it is particularly disturbing to hear our very own Secretary of State, who is supposed to be our ambassador to the world and represent our values, embrace the delegitimization rhetoric of those who seek harm to Israel. Secretary Kerry's remarks about Israel simply should not be tolerated" (Josh Rogin, "Exclusive: Kerry Warns Israel Could Become 'An Apartheid State,'" *Daily Beast*, April 27, 2014, www .thedailybeast.com/articles/2014/04/27/exclusive-kerry-warns-israel-could-become -an-apartheid-state.html; Lynn Sweet, "Dold on Kerry Israel 'Apartheid' Comment: Should Not Be Tolerated," *Chicago Sun-Times*, May 1, 2014, politics.suntimes.com/article/washington /dold-kerry-israel-apartheid-comment-should-not-be-tolerated/thu-05012014-402pm).

28. The Reut Institute is an Israel-based think tank that works closely with the Israeli government to "[provide] a variety of decision-support services to Israel's decision makers and government agencies." See Reut Institute, "Services and Products," reut-institute.org/Content .aspx?Page=Services. For a summary of the report, see Reut Institute, "The Delegitimization Challenge: Creating a Political Firewall," February 14, 2010, reut-institute.org/Publication .aspx?Public, paper submitted to the Tenth Herzliya Conference, March 2010, reut -institute.org/data/uploads/PDFVer/20100310%20Delegitimacy%20Eng.pdf.

29. Ibid.

30. Ali Abunimah, "Israel's New Strategy: 'Sabotage' and 'Attack' the Global Justice Movement," *Electronic Intifada*, February 16, 2010, electronicintifada.net/content/israels-new-strategy -sabotage-and-attack-global-justice-movement/8683. The article includes a photograph of the Reut Institute presentation.

31. Jewish Federation of Central Massachusetts, "The Launch of the Israel Action Network," *Jewish Central Voice*, February 2011, jewishcentralvoice.com/2011/02/the-launch-of-the -israel-action-network/.

32. The Jewish Agency has focused on bringing Jews from across the world to Israel since its founding before the establishment of the Israeli state. See Jewish Agency for Israel, "About Us," November 16, 2013, www.jewishagency.org/content/4916; Josh Nathan-Kazis, "Jewish Agency Plans $300M-a-Year Push for Israel," *Haaretz*, August 15, 2013, forward.com /articles/182354/jewish-agency-plans-m-a-year-push-for-israel/?p=all.

33. Nathan Guttman, "Secret Sheldon Adelson Summit Raises up to $50M for Strident Anti-BDS Push," *The Forward*, June 9, 2015, forward.com/news/israel/309676 /secret-sheldon-adelson-summit-raises-up-to-50m-for-strident-anti-bds-push/.

34. Herb Keinon, "Netanyahu: Israel Need Not Engage in Self-Flagellation over Delegitimization Efforts," *Jerusalem Post*, May 31, 2015, www.jpost.com/Israel-News/Politics -And-Diplomacy/Netanyahu-Israel-need-not-engage-in-self-flagellation-over-delegiti mization-efforts-404600; Itamar Eichner, "Israel to Allocate NIS 100 Million for BDS Battle," *Ynet*, June 7, 2015, www.ynetnews.com/articles/0,7340,L-4665676,00.html.

35. Herb Keinon, "Netanyahu Convenes Strategy Meeting to Fight Boycotts," *Jerusalem Post*, February 10, 2014, www.jpost.com/National-News/Netanyahu-convenes-strategy -meeting-to-fight-boycotts-340904.

36. Ibid.

37. Rahim Kurwa, "Submission: Anti-Divestment Groups Resort to Personal Attacks in Lieu of Logical Argument," *Daily Bruin*, February 11, 2015, dailybruin.com/2015 /02/11/submission-anti-divestment-groups-resort-to-personal-attacks-in-lieu-of -logical-argument/.

38. White, "Israeli Think Tank Holds Anti-BDS 'Hackathon.'" StandWithUs, J Street, and the Israel Campus Coalition attended the gathering.

39. Reut Institute, "Contending with BDS and the Assault on Israel's Legitimacy," June 2015, reut-institute.org/en/Publication.aspx?PublicationId=4224.

40. Canary Mission, "About," n.d., www.canarymission.org/about/. See also Josh Nathan-Kazis, "Shadowy Web Site Creates Blacklist of Pro-Palestinian Activists," *The Forward*, May 27, 2015, forward.com/news/308902/shadowy-web-site-creates-black-list-of-pro-palestinian -activists/; Amanda Holpuch, "Website Targets Pro-Palestinian Students in Effort to Harm Job Prospects," *Guardian*, May 27, 2015, www.theguardian.com/us-news/2015/may/27 /website-targets-pro-palestinian-students-harm-job-prospects; Lyanne Melendez, "Web site Publicizes Actions of Politically Active Students," ABC7 News, May 29, 2015, abc7news.com/politics/website-publicizes-actions-of-politically-active-college-students

-/747121/.

41. Campus Watch, "About Campus Watch," 2015, www.campus-watch.org/about.php.

42. Kane, "Israel Lobby Group."

43. Palestine Legal interview with (name withheld), April 8, 2015; CCR interview with Shezza Abboushi Dallal, July 31, 2015.

44. Palestine Legal interview with student (name withheld), January 2014; Palestine Legal interview with student (name withheld), June 2015; Asa Winstanley and Nora Barrows-Friedman, "Documents Reveal Zionist Group Spied on US Student Delegation to Palestine," *Electronic Intifada*, January 29, 2014, electronicintifada.net/content/documents -reveal-zionist-group-spied-us-student-delegation-palestine/13130.

45. Kristen Mott, "University of Toledo Students Closer to Divestment Vote," *Cleveland Jewish News,* April 8, 2015, www.clevelandjewishnews.com/news/local_news/university-of -toledo-students-closer-to-divestment-vote/article_2280e6d4-de0f-11e49–ed0-d7177f272115 .html; Lauren Lindstrom, "UT Student Senate Tosses Divestment Proposal," *Toledo Blade*, February 18, 2015, www.toledoblade.com/Education/2015/02/18/Student-senate -tables-idea-of-UT-divestment.html; Vanessa McCray, "UT Student Senate Considers Call for Israeli Divestment," *Toledo Blade*, February 17, 2015, www.toledoblade.com /Education/2015/02/17/UT-student-senate-to-issue-call-for-Israeli-divestment.html.

46. Anti-Defamation League, "BDS Resolution Defeated at Northeastern University," March 20, 2015, newengland.adl.org/2015/03/20/bds-resolution-defeated-at-northeastern -university/.

47. Tina Matar, "Palestine & Israel: Settler-Colonialism and Apartheid," course syllabus, on file with Palestine Legal and available at media.wix.com/ugd/2a8cf7_bea6acfca35445e8823cf31a28a1af4a .docx?dn=IsraelandPalestine.docx.

48. AMCHA Initiative et al., "20 Groups Write to Chancellor Wilcox Regarding Serious Concerns about Political Indoctrination in UCR Course," April 16, 2015, www .amchainitiative.org/serious-concerns-about-political-indoctrination-in-ucr-course.

49. For example, the student received an email that read, "Since the palestinians weren't a people, but an islamo-nazi invention for the annihilation of Jews, then anything can be taught in colleges. Like hamas baby shields, college baby brains are a great weapon." Email from (name withheld) to Tina Matar, April 25, 2015, on file with Palestine Legal. A misogynist blogger who criticized the course posted a picture of a woman in a sexually provocative position, suggesting it was the student instructor, and wrote, "The chick looks like an attention-whore. . . . Sorry about my little 'micro-agression' in calling her a whore. Actually, that might not be a micro-aggression at all. That may be a full-on rape. You'd have to clue me in. If it is a rape, does that mean this Muslima is subject to Honor Killing? God, I hope not. She is pretty fuckin' hot." User "Pastorius," "Antisemitic Class Taught at UC Riverside Is Not Being Pulled," Infidel Bloggers Alliance, April 25, 2015, ibloga.blogspot.com/2015/04/antisemitic-class-taught-at-uc.html.

50. UCLA Academic Senate Committee on Academic Freedom, letter to Professor David Delgado Shorter, July 9, 2012, amchainitiative.org/letter-from-ucla-academic-senate -committee-on-academic-freedom-to-professor-david-delgado-shorter/.

51. Larry Gordon, "UCLA Professor Told Not to Link Class Material to Anti-Israel Campaign," *Los Angeles Times,* April 16, 2012, latimesblogs.latimes.com/lanow/2012/04/ucla -professor-told-not-to-link-class-material-to-an-anti-israel-campaign.html; Peter Schmidt, "Movement to Protest Israel's Policies Triggers Bitter Fights Over US Scholars' Speech," *Chronicle of Higher Education,* May 4, 2012, www.chronicle.com/article/ Clashes-Over-Israeli-Policies/131778/; Kaustuv Basu, "A Link Too Far," *Inside Higher*

Ed, April 16, 2012, www.insidehighered.com/news/2012/04/16/ucla-professor-counseled
-after-linking-course-page-political-petition; Nora Barrows-Friedman, "LA Professor
Wakes Up to Hate Mail for Linking to Anti-Zionist Material," *Electronic Intifada,* August
1, 2012, electronicintifada.net/content/la-professor-wakes-hate-mail-linking-anti-zionist
-material/11547.

52. Interview with Palestine Legal, October 25, 2013.

53. The definition was formerly known as the European Union Monitoring Centre (EU-MC)'s working definition of antisemitism. EUMC originally formulated the definition to facilitate data collection efforts (Ken Stern, "The Working Definition: A Reappraisal," Address at Stephen Roth Institute for Study of Contemporary Antisemitism and Racism, Tel Aviv University, "The Working Definition of Antisemitism— Six Years After" conference, August 31, 2010, kantorcenter.tau.ac.il/sites/default/files /proceeding-all_3.pdf. In 2013, the successor European civil rights agency removed the definition from its website "together with other non-official documents," to the consternation of Israeli officials and US-based Israel advocacy groups, including the AJC and SWC, which called on the agency to restore the working definition to its website. Jewish Telegraphic Agency, "EU Drops Its 'Working Definition' of Antisemitism," *The Times of Israel,* December 5, 2013, www.timesofisrael.com/eu-drops-its-working-definition -of-anti-semitism/#ixzz37qJRBuJL; Simon Wiesenthal Center, "SWC to EU Baroness Ashton: Return Antisemitism Definition Document to EU Fundamental Rights Agency Website," press release, November 6, 2013, www.wiesenthal.com/site/apps/nlnet /content.aspx?c=lsKWLbPJLnF&b=8776547&ct=13381863.

54. US State Department, "Defining Antisemitism," June 8, 2010, www.state.gov/j/drl /rls/fs/2010/122352.htm; Palestine Legal, "FAQ: What to Know about Efforts to Redefine Antisemitism to Silence Criticism of Israel," n.d., static1.squarespace.com /static/548748b1e4b083fc03ebf70e/t/556490f5e4b0658666cfe867/1432654069359/6 .+FAQ-onDefinition-of-Anti-Semitism-3-9-15.pdf. The State Department definition, designed to identify instances of global antisemitism, would violate the First Amendment if applied to restrict speech in the United States and therefore has limited legal effect. The State Department's use of the definition in its reporting on global antisemitism seems to acknowledge this, noting that "while the report describes many measures that foreign governments have adopted to combat antisemitism, it does not endorse any such measures that prohibit conduct that would be protected under the U.S. Constitution." See US State Department, *2008 Contemporary Global Antisemitism Report* (Washington, DC: US State Department, 2008), 2, www.state.gov/documents/organization/102301.pdf.

55. Larry Gordon, "Definition of Antisemitism Provokes Campus Debates," *Los Angeles Times,* May 18, 2015, www.latimes.com/local/education/la-me-ln-campuses-israel-20150518 -story.html.

56. Ibid.

57. AMCHA Initiative et al., "26 Groups Write to Stanford President Hennessy Regarding University Response to Swastikas & Ask Stanford to Adopt U.S. State Dep't Definition of Antisemitism," April 28, 2015, www.amchainitiative.org/letter-to-stanford-president-re -swastikas.

58. AMCHA Initiative et al., letter to Morton Schapiro, April 21, 2015, www.amchainitiative .org/wp-content/uploads/2015/04/President-Morton-Schapiro-Letter-re-swastikas-4 .21.15.pdf.

59. Brandeis Center et al., "Antisemitism at Northeastern University," April 6, 2015, brandeiscenter.com/blog/anti-semitism-at-northeastern-university.

60. Nathan Guttman, "Could California Ban Anti-Israel Campus Protests as 'Antisemitic' Hate?," *The Forward*, June 10, 2015. forward.com/news/national/309450/what-is-anti-semitism/.

61. Jonathan Molina, "After Condemning Antisemitism, UCSB Student Senate Rejects BDS Resolution," Brandeis Center, April 23, 2015, brandeiscenter.com/blog/after-condemning -anti-semitism-ucsb-votes-down-a-bds-resolution/.

62. Palestine Legal, "In Rightfully Condemning Antisemitism, UCLA Student Council Tacitly Silences Critics of Israel," March 11, 2015, palestinelegalsupport.org/2015 /03/11/in-rightfully-condemning-anti-semitism-ucla-student-council-tacitly-silences -critics-of-israel/; Jewish Voice for Peace, "UCLA Resolution on Antisemitism Creates Dangerous Precedent," March 11, 2015, jewishvoiceforpeace.org/blog/ucla-resolution -on-anti-semitism-creates-dangerous-precedent; Roii Ball, "USAC Resolution Fails to Distinguish Antisemitism, Criticism of Israel," *Daily Bruin*, March 18, 2015, daily-bruin.com/2015/03/17/submission-usac-resolution-fails-to-distinguish-anti-semitism -criticism-of-israel/.

63. California State Assembly, House Resolution No. 35, adopted August 28, 2012. The bill, available at leginfo.legislature.ca.gov/faces/billTextClient.xhtml?bill_id=201120120HR35, purports to provide evidence of antisemitism on campus, but the examples provided were replete with false information, exaggerations, and assumptions that criticism of Israeli policy is antisemitic. The bill's text evidences the latter by conflating a number of activities: "(2) speakers, films, and exhibits sponsored by student, faculty, and community groups that engage in antisemitic discourse or use antisemitic imagery and language to falsely describe Israel, Zionists, and Jews, including that Israel is a racist, apartheid, or Nazi state, that Israel is guilty of heinous crimes against humanity such as ethnic cleansing and genocide, that the Jewish state should be destroyed, that violence against Jews is justified, that Jews exaggerate the Holocaust as a tool of Zionist propaganda, and that Jews in America wield excessive power over American foreign policy; (3) swastikas and other antisemitic graffiti in residential halls, public areas on campus, and Hillel houses; (4) student- and faculty-sponsored boycott, divestment, and sanction campaigns against Israel that are a means of demonizing Israel and seek to harm the Jewish state; . . . (6) suppression and disruption of free speech that present Israel's point of view." By pairing on a continuum real instances of antisemitism (such as swastika graffiti) with Palestinian rights advocacy, with which there was no documented relationship, the bill irresponsibly implies that critics of Israel were responsible for the bona fide antisemitic acts.

64. Ibid.

65. Ibid.

66. Dexter Van Zile, "JVP an Accessory to the Spread of Antisemitism in the US," *The Times of Israel*, July 16, 2014, blogs.timesofisrael.com/jvp-an-accessory-to-the-spread-of -antisemitism-in-u-s/; Zach Stern, "'Open Hillel' Legitimizes Antisemitism," Zionist Organization of America, October 27, 2014, zoa.org/2014/10/10264067-zoa-campus -professional-zach-stern-article-about-anti-israel-open-hillel/; Philip Weiss, "Congressman with Ties to Netanyahu Calls J Street 'Anti-Semitic,'" *Mondoweiss*, July 13, 2012, mondoweiss.net/2012/07/congressman-with-ties-to-netanyahu-calls-j-street-anti-semitic.

67. Anti-Defamation League, "News: Ranking the Top 10 Anti-Israel Groups in 2013," press release, October 21, 2013, www.adl.org/press-center/press-releases/israel-middle-east/adl -lists-top-ten-anti-israel-groups-in-america.html.

68. CCR interview with NYU SJP former president Ellis Garey, July 31, 2015.

69. Moses Hetfield, "Abusing the Term 'Antisemitism,'" *Stanford Daily*, April 21, 2015, www .stanforddaily.com/2015/04/21/abusing-the-term-anti-semitism/. The editorial responded to a campus controversy in which Israel advocacy organizations accused supporters of

divestment from Israel of antisemitic comments.

Let the Semites End the World!

Frantz Fanon, *Black Skin, White Masks*, Richard Philcox, trans. (New York: Grove Press, 2008).

1. Lewis Gordon, Ramón Grosfoguel, and Eric Mielants, "Global Anti-Semitism in World-Historical Perspective: An Introduction," *Human Architecture* 7, no. 2 (Spring 2009): 3.

2. Hernan Cortés, *The Dispatches of Hernando Cortés, The Conqueror of Mexico, Addressed to the Emperor Charles V, Written during the Conquest, and Containing a Narrative of Its Events* (New York: Wiley and Putnam, 1843), accessed online December 6, 2014, mith.umd.edu/eada/html/display.php?docs=cortez_letter2.xml.

3. Kenneth Mills, William B. Taylor, and Sandra Lauderdale Graham, *Colonial Latin America: A Documentary History* (Wilmington, DE: Scholarly Resources, 2002), 129–30.

4. Kimberlé Crenshaw, "Demarginalizing the Intersection of Race and Sex: A Black Feminist Critique of Antidiscrimination Doctrine, Feminist Theory and Antiracist Politics," *University of Chicago Legal Forum* (1989): 139–67.

5. Audre Lorde, *Sister Outsider: Essays & Speeches by Audre Lorde* (Berkeley: Crossing Press, 2007), 138.

6. Ramón Grosfoguel, "Decolonizing Post-Colonial Studies and Paradigms of Political Economy: Transmodernity, Decolonial Thinking, and Global Coloniality," *TRANSMODERNITY: Journal of Peripheral Cultural Production of the Luso-Hispanic World* 1, no. 1 (2011): 1–37.

7. Ibid.

8. Of course, there are contextualized exceptions to the colonial matrix of power depending on geopolitical location. The Brahmin supremacist caste system in India—which is over two thousand years old, pre-dating European colonialism—is one example of a still very vibrant premodern system of oppression that adds an additional sub-systemic hierarchy to the colonial matrix of power in that context.

9. Lewis Gordon, "Through the Zone of Nonbeing: A Reading of Black Skin, White Masks in Celebration of Fanon's Eightieth Birthday," *The C.L.R. James Journal* 11, no. 1 (2005): 1–43.

10. Gloria Anzaldúa, *Borderlands/La Frontera: The New Mestiza* (San Francisco: Spinsters/Aunt Lute, 1987).

Building toward the Next World

1. The Torah is the central book of the Jewish religion, where the Talmud is the book of commentary on the Torah by Rabbinical leaders. Together, the two make up Jewish law and custom. The Bund was a secular Jewish socialist party active in the Russian Empire between 1897 and 1920. Matzpen was an Israeli revolutionary socialist and anti-Zionist organization active from 1962 to the 1980s.

JVP Statements on Antisemitism

1. The term "Ashkenazi" (plural: Ashkenazim) refers to Jews who descend from communities who lived in Central and Western Europe and primarily spoke various dialects of Yiddish. "Sephardi" (plural: Sephardim) refers to Jews who descend from communities who lived in the Iberian Peninsula and spoke Spanish and Ladino. "Ashkenazi" and "Sephardi" are also used to distinguish between the different religious practices, melodies, and ritual foods that each group uses. "Mizrahi" (plural: Mizrahim) is an umbrella term for Jews who descend from the Middle East and North Africa, including but not limited to Morocco, Tunisia, Iran, Iraq, Afghanistan, Yemen, Uzbekistan, Lebanon, Turkey, In-

dia, and Pakistan. The word "Mizrahi" is the Hebrew word for "East" or "Oriental," and thus has been a controversial term that many are choosing to reclaim. We understand that these terms do not and cannot encapsulate the multiplicity of Jewish difference and experience, and acknowledge that these identities overlap, but we want to name them as important to our understanding of antisemitism.

2.   Jews, Muslims, Buddhists, Hindus, and other non-Christian faiths together make up just 6 percent of the U.S. population.

3.   For example, these antisemitic interpretations were part of the Catholic Church's theology and practices up until the Vatican II congress in the 1960s. These interpretations are by no means limited to the Catholic Church. For more, please see Norman A. Beck, *Mature Christianity in the 21st Century: The Recognition and Repudiation of the Anti-Jewish Polemic of the New Testament* (Ann Arbor: University of Michigan Press, 1994).

4.   For more on racialization, see Michael Omi and Howard Winant, *Racial Formation in the United States: From the 1960s to the 1980s* (New York: Routledge University Press, 1989). For more on Jewish racialization, see Karen Brodkin, *How Jews Became White Folks and What That Says about Race in America* (New Brunswick, NJ: Rutgers University Press, 1998).

5.   The most notable example of this is *The Protocols of the Elders of Zion*, an antisemitic text from 1903 that fabricated a Jewish plan for global domination.

6.   Wilson Dizard, "A Look at Breitbart's 'Alt-Right Lite' Plan for Israel/Palestine," *Mondoweiss*, August 23, 2016.

7.   The term "microaggressions" describes brief and commonplace comments or actions that intentionally or unintentionally perpetuate bigoted environments. See Derald Wing Sue, *Microaggressions in Everyday Life* (Hoboken, NJ: Wiley and Sons, 2010).

8.   For example, in February 2015, swastikas were found at a Jewish fraternity at UC Davis. Press outlets, especially conservative ones, suggested without evidence that Students for Justice in Palestine were directly or indirectly responsible. Another example would be New York governor Andrew Cuomo's anti-BDS executive order, signed in June 2016, which argued that boycotting Israel was discriminatory.

Index

About Jewish Voice for Peace

Jewish Voice for Peace (www.jewishvoiceforpeace.org) is a national, grass-roots organization inspired by Jewish tradition to work for a just and lasting peace according to principles of human rights, equality, and international law for all the people of Israel and Palestine.

Started in 1996 in the San Francisco Bay Area by three UC Berkeley undergrads as an all-volunteer Israel and Palestine peace group, today, JVP is a national organization powered by a growing grassroots base. We have over ten thousand members and over sixty chapters across the United States, a Rabbinic Council, an Artists' Council, an Academic Advisory Council, a Student Network, and an Advisory Board consisting of some of the best-known Jewish thinkers of our time.

About Haymarket Books

Haymarket Books is a nonprofit, progressive book distributor and publisher, a project of the Center for Economic Research and Social Change. We believe that activists need to take ideas, history, and politics into the many struggles for social justice today. Learning the lessons of past victories, as well as defeats, can arm a new generation of fighters for a better world. As Karl Marx said, "The philosophers have merely interpreted the world; the point, however, is to change it."

We take inspiration and courage from our namesakes, the Haymarket martyrs, who gave their lives fighting for a better world. Their 1886 struggle for the eight-hour day reminds workers around the world that ordinary people can organize and struggle for their own liberation.

For more information and to shop our complete catalog of titles, visit us online at www.haymarketbooks.org.